Closing the African American Achievement Gap in Higher Education

Closing the African American Achievement Gap in Higher Education

EDITED BY

Alfred P. Rovai
Louis B. Gallien Jr.
Helen R. Stiff-Williams

TEACHERS COLLEGE
COLUMBIA UNIVERSITY
NEW YORK AND LONDON

Published by Teachers College Press, 1234 Amsterdam Avenue, New York, NY 10027

Library of Congress Cataloging-in-Publication Data

Closing the African American achievement gap in higher education / edited by Alfred P. Rovai, Louis B. Gallien Jr., and Helen R. Stiff-Williams.
    p. cm.
  Includes bibliographical references and index.
  ISBN 978-0-8077-4778-0 (cloth : alk. paper)
  1. African Americans—Education (Higher) 2. Academic achievement—United States.
I. Rovai, Alfred P. II. Gallien, Louis B. Jr. III. Stiff-Williams, Helen R.
  LC2781.C54 2007
  378.1'982996073—dc22

2007010659

ISBN 978-0-8077-4778-0 (cloth)

Printed on acid-free paper

Manufactured in the United States of America

14 13 12 11 10 09 08 07   8 7 6 5 4 3 2 1

Contents

Preface

The African American achievement gap is one of the most pressing and confounding problems in U.S. education today, and sustained systematic research is needed to gain a better understanding of the persistent academic underachievement of many Black students. The No Child Left Behind Act, signed into law by President George W. Bush in January 2002, greatly increases pressure on states to address the achievement gap in public schools, requiring them to publish test scores separately for racial and ethnic groups and to work to eliminate gaps in achievement. Although many of the educational research efforts are aimed at examining achievement in the K–12 school environment, the United States also struggles to reduce the achievement gap in higher education, the focus of this book.

Although some Black students are doing well academically on predominantly White college campuses, many often exhibit a marked decrease in performance from their high school grades over and beyond what is generally expected for adjustment to college level work. Additionally, graduation rates are lower and the overall college experience is often less satisfying for African American students. In particular, African American males face substantial barriers to their educational development. In 2000, nearly two-thirds of Black students on college campuses were female, which raises issues regarding Black males and the existence of a Black gender gap in higher education. Moreover, the high visibility of Black male athletes on these campuses fosters the racial stereotype that Black males excel in athletics but not in academics.

The professional literature and popular press have suggested that the achievement gap is related to factors ranging from differences in academic preparation to genetics. Yet research has shown that even where grades and test scores are equal, many minority African American students still may underperform, raising serious questions about the quality of instruction and institutional factors that appear to undermine the success of these students. Consequently, a growing number of educators are opting to use the expression "opportunity gap" instead of achievement gap to more accurately reflect the larger role of schools and society, rather than to blame students, in explaining differences in achievement.

Evidence of this opportunity gap can be found in the underrepresentation of African American secondary students in gifted/talented programs and advanced placement classes and overrepresentation in special education classes and low-track placements. Moreover, public schools in poor neighborhoods that serve large numbers of Black children are often bereft of the best-prepared teachers and counselors, and lack many of the educational resources and facilities needed for the most effective learning to take place. Nonetheless, some educators also place part of the blame on the African Americans students themselves, citing factors such as inadequate study habits, lack of motivation, and the failure to take on challenging academic coursework. Regardless of the source of the achievement gap, this book offers strategies that are intended to contribute to the improvement of African American student achievement in institutions of higher education.

PURPOSE AND ORGANIZATION

This book was written based on the following research-based suppositions:

1. The achievement gap (i.e., the difference in school performance tied to race and ethnicity) does not appear to be closing, although there are numerous exemplary programs where substantial progress has been achieved.
2. Inequities persist in our society and in our educational institutions that help explain the achievement gap as an actual opportunity gap.
3. All individuals do not learn best via the same pedagogical methods and strategies. Teachers must develop a variety of means to accomplish learning outcomes that reflect the cultural and learning style preferences of a wide variety of groups and individuals.
4. African Americans are not monolithic regarding their personal characteristics and preferences. Although many African Americans have similar learning styles and cognitive preferences, these preferences are not universal among all African Americans.
5. The achievement gap represents a complex problem with many causes, both internal and external to the school.
6. Understanding and responding to the cultural diversity of students are important steps that will contribute to increased academic achievement among all students.

The major responsibility is on educational institutions to ensure that all students have equitable opportunities to achieve academic success. The achievement gap can be reduced and possibly eliminated through changes that foster supportive institutional cultures, the use of academic support programs that respond to the opportunity gap, and high-quality classroom instruction that engages all learners.

Research provides valuable insights that suggest some key strategies to help close the achievement gap. Moreover, there are numerous exemplars of successful educational programs in adult education. This book provides a fresh look at research regarding the learning characteristics of adult African American college students and their traditional and online distance education experiences. It seeks to increase awareness of cultural issues and related best practices among higher education faculty members, administrators, and staff personnel who can influence the achievement levels of students. It accomplishes this purpose by summarizing relevant research, identifying the major challenges to African American achievement, fostering new and productive inquiry and educational activities, and drawing from the experiences and resources of various researchers and educational practitioners to identify promising strategies.

This book can be used as a core text or as a supplemental volume for university-level adult education, distance education, and multicultural education courses. It can also serve as a useful reference for higher education faculty, professional development staff, and designers of traditional and distributed courses. It will also be of interest to educational researchers and to those who have an interest in learning more about adult education and closing the African American achievement gap. Readers who are especially interested in a summary of the book are invited to go directly to Chapter 11—Summary and Conclusions.

Acknowledgments

Preparation of this book was a labor of love aided by the collected wisdom of the many social science researchers whose works are cited in this book. We are especially grateful to the chapter authors who were able to take the original book prospectus and develop their chapters. We also acknowledge the gracious and valuable comments we received at the April 2006 Annual Conference of the American Educational Research Association during our interactive symposium on Closing the African American Achievement Gap in Higher Education. We also extend thanks to Regent University for a faculty research grant that helped defray the costs associated with developing this book. In addition, we acknowledge the work of Alice Ledford and Lakisha Armstrong, Regent University graduates who worked as research assistants providing support for this book; and Mohamed Barrie, a doctoral fellow at Regent University during the 2006–2007 academic year, who assisted us in accomplishing various editorial tasks. Finally, we extend thanks to the professional staff at Teachers College Press for their encouragement, valuable feedback, and support.

ONE

The African American Achievement Gap

Helen R. Stiff-Williams

PURPOSE

The purpose of this chapter is to provide the background and context for the rest of the book by defining and discussing the African American achievement gap, describing its impact on both Blacks and American society, and presenting a theoretical basis for this phenomenon. Subsequent chapters identify the major challenges to high achievement by Black collegians in both the traditional campus classroom and in the virtual one. Additionally, promising research-based strategies that can promote greater achievement among African Americans in higher education are discussed.

BACKGROUND

Achievement refers to the extent to which learners acquire the knowledge, skills, and proficiencies that the instructor seeks to teach or assign (Salvia & Ysseldyke, 2000). In the classroom, the instructor typically designs the approaches or develops the instruments for measuring the extent of learning within the classroom. To permit comparisons of student learning beyond the classroom, such as state-wide or nationally, standardized tests are utilized. Widely identified as achievement tests, these instruments, according to Salvia and Ysseldyke (2000), provide a global estimate of academic skill development.

However, not all students achieve at the same level, and differences often exist between individuals as well as groups. The African American achievement gap is the observed difference in academic achievement between Blacks and Whites and is present before children begin school, throughout their K–12 experiences, and continues in institutions of higher education. Kober (2001) reports that African American and Hispanic students score significantly lower, on average, than White and Asian students. This gap has stubbornly resisted closing over the years and is among the most urgent contemporary problems in education and society. However, Kober also suggests it is wrong to assume that the quality of schools is declining because of the achievement gap. She claims that over the past 25 to 30 years, every subgroup of students, including African Americans, has increased its average achievement. Consequently, the achievement of African American students must be increased markedly in order to close the gap.

It is important to understand that the term *achievement gap* does not refer to one single gap, but to many interrelated gaps. "Achievement gap" is a contemporary expression used to refer to the differences in the academic performance of subpopulations of students. For specific academic areas of study, achievement gaps are known to exist, for example, between males and females; high, middle, and low socioeconomic groups; African Americans and Whites; and rural, suburban, and urban groups. Furthermore, data analyses have shown that there are multiple and varied gaps within and across groups as differences are measured using group means.

For purposes of discussion in this book, the writers refer to the multiple and varied gaps apparent in the comparison of the achievement of African American students with other student ethnicities, and, most commonly, with White students who are members of the dominant culture in American society. Between these two groups, multiple and diverse gaps are pronounced and sustained. These gaps address differences in aspects of higher education such as college applications, college enrollment, course grades, grades on standardized achievement tests, college graduation, and pursuit of advanced degrees. As is common in the professional literature, the term *achievement gap* will be used with the understanding that the discussion is actually about multiple and varied types of academic gaps.

THE AFRICAN AMERICAN ACHIEVEMENT GAP

Preschool and K–12

Gaps between African American and White children have been measured as early as preschool age. Duncan and Magnuson (2005) report that, as children begin school, African American children, on average, lag in academic preparedness in comparison to White children. Consequently, many African American students arrive at kindergarten considerably behind their White peers in measurable cognitive skills (Nettles, Millett, & Ready, 2003).

National Assessment of Educational Progress (NAEP) statistics reveal that African American students by the fourth grade perform two years behind White students (Robelen, 2002). Furthermore, according to a 1999 report of the National Center for Education Statistics (NCES), African American students by the end of high school have major reading deficiencies to the extent that only one in 100 can read and comprehend specialized text such as the science section of a newspaper (Reynolds, 2002). In comparison, among White students graduating from high school, one out of every 12 students can read and comprehend the specialized text. This report also indicates that only 20% of African American students can read less specialized text, while more than 50% of White students can complete the same reading task. Reynolds (2002) reports that the gap in test results is equally dismal for mathematics and science.

To further illustrate the gap, Chubb and Loveless (2002) declare, "The average black or Hispanic student, in elementary, middle, or high school, currently achieves at about the same level as the average white student in the lowest quartile of White achievement" (p. 1). Based on NAEP test results, Chubb and Loveless (2002) report that by age 17, Black and Hispanic students are testing on average approximately four years below White students.

Higher Education

The gaps that persist in all grades of public schools also appear in different forms and are just as pervasive in the nation's institutions of higher education. Table 1.1 compares selective enrollment and school completion rates by ethnic group. Clearly, Black students are less likely to enroll in postsecondary schools than are their White peers and, once enrolled, are less likely to obtain a degree. However, the averages depicted for completion rates in Table 1.1 do not depict the large variation in graduation rates by school. Carey (2004), describing data collected annually by the U.S. Department of Education's Graduation Rate Survey, a component of the Integrated Postsecondary Education Data System (IPEDS), reports large variations in graduation rates by school. In particular, he writes that of the 772 colleges and universities in the United States where at least 5% of the full-time undergraduates are African American:

- 299 have a graduation rate for African American students under 30%,
- 164 have a graduation rate for African American students under 20%, and
- 68 have a graduation rate for African American students under 10%.

Table 1.2 summarizes the number of degrees conferred by gender and ethnic group by U.S. colleges and universities during the 2002–2003 academic year. It clearly shows that Black men trail Black women in educational attainment. For African Americans, females earn approximately twice the number of bachelor's and master's degrees that males do. This disparity

Table 1.1. Higher Education Enrollment and Completion Rates by Ethnic Group

	Black students	White students
Enrollment in college immediately after high school graduation in 2004	62.5%	68.8%
Enrollment rates of 18- to 24-year-olds in degree-granting institutions in 2004	31.8%	41.7%
Persons age 25 and over, bachelor's degree completion or beyond in 2005	17.7%	30.5%
Bachelor's degree completion status in 2001 of first-time postsecondary students starting during the 1995-1996 academic year	43.4%	61.9%
Dropouts in 2001 of first-time postsecondary students starting during the 1995-1996 academic year	28.2%	19.4%
Distribution of 1990 high school sophomores through 2000: bachelor's degree completion	15.4%	29.4%
Distribution of 1990 high school sophomores through 2000: master's degree completion	0.8%	3.5%

Source: *Digest of Education Statistics*, 2005, Tables 6, 181, 184, 306, and 310.

between the number of Black females and males earning academic degrees is a serious problem, even after considering that the 2000 U.S. census shows the White population is 49.10% male and 50.90% female, while for Blacks the population is 47.5% male and 52.5% female (Cuyjet, 2006). Even socioeconomic status fails to correct this trend. Middle-class African American males also lag significantly behind White peers on both grade point average and standardized tests (Jencks & Phillips, 1998; Noguera, 2001).

This African American gender gap also exists at community colleges. Bush and Bush (2005) report that a review of California community college data reveals that African American males are the lowest-performing subgroup in the percentage of degrees earned, persistence rates, and average cumulative grade point average.

Table 1.3 shows that the achievement gap also extends to course grades. Almost one-half of Black students earn course grades of C's, D's, or lower, compared to less than one-third of White students. The research literature provides substantial evidence of similar differences in college grades between Black and White college students over time. Kane (1998), using data from the High School and Beyond (HSB) study, investigated differences in the educational performance of minority and White students. The HSB data pertain to a sample of students in the graduating class of 1982 from more

Table 1.2. Higher Education Earned Degrees (and Percentages) Conferred by Gender and Ethnic Group, 2002–2003

	Black students	White students
	BACHELOR'S DEGREES	
Females	82,769 (16.1%)	430,024 (83.9%)
Males	41,472 (6.9%)	564,210 (93.1%)
	MASTER'S DEGREES	
Females	31,467 (13.1%)	208,515 (86.9%)
Males	12,805 (8.8%)	133,220 (91.2%)
	DOCTORATE DEGREES	
Females	1,604 (10.1%)	14,228 (89.9%)
Males	913 (6.4%)	13,470 (93.6%)
	PROFESSIONAL DEGREES	
Females	3,543 (11.6%)	27,082 (88.4%)
Males	2,172 (6.4%)	31,596 (93.6%)

Source: 2005–2006 Almanac. (2005). *The Chronicle of Higher Education Almanac, 52*(1), 20.

than 1,000 public and private high schools in the United States who were periodically resurveyed over the next 10 years. Kane reports that Black students scored from 0.3 to 0.4 of a letter grade lower in college grade point average (on a four-point scale), compared to White students.

The achievement gap also extends to standardized test results. The American College Test (ACT) and the Scholastic Aptitude Test (SAT) assess

Table 1.3. Undergraduate Grades by Ethnic Group, 1999–2002

	Black students	White students
Mostly A's	7.3%	16.5%
A's and B's	7.5%	11.7%
Mostly B's	20.3%	25.3%
B's and C's	16.0%	16.2%
C's and D's or lower	48.9%	30.3%

Source: 2004–2005 Almanac. *The Chronicle of Higher Education Almanac, 51*(1), 13.

high school students' general educational development and their ability to complete college-level work. They are voluntarily taken mainly by students who plan to matriculate to college. The professional literature shows that scores on standardized tests such as the ACT (the ACT has a scale of 1 to 36) or the SAT (the SAT has a scale of 200 to 800) are generally strong predictors of student success in college for students of all ethnicities. Scores of 20 on the ACT and 500 on the SAT represent the 50th percentile.

Table 1.4 compares Black and White student performance on the ACT and the SAT. African Americans score, on average, significantly less than their White peer group on both tests. The difference in ACT scores is 4.9 points, which is almost one standard deviation on the ACT scale. The difference in SAT scores is approximately 100 points on each of the verbal and mathematical sections, which equates to about one standard deviation. Moreover, Bridgeman and Wendler (2005) report that 21% of African American SAT test takers score 500 or more on the verbal section, compared to 59% of Whites. For the mathematical section the gap is even greater: 20% of African Americans versus 60% of Whites. The SAT scores for national samples of college-bound seniors in the classes of 2001 to 2005 have held steady. However, Kober (2001) points out that SAT scores have increased for Black and White students over time. The average composite SAT score of Black students has increased from 686 in 1976 to 860 in 2000. The average ACT composite score for Black students has increased from 15.1 in 1976 to 17.0 in 2000 (Kober, 2001).

Tables 1.3 and 1.4 suggest that there is a direct relationship between course grades and ACT/SAT scores. Bridgeman and Wendler (2005) sup-

Table 1.4. ACT and SAT Test Scores by Ethnic Group

	Black students	White students
AVERAGE ACT SCORES		
Score	17.0	21.9
1-year change	-0.1	+0.1
AVERAGE SAT SCORES		
Verbal section score	430	528
1-year change	-1.0	-1.0
Mathematical section score	427	531
1-year change	+1.0	-3.0

Source: 2005–2006 Almanac. *The Chronicle of Higher Education Almanac, 52*(1), 12.

port this view and point out that students who excel in rigorous courses tend to obtain high SAT scores, and students who get high SAT scores tend to take and excel in rigorous courses. Low test scores for many African American students limit access to upper-tier colleges and universities where research shows that minority students are more likely to graduate. Instead, minority students gain access to the colleges and universities where Black graduation rates are low. Carey (2005) summarizes the condition in this way:

> African American students are more than four times as likely to enter college at an institution where at least 70% of black students fail to graduate as they are to begin at an institution where at least 70% of black students succeed. (p. 14)

Bridgeman and Wendler (2005) report that relatively few high-achieving Black students, and especially high-achieving males, select education majors. Less than half a percent of African American high-achieving men choose education majors. They also claim that education is a popular major among students in the lowest achievement group. Such a situation cannot be helpful in promoting outstanding African American teachers for our urban schools.

CONSEQUENCES OF THE ACHIEVEMENT GAP

Jamie Merisotis (2003), president of the Institute for Higher Education Policy, argues that promoting access to higher education remains one of the most critical responsibilities of the federal government in ensuring public, private, social, and economic stability and prosperity. The major benefits that accrue to society as a result of a postsecondary education are identified in Figure 1.1.

The link between education and earning power is confirmed by research and U.S. government statistics. The requirements of the information age, the growth in technology-driven industry, and the new economy place added emphasis on the need for an educated workforce. According to the U.S. Department of Commerce, Bureau of the Census (2001), in 1999 a person with a high school diploma earned, on average, $24,572 a year. A bachelor's degree nearly doubled income potential, to $45,600. A master's degree raised income to $55,600, and a professional degree resulted in income over $100,000. As a result, there is a growing disparity in our society between those with an education and earning power (i.e., possessing human capital) and those who must rely on others for support.

Figure 1.1. Benefits of Higher Education

	Public	*Private*
ECONOMIC	Increased tax revenues Greater productivity Increased consumption Increased workforce flexibility Decreased reliance on government support	Higher salaries and benefits Employment Increased savings Improved working conditions Personal/professional mobility
SOCIAL	Reduced crime Increased charitable giving, service Increased quality of civic life Social cohesion, appreciation of diversity Improved technology access and use	Improved health Improved quality of life for offspring Better consumer decision-making Increased personal status More hobbies, leisure activities

Source: Merisotis, 2003, p. 11.

Human Capital Theory is a model that suggests workers and employers try to maximize their earnings. Proponents of this theory, such as Becker (1994), argue that inequality in employment exists, in part, because some workers are more productive than others. Productive workers are more productive, in part, because they acquire more human capital in endeavors such as advanced schooling, health care, and other activities that can increase their earning potential. According to this theory, the same level of human capital results in more talented workers being more productive than their less talented peers. If employers do not hire the most productive workers, their competitors will hire them and thereby will be in a position to offer their goods and services at lower prices. Earning power is therefore directly related to human capital. However, this theory does not take into consideration that some employers will behave nonrationally and bypass African Americans because of discriminatory practices.

The impact of the influence of education on earning power and human capital is underscored by research conducted by Johnson and Neal (1998). Their study reveals that the only parity in annual wages between African Americans and Whites occurs when African Americans are college graduates. Yet, as noted above, the African American achievement gap entails less access to a college education on the part of Blacks and, once enrolled, they are less likely to graduate. The consequences include negative effects on Black employment and occupational attainment.

The *Monthly Labor Review* (2004) provides some insight into the effects of education on unemployment rates, see Table 1.5. Although the unemployment rates are higher for Blacks than Whites at each education level, the average expected Black unemployment rate for college graduates is less than half that of Blacks with only a high school diploma.

Not only is employment status affected by the level of educational attainment, but research also indicates that the annual income and projected lifetime earnings are dramatically impacted by one's educational level. Drawing on U.S. Census Bureau data, high school graduates earn an average of $1.2 million over an adult's working life, while bachelor's degree holders earn about $2.1 million (Day & Newburger, 2002). The NAACP Legal Defense and Education Fund (2005) uses the expression "the million dollar gap" to reference this huge income difference.

According to a report by Editorial Projects in Education (2006), the cumulative costs to the nation for school dropouts are calculated to be in the billions of dollars because of lost tax revenue and substantial spending required for social programs. According to this report, the result of the loss in earnings is an aggregated tax loss of about $192 billion, equal to 1.6% of the national gross domestic product for a cohort of 18-year-olds who do not earn a high school diploma.

Beyond the consequences of the achievement gap to individuals and families, the federal, state, and local governments are further impacted through higher costs for health, welfare spending, public housing, food stamps, medical care, incarceration, and so forth. For example, Harlow (2003) reports that the 1997 incarceration rate for individuals with only a high school diploma is 1.2%, while the rate for those who hold a bachelor's degree is 0.1%. Harlow also reports that approximately 40% of inmates in state prisons are not high school graduates. Economist Enrico Moretti also supports the linkage of education with incarceration. According to Richard

Table 1.5. Unemployment Rates by Education Level and Ethnicity

	Black adults	*White adults*
High school dropout	13.9%	7.8%
High school graduate	9.3%	4.8%
Some college	7.9%	4.2%
College graduate	4.5%	2.8%

Source: *Monthly Labor Review*, 2004, p. 6.

(2005), Moretti determined that high school dropouts have a higher propensity for committing crimes and being jailed than persons who graduate from high school and have more education. Moretti projects that if there were a 1% increase in the high school completion rate of males between ages 20 and 60, the result would be a savings of $1.4 billion annually through reduced crime and victimization in the nation.

Vernez, Krop, and Rydell (1999) report the effects of increased education on public expenditures for programs such as welfare, see Table 1.6. According to these statistics, if a Black high school student can be encouraged to graduate from high school and to subsequently attend college and graduate, by the time he or she is 30 years old, the individual will have saved the nation almost $5,800 in support from social programs. Moreover, he or she will have paid more in taxes and would have been able to spend from earnings because of the additional disposable income.

Research also shows a positive correlation between completion of higher education and good health, another factor that increases human capital. For every income level, the percentage of adults perceiving themselves as healthy or very healthy increases with higher levels of education. For example, Baum and Payea (2005) use National Center for Health Statistics data to report that 73% of college graduates with incomes between $35,000 and $54,999 feel they are in excellent or very good health, compared to 62% of high school graduates in the same income bracket. Cohn and Geske (1992) support this view, and also report that parents' schooling levels are directly related to the health status of their children. As an added health bonus, Baum and Payea (2005) provide evidence that college graduates smoke much less than individuals who have not progressed beyond high school graduation. In 2000, Baum and Payea report 14% of college graduates and 28% of high school graduates smoke.

Other researchers and scholars identify additional social problems that could be contained through increased educational attainment in the United

Table 1.6. Effects of Increased Education on Annual Savings on Social Programs for 30-Year-Old Men and Women by Ethnicity

	Black adults	White adults
High school dropout to high school completion	$3,300	$1,600
High school graduate to some college	$1,300	$500
Some college to college graduate	$1,200	$300
Total saving—High school dropout to college graduate	$5,800	$2,400

Source: Vernez, Krop, and Rydell, 1999, p. 30.

States. For example, Chubb and Loveless (2002) wrote: "If the achievement gap could be reduced, the fortunes of Blacks and Hispanics would not only be raised, but the social and economic differences that intensify the country's racial tensions would also be ameliorated" (p. 1).

Although postsecondary education and educational attainment has increased among the adult population, African American males cluster at the bottom of almost every academic performance indicator. In 2000–2001, African American males represented 8.6% of the national public school population, but comprised a disproportionate number of those with special education, suspended, and/or expelled status. Middle-class African American males also lag significantly behind White male peers on grade point average and standardized tests (Jencks & Phillips, 1998; Noguera, 2001).

Additionally, African American males have not been performing as well as their Black female counterparts in higher education. According to Cuyjet (2006), when the number of Black men on campus fails to achieve a critical mass, which he describes as a population of African American men large enough to sustain their cultural identity and peer support, the college community is seen as deficient because Black males fail to find a level of cultural comfort in the campus community. Cuyjet also notes that the high visibility of Black male athletes and the corresponding invisibility of the Black male nonathlete students contribute to the racial stereotype of African American men as being nonintellectual. Ogbu (1991) points out that because of a history of discrimination and roadblocks that limit the academic and employment pursuits of African American males, this group has sought to demonstrate its prowess in athletic activities. In following Ogbu's explanation for the direction chosen by many African American males, it becomes critical to confront barriers within the U.S. educational system that undermine or deter their academic pursuits.

The relatively low numbers of Black males on campus can also negatively influence the social lives of Black females (Cuyjet, 2006). In particular, a significant gender imbalance makes normal social interactions, particularly dating opportunities, difficult within the African American college community. Moreover, the smaller numbers of Black men with college degrees has a negative impact on the social life of African American female college graduates who seek compatible partners.

Kaba (2005) suggests that as a result of this Black gender gap, females are in a position to take on more leadership positions within the African American community. The National Council on Education and the National Urban League both maintain that involving African American males in the higher education system is critical to reversing economic trends for American society (Polite & Davis, 1999).

From a global perspective, the scope of the achievement deficit of African American students has a negative impact upon U.S. economic status.

Citing information from the Organisation for Economic Co-operation and Development, Carey (2005), points out:

> Recent data show that competitors in the industrialized world are catching up— fast. A generation ago, countries like Canada, Japan, Great Britain, and Korea ranked far below the United States in terms of the percent of young adults with a four-year college degree. Since then, each of these countries has increased its B. A. attainment rate significantly, while the American rate has stayed virtually unchanged. (p. 2)

A THEORETICAL FRAMEWORK OF CAUSES AND EFFECTS

Foley (1991) describes the various research tendencies that help explain the ethnic minority achievement gap. These tendencies fall into camps characterized by either microethnography or macroethnography. Those in the microethnographic camp attribute the achievement gap largely to differences between ethnic minority and majority cultures and in how minority students are treated in the classroom, e.g., receiving less counseling and less attention. This microethnographic approach focuses on cultural language differences in the classroom to help explain the achievement gap. Although associated research has produced valuable insights, this approach has been criticized because of its behaviorist and deterministic tendencies (Erickson, 1987; Foley, 1991) and its narrowness and decontextualized nature (Ogbu, 1987). The macroethnographic approach, on the other hand, is best represented by John Ogbu's Cultural-Ecological Theory of School Performance (e.g., Ogbu, 1987, 1989; Ogbu & Simons, 1998). This theory does not dismiss the importance of cultural differences at the micro level, but focuses more on the macro level and how group members view themselves and their positions in relation to mainstream society.

According to cultural-ecological theory, cultural groups are categorized as either voluntary settlers, known as immigrants, or involuntary settlers, referred to as nonimmigrants who are brought into a dominant society by force, such as enslavement, colonization, or subjugation. Voluntarily immigrating minorities tend to view their cultural and language barriers in school and in society as temporary barriers to be overcome in order to achieve their goals. Involuntarily immigrating minorities, having emerged from a history of enslavement, generations of legal segregation, and continuing discrimination, perceive society as being structured to limit their opportunities for advancement. As a result, involuntary minorities, because of generations of oppression, act in defiant or oppositional ways, even if the outcome works against their collective and individual well-being.

Ogbu explains that many African Americans, after having lived for generations as oppressed people, reject aspects of the dominant culture as a means of asserting their independence, retaining power over their lives, and maintaining a sense of control over their destiny. The oppositional behaviors such as rejecting advanced course work because it would be "acting White" represent the actions of involuntary minorities in their attempts to assert independence and self-direction as a result of historical oppression and perceived lack of control over their destiny (Ogbu, 1991).

Foley (1991) summarizes the differences between voluntary and involuntary minorities as follows:

> Given the logic of cultural inversion, voluntary minorities come to understand being successful in school as acting white and adopting a white style of speech and cultural expression. This sort of oppositional logic dictates that they must choose between being occupationally successful (white) and culturally successful (black). Quite ironically, the battle to preserve their ethnic culture becomes the very thing that dooms [involuntary] minorities of color, to academic failure. (p. 66)

Cultural-ecological theory places importance on system forces (e.g., how minorities are treated by society and its institutions) and community forces (e.g., how minorities interpret and respond to the treatment) as factors that influence student academic performance. Therefore, this theory, while recognizing the existence of systematic discrimination that generates substantial distrust of schools and their agents on the part of Blacks, also recognizes the existence of minority agency. Hence, Ogbu (1987) recognized a need for the study of community forces to complement analyses of system forces. Community forces that can contribute to the achievement gap include minority student responses to lowered teachers' expectations, the various manifestations of racial stereotyping, the labeling of minority students with academic problems as handicapped, the belittlement of minority cultures, the presence of pervading beliefs held by the majority in the inferiority of the minority culture, and the cultural differences between students and teachers (Ogbu, 2003).

According to Ogbu (1987), cultural-ecological theory also suggests that the system force of institutionalized discrimination suppresses the commitment of Black students to school norms since they tend to identify the school as a White domain that forces them to think and act White. Ogbu suggests that involuntary immigrants often find it difficult to withstand the psychological pressures needed to cross cultural borders. Consequently, Ogbu and Fordham (1986) theorize that some Black students underperform in school because of their cultural opposition to acting White, which is acting in defiance of their perceptions of majority efforts to control their destiny. Of course, Ogbu's "acting White" phenomenon may be more relevant in a K–12 school environment where school attendance is mandatory than in higher education where adults enroll based on their desire for continued education and to earn a college degree. Lundy (2003) argues that instead of rejecting academic success, many Black students view high academic achievement as cultural agency to resist White supremacy. Additionally, Carter (2003) provides research evidence that the burden of acting White is more related to speech, dress, musical tastes, and styles of interaction than to academic achievement.

Foley (1991) and others identify the need to synthesize the micro- and macroethnographic approaches in explaining the ethnic minority achievement gap. This approach is consistent with that of Erickson (1987), who suggests that one should consider all of the variances possible in order to approach students in a culturally respectful and aware manner. Consequently, the following chapters of this book draw from research conducted by both camps to explain possible causes for the African American achievement gap.

CONCLUSION

This chapter aimed to define the achievement gap as the measured difference in the achievement of African American students and their White counterparts. From the research, it is apparent that the African American achievement gap is measurable as early as the preschool age, continues throughout the K–12 educational program, and extends into the college years and beyond. The gap between African American and White student performance is evident in a variety of measures.

As African American students advance through the educational system, the research indicates that they are more likely to be taught by teachers who are less qualified than the teachers of majority students. Further, according to Ferguson (2003), African American students are likely to experience biased perceptions on the part of the teacher, generally manifested as low expectations for achievement as compared to expectations for White students. Other in-school conditions identified as causes for the achievement gap include poor-quality curriculum that does not challenge students; tracking, grouping, and advising practices that place students in or allow students to take courses that do not provide appropriately rigorous academic experiences; weak school leaders who do not address equity issues; poorly maintained and aged educational facilities (particularly in high-poverty, high-minority school districts); and inadequate instructional resources.

According to the research, many of the conditions associated with the achievement gap in pre-K through 12 educational settings form the foundation for the achievement gap in higher education. Many scholars and researchers agree that factors such as family poverty, poor-quality teachers, and poor-quality curriculum contribute to this gap in higher education. Beyond these inherent factors, institutional factors such as a less than supportive culture, inadequate advising and mentoring, a lack of financial resources, and mismatched pedagogical practices have been identified as contributors to the achievement gap in higher education.

The statistics presented in this chapter largely reflect gaps in educational outcomes, e.g., differences in average college completions, course grades, and standardized test results. If one takes a systems view of education, then education is a process with inputs as well as outputs. Students are inputs, but so are resources and teachers. One can therefore expect outcomes to be related to both system inputs and processes. In this regard, the notion of an opportunity gap has emerged—K–12 schools serving mostly affluent White communities have the best and most experienced teachers, modern technology and facilities, smaller classes, and other advantages, while schools serving mostly the poor must often work with less. Therefore, it is not surprising that such differences in opportunities to learn result in different learning outcomes, which in turn result in differences in college preparation for those students with the potential to succeed in higher education. Many Black students, as measured by the ACT and SAT scales, arrive at colleges and universities largely unequipped to fully engage in postsecondary education. Yet we know from research in cognitive science that all racial/ethnic groups have the same innate cognitive abilities. The attitude of policy makers, administrators, and educators must move away from a deficit and pathological view regarding African Americans and instead focus on inequities in their institutions by removing those obstacles that stand in the way of Black student progress.

Given the research, there is a preponderance of evidence that many of the causes for the African American achievement gap are rooted in poverty. Factors such as the high mobility or the transience of families, lack of developmentally appropriate cognitive experiences, excessive television watching, the "summer effect" in which students lose academic ground during the summer months, are all directly related to conditions of poverty in which too many African Americans exist. The research has established that conditions of poverty and discrimination limit the opportunities of many African Americans and reduce opportunities throughout the educational process.

Acknowledgement of the economic and social impact of lost human capital on the nation's economy is not new. Almost a century ago, economist Alfred Marshall (1920) summed up the situation with the following remark that still rings true today:

> There is no extravagance more prejudicial to growth of national wealth than that wasteful negligence which allows genius that happens to be born of lowly parentage to expend itself in lowly work. No change would conduce so much to a rapid increase of material wealth as an improvement in our schools, and

especially those of the middle grades, provided it be combined with an extensive system of scholarships, which will enable the clever son of a working man to rise gradually from school to school till he has the best theoretical and practical education which the age can give. (p. 176)

The chapters that follow expound upon the background issues associated with the African American achievement gap. These chapters aim to provide the background necessary for understanding the origin, the causes, and the challenges of this gap. Subsequent chapters provide research-based strategies to eliminate these barriers to Black student learning and educational attainment.

DISCUSSION TOPICS

1. To what extent do policy makers, the leadership, and faculty members at your institution know and understand the causes of the African American achievement gap?
2. To what extent have policy makers, the leadership, and faculty members identified the types of gaps in achievement at your institution?
3. Given the presumed identification of the various gaps at your institution, what steps have been taken at the different levels within your institution to address these achievement gaps?
4. To what extent do policy makers and leaders understand the consequences of not addressing the achievement gaps within your institution?
5. To what extent is there an organized system-wide approach to address the multiple and varied African American achievement gaps within your institution in areas such as recruitment, retention, and graduation rates?
6. If efforts have been under way to address the African American achievement gap in your institution, what results are evident from the efforts that have been completed? What data exist to direct the next steps to be taken at your institution to address the achievement gap?

REFERENCES

2004–5 Almanac. (2004). *The Chronicle of Higher Education Almanac, 51*(1). Retrieved November 29, 2006, from http://chronicle.com/free/almanac/2004/notes/notes.htm

2005–6 Almanac. (2005). *The Chronicle of Higher Education Almanac, 52*(1). Retrieved November 29, 2006, from http://chronicle.com/free/almanac/2005/notes/notes.htm

Baum, S., & Payea, K. (2005). *Education pays 2004: The benefits of higher education for individuals and society.* Washington, DC: The College Board.

Becker, G. S. (1994). *Human capital: A theoretical and empirical analysis, with special reference to education* (3rd ed.). Chicago: University of Chicago Press.

Bridgeman, B., & Wendler, C. (2005). *Policy information report: Characteristics of minority students who excel on the SAT and in the classroom.* Princeton, NJ: Educational Testing Service.

Bush, E. C., & Bush, L. (2005). Black male achievement and the community college. *Black Issues in Higher Education, 22*(2), 44.

Carey, K. (2004). *A matter of degrees: Improving graduation rates in four-year colleges and universities.* Washington, DC: The Education Trust.

Carey, K. (2005). *One step from the finish line: Higher college graduation rates are within our reach.* Washington, DC: The Education Trust.

Carter, P. I. (2003). *Balancing "acts": Issues of identity and cultural resistance in the social and educational behaviors of minority youth.* Unpublished doctoral dissertation, Columbia University, New York. (Digital Dissertations No. AAT 9948950).

Chubb, J. E., & Loveless, T. (Eds.) (2002). *Bridging the achievement gap.* Washington, DC: Brookings Institution Press.

Cohn, E., & Geske, T. G. (1992). Private nonmonetary returns to investment in higher education. In W. E. Becker Jr., & D. R. Lewis (Eds.), *The economics of American higher education* (pp. 173–195). Boston: Kluwer Academic Publishers.

Cuyjet, M. J. (Ed.) (2006). *African American men in college.* New York: Jossey-Bass.

Day, J. C., & Newburger, E. C. (2002). *The big payoff: Educational attainment and synthetic estimates of work life earnings.* (Current Population Reports, Special Studies, P23-210). Washington, DC: Commerce Department, Economics and Statistics Administration, Census Bureau.

Digest of Education Statistics. (2005). Washington, DC: U.S. Department of Education, National Center for Education Statistics. Retrieved November 29, 2006, from http://nces.ed.gov/programs/digest/d05/

Duncan, G. J., & Magnuson, K. A. (2005). Can family socioeconomic resources account for racial and ethnic test score gaps? *The Future of Children, 15*(1), 35–54.

Editorial Projects in Education. (2006, June). *Diplomas count: An essential guide to graduation policy and rates.* Bethesda, MD: Author.

Erickson, F. (1987). Transformation and school success: The politics of culture and educational achievement. *Anthropology and Education Quarterly, 18*(4), 335–356.

Ferguson, R. (2003). Teachers' perceptions and expectations and the black-white test score gap. *Urban Education, 38*(4), 460–507.

Foley, D. E. (1991). Reconsidering anthropological explanations of ethnic school failure. *Anthropology & Education Quarterly, 22*(1), 60–86.

Harlow, C. W. (2003). *Education and correctional populations.* Washington, DC: Bureau of Justice Statistics, Department of Justice.

Jencks, C., & Phillips, M. (Eds.). (1998). *The black-white test score gap.* Washington, DC: Brookings Institution Press.

Johnson, W. R., & Neal, D. (1998). Basic skills and the black-white earnings gap. In C. Jencks & M. Phillips (Eds.), *The black-white test score gap* (pp. 480–497). Washington, DC: Brookings Institution Press.

Kaba, A. (2005). Progress of African Americans in higher education: The widening gender gap and its current and future implications. *Education Policy Analysis Archives, 13*(25), 1–32.

Kane, T. J. (1998). Racial and ethnic preferences in college admissions. In C. Jencks & M. Phillips (Eds.), *The black-white test score gap* (pp. 431–456). Washington, DC: Brookings Institution Press.

Kober, N. (2001). *It takes more than testing: Closing the achievement gap.* Washington, DC: Center on Education Policy.

Lundy, G. (2003). The myths of oppositional culture. *Journal of Black Studies, 33*(4), 450–467.

Marshall, A. (1920). *Principles of economics* (8th ed.). London: Macmillan.

Merisotis, J. P. (2003, October 16). Testimony of Jamie P. Merisotis. Hearing on promoting access to postsecondary education: Issues for the Reauthorization of the Higher Education Act, United States Senate, Committee on Health, Education, Labor, and Pensions. Retrieved November 29, 2006, from http://www.ihep.org/Organization/Press/Testimony20031016.pdf

Monthly Labor Review. (2004). A visual essay: Blacks, Asians, and Hispanics in the civilian labor force. *Monthly Labor Review, 127*(6), 69–76. Retrieved November 29, 2006, from http://www.bls.gov/opub/mlr/2004/06/ressum.htm

NAACP Legal Defense and Education Fund, Inc. (2005, June). *Moving from rhetoric to reality in opening doors to higher education for African American students.* Retrieved November 29, 2006, from http://www.naacpldf.org/landing.aspx?sub=52

Nettles, M. T., Millett, C. M., & Ready, D. D. (2003). Attacking the African American-White-achievement gap on college admissions tests. In D. Ravitch (Ed.), *Brookings papers on education policy* (pp. 215–238). Retrieved November 29, 2006, from http://muse.jhu.edu/journals/brookings_papers_on_education_ policy/toc/pep2003.1.html

Noguera, P. A. (2001). Racial politics and the elusive quest for excellence and equity in education. *Education and Urban Society, 34*(1), 18–41.

Ogbu, J. U. (1987). Variability in minority school performance: A problem in search of an explanation. *Anthropology and Education Quarterly, 18*(4), 312–334.

Ogbu, J. U. (1989). The individual in collective adaptation: A framework for focusing on academic underperformance and dropping out among involuntary minorities. In L. Weis, E. Farrar, & H. G. Petrie (Eds.), *Dropouts from school: Issues, dilemmas, and solutions* (pp. 181–204). Albany, NY: State University of New York Press.

Ogbu, J. U. (1991). Minority coping responses and school experience. *Journal of Psychohistory, 18*(4), 433–456.

Ogbu, J. U. (2003). *Black American students in an affluent suburb: A study of academic disengagement.* Mahwah, NJ: Lawrence Erlbaum.

Ogbu, J. U., & Fordham, S. (1986). African American students' school success: Coping with the burden of "acting white." *Urban Review, 18*(3), 176–206.

Ogbu, J. U., & Simons, H. D. (1998). Voluntary and involuntary minorities: A cultural-ecological theory of school performance with some implications for education. *Anthropology and Education Quarterly, 29*(2), 155–188.

Polite, V. C., & Davis, J. E. (1999). *African American males in school and society: Practices and policies for effective education.* New York: Teachers College Press.

Reynolds, G. M. (2002). Identifying and eliminating the achievement gaps: A research-based approach. In A. Alson, D. Carnahan, P. Kimmelman, M. Johnson, R. Legler, & S. Robinson (Reviewers), *Bridging the great divide: Broadening perspectives on closing the achievement gaps* (pp. 3–12). Naperville, IL: North Central Regional Educational Laboratory.

Richard, A. (2005, November). *Researchers tally costs of education failing.* New York: Teachers College. Retrieved November 29, 2006, from http://www.tc.columbia.edu/news/article.htm?id=5343

Robelen, E. W. (2002). *Taking on the achievement gap.* Naperville, IL: North Central Regional Educational Laboratory.

Salvia, J., & Ysseldyke, J. E. (2000). *Assessment* (8th ed.). New York: Houghton Mifflin.

U.S. Department of Commerce, Bureau of the Census. (2001). *Current population reports, Series P-60.* Washington, DC: U.S. Government Printing Office.

Vernez, G., Krop, R. A., & Rydell, C. P. (1999). *Closing the education gap.* Santa Monica, CA: Rand Corporation.

TWO

African American and Hip-Hop Cultural Influences

Emery M. Petchauer

PURPOSE

The purpose of this chapter is to discuss two cultural influences on African American learning and achievement in higher education: African American culture and hip-hop culture. Although the educational implications of African American culture have received scholarly attention in the past decades (e.g., Gallien & Peterson, 2004; Hale-Benson 1986; Irvine, 1990), hip-hop has emerged more recently as an important domain of inquiry in numerous disciplines, including education (Baker, 1995; Ginwright, 2004; West, 2005).

BACKGROUND

Definitions of culture in social science literature generally center on learned systems of values, beliefs, meanings, symbols, and behavior imprinted on individuals by family and community beginning at birth (e.g., Lewis, 2002). Such constructed systems may pertain to groups organized around geographical locations, professional sports teams, music genres, ethnicities, and so forth. Though culture is often considered a fixed, static domain that individuals occupy, Lewis (2002) highlights that this is not the case:

> The imaginings and meanings [of culture], however, can never be fixed or solidified, but remain assemblages that can be dismantled through time, space and human action. That is, the "system" into which meanings are formed is far from absolute and immutable. (p. 13)

McCarthy (1998) amplifies the potentially problematic nature of culture by positing rather straightforwardly, "to study race, identity, culture, and to intervene in their fields of effects, one must be prepared to live with extraordinary complexity and variability of meaning" (p. 6).

One of the "fields of effects" necessitating intervention to which McCarthy alludes is higher education, or, more specifically, the learning and achievement of African American college students. Gay (2000) suggests that "culture is at the heart of all we do in the name of education, whether that is curriculum, instruction, administration, or performance assessment" (p. 8). Ladson-Billings (2001) writes that much of what educators know about the intersection of culture and education is not definite and, thus, further inquiry is needed. Spindler and Spindler (2000) highlight the range of cultural influence in educational settings: "As a teacher, a student, a delinquent, a superlatively good student, or a miserably inept student, or an antagonistic, alienated, or resistive student, we are caught up in the cultural process" (p. 365).

The cultural debates over hip-hop (e.g., Boyd, 2003; Kilson, 2003) suggest that African American and hip-hop cultures are neither identical nor completely separate entities. Although hip-hop in many ways is a subset of Black culture—exhibiting many characteristics of African American culture, maintaining some of the ideological underpinnings of the civil rights and Black power movements, and having been assembled by marginalized African American and Latino youth—participation and cultural membership in hip-hop in the 21st century is not limited to individuals who are phenotypically Black (Kitwana, 2006). African American and hip-hop cultures satisfy Lewis's (2002) description of simultaneously being "consonant, disjunctive, overlapping, [and] contentious" (p. 15), and consequently necessitate conjoined inquiry in the context of learning and achievement for African American students in higher education.

INFLUENCES OF AFRICAN AMERICAN CULTURE ON STUDENT LEARNING

It is important to make a clear distinction between African American culture in terms of ethnicity and race. Hilliard (2001) argues that *ethnicity* is a more appropriate term than *race* when discussing culture and education. According to Hilliard, ethnicity includes facets such as history, language, communal beliefs, values, and rituals.

Individuals are born into an ethnic culture and make choices and/or are socialized throughout their lives in manners that affect degrees of ethnic affiliation. As Lee (2001) notes, "people who are classified as black in western culture sometimes choose to cross ethnic identity borders, and to live—in terms of language, beliefs, and social practices—as members of other ethnic groups than that to which they were born" (p. 90). Likewise, an individual of Euro-American ancestry who adopts linguistic and kinesthetic character-istics of Black culture makes a similar choice. The borders between ethnicities are more permeable than they are fixed, as is suggested by the fluidity en-demic to cultural classifications (Lewis, 2002). Hilliard (2001) argues that race, although related to ethnicity, is problematic because it is a biologically and phenotypically oriented construct infused with political and social ide-ology. Race obfuscates more than it clarifies and thus is a less useful con-struct with which to discuss African American culture, learning, and achievement.

It must be noted, too, that African American culture, like all cultures, is not monolithic. All cultures contain degrees of hybridism, and discussions of cultures and their implications necessarily operate upon idealizations of those cultures—heuristic cultural categories—that must adequately account for other, conflated cultural influences (e.g., socioeconomic class). This point is emblematic of the flexibility and variability of culture suggested by McCarthy (1998) at the start of this chapter.

Gay (2000) offers a model that accounts for cultural influences upon education and behavioral expressions to clarify the conflated influences of ethnicity and other cultural influences (see Figure 2.1). She argues that mem-bers of ethnic groups share some common cultural characteristics that are expressed through behaviors such as thinking, reading, speaking, writing, learning, and so forth. Groups of African American students with high eth-nic identities, for example, have been observed to be field-dependent and high-context learners (e.g., Ibarra, 2001; Irvine, 1990), as will be discussed below. Although not all members of an ethnic group will demonstrate these cultural characteristics to the same levels, there exists a set of model characteristics that can be found in given samples of an ethnic population. The variability of these expressions depends upon one's degree of ethnic identification and the influence of other mitigating variables (i.e., other cultural influences). In-fluential mitigating variables include gender, age, socioeconomic class, edu-cational background and level of attainment, geographical location, and so on. Gay's (2000) model gives primacy to ethnicity over other cultural ele-ments, such as religion, as influential to learning and achievement and yet maintains the tenet that African American culture, like other cultures, is not monolithic in identification and expression.

Although there is general consensus among culturally responsive peda-gogues that both ethnic culture and socioeconomic class are powerful influ-ences upon student learning and achievement, the primacy that Gay's (2000) model gives to ethnic affiliation is supported by other researchers. Hale-Benson (1986) suggests that for middle- and lower-class students, ethnicity is a greater influence upon cognitive achievement than is social class. Thernstrom and Thernstrom's (2004) study of the influence of class and ethnicity supports this conclusion. Bennett (2006) and Hernandez (2000)

Figure 2.1. Interaction of Ethnic Culture, Mitigating Variables, and Expressive Behaviors

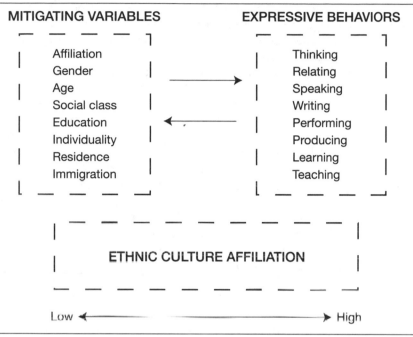

MITIGATING VARIABLES

- Affiliation
- Gender
- Age
- Social class
- Education
- Individuality
- Residence
- Immigration

EXPRESSIVE BEHAVIORS

- Thinking
- Relating
- Speaking
- Writing
- Performing
- Producing
- Learning
- Teaching

ETHNIC CULTURE AFFILIATION

Low ◄─────────────────► High

Source: Adapted from Gay, 2000, p. 11.

draw similar conclusions, linking ethnic culture and learning-style preferences. Although some other studies (e.g., Gadzella, Masten, & Huang, 1999) suggest no significant difference between ethnicity and learning-style preference, uncontrolled mitigating variables such as the ones recognized by Gay (2000) could explain the difference in results.

The idea that there are preferences, orientations, and characteristics endemic to ethnicity that implicate African American learning and achievement is based upon the notion that such characteristics have been transmitted within African American communities since the African Diaspora. Hale-Benson (1986) and others synthesize this body of literature to identify West Africa as the source of model characteristics for most African Americans. Consistent with the framework provided by Gay (2000), Hale-Benson acknowledges that less majority culture contact and lower socioeconomic status (i.e., fewer mitigating variables, fewer opportunities for acculturation) increase the likelihood that West African–derived values, orientations, and characteristics are transmitted to subsequent generations of African Americans.

Bennett (2006) describes five aspects of ethnicity that implicate learning environments: verbal communication, nonverbal communication, orientation modes, social values, and intellectual modes. These aspects are evident among the abiding cultural characteristics that numerous researchers (e.g., Boykin, 1985; Karenga, 2003; Ladner, 2000) have framed among African Americans (see Figure 2.2).

These overlapping characteristics fit into the larger description of a holistic African (American) worldview. Paris (1995) suggests that an African American worldview is not simply an extension of an African worldview but rather a preservation and adaptation of that worldview through an amalgamation with U.S. elements. Paris highlights that the central feature of an African worldview is a cosmological whole where unity exists among all realms, such as humanity, spirit, nature, and history. "The African universe is conceived as a unified spiritual totality . . . [where] all being is organically interrelated and interdependent" (Richards, 1989, p. 210).

It is important to reiterate that these West African–derived characteristics (as well as their implications in learning environments, discussed next) are presented as traits of modal personality. Nowhere do the researchers cited above posit that these traits are present among all African Americans at all times. Numerous mitigating variables as well as levels of majority (i.e., non-Black) culture contact and socialization implicate the manifestation of these characteristics (Bennett, 2006). In light of this, it may be helpful to consider such facets of identity as performed (McCarthy, 1998). Such a conceptualization of (ethnic) identity highlights that these and other facets are, indeed, never fixed. In addition, it is certainly the case that the behaviors described above would be more easily evoked among some contexts and suppressed

Figure 2.2. Abiding African American Cultural Characteristics

Boykin (1985)	Karenga (2003)	Ladner (2000)
Spirituality	Unity	Identity
Harmony	Self-determination	Faith in god
Movement	Collectivity	Respect
Verve	Cooperation	Honesty
Affect	Purpose	Responsibility
Communalism	Creativity	Self-reliance
Expressive individualism	Faith	Hard work
Oral tradition		Resourcefulness
Social time perspective		Education
		Courage
		Integrity

among others. This reiteration does not nullify the relevance of the research cited above. Rather, to draw from Gay (2000) once more, "descriptions of culture are approximations of reality—templates, if you will—through which actual behaviors of individuals can be filtered in search of alternative explanations and deeper meanings" (p. 12).

CHARACTERISTICS OF AFRICAN AMERICAN ACCULTURATED LEARNERS

Many of the recognized characteristics of African American learners are clearly related to the cultural characteristics described above. Although controversial (e.g., Frisby, 1993), they have received much attention among culturally responsive educational researchers such as Fordham and Ogbu (1986), Hilliard (1998), and Hale-Benson (1986). While an in-depth account of these characteristics and the intricate interplay of mitigating variables are beyond the scope of this section, it is worthwhile to review some of the more substantial characteristics as indicated by the existing literature.

Perry, Steele, and Hilliard (2004) posit that African American students are more successful in learning environments characterized by harmony, cooperation, affect, socialization, and community. The communal maxim "lift as we climb" that often serves as a mantra in African American learning environments (e.g., historically Black colleges and universities) implies many of these characteristics (Gallien & Peterson, 2004). African American learners are inclined to engage in learning in a holistic manner, compared to the compartmentalized and analytical manner of many Euro-American students and institutions (Hale-Benson, 1986). Similar to a relational style of learning (Hale-Benson, 1986), holistically inclined learners attend best when material is relevant to their own experiences and embedded in context. Additionally, such students are oriented toward learning that emphasizes divergent and inductive thinking (Irvine, 1990).

Field Characteristics

Field Theory (Witkin, Moore, Goodenough, & Cox, 1977) and its notion of field-independent and field-dependent (i.e., field-sensitive) cognitive styles have been used to describe two different learning orientations, and further clarifies some of the above characteristics. Many researchers, such as Ibarra (2001) and Shade (1982), suggest that African American students demonstrate characteristics of field-dependency and approach learning from a global perspective that does not compartmentalize or separate interrelated components of learning for the sake of analysis. Asa Hilliard, as cited in Hale-Benson (1986), makes this distinction clear:

> Afro-American people tend to respond to things in terms of the whole picture instead of its parts. The Euro-American tends to believe that anything can be divided and subdivided into pieces and that these pieces add up to a whole. (p. 42)

Learners demonstrating field-dependence often have highly developed social skills and are sensitive to the social elements of the learning environment. They often benefit from a dialogical learning environment and educators who forge supportive, caring relationships with students beyond the classroom context (Delpit, 1996). Field-dependent learners also benefit from examples and contextual and cooperative learning environments that relate learning materials to students' personal experiences rather than casting them in an abstract, decontextualized manner (Gay, 2000; Ibarra, 2001).

Such characteristics contrast with those of field-independent learners who demonstrate success in individualistic, competitive, and more decontextualized learning environments (Ibarra, 2001). Field-independent learners approach learning more as an independent activity rather than a social or communal activity. Consequently, they may be inattentive to relational and affective aspects of the learning environment, and their strength often lies in abstraction (Bennett, 2006). It is important to note that such characteristics, particularly in terms of affective influence, do not deemphasize the importance of cognition, but instead highlight that such learners employ the affective domain as well as the cognitive domain during the learning process (Pasteur & Toldson, 1982).

Communicative Characteristics

Communication patterns and inclinations among African American learners also implicate the manners in which they approach learning. Murrell (2002) emphasizes this perspective by noting that "the uses of language and forms of discourse are critical determinants of the degree to which children can participate in the social-interactional dynamics of learning" (p. 129).

Bennett (2006) highlights that many African American students are socialized to thrive in communicative environments where there is an active and improvisational interchange between speaker and audience instead of one in which there exists a prescribed (or implied) rigid structure of communication. Peterson (2004) describes these modes as interactive and participatory, or what is often referred to as call-and-response. Consistent with the characteristics identified by Perry, Steele, and Hilliard (2004), call-and-response and other such modes of communication reflect oneness, interdependence, and participation (Peterson, 2004).

Many researchers (e.g., Smitherman, 1986) have discussed the grammatical and syntactical linguistic differences that some African American students bring into learning environments, but nonverbal means of communication are also relevant. Peterson (2004) highlights that many nonverbal communicative cues, such as tone, facial expression, eye contact, and body posture, are central aspects of classroom communication, along with the "literal" meanings of the spoken word. That is, many African American students are sensitized to derive and communicate meaning from these nonverbal modes of communication (i.e., the context of communication) along with the spoken word.

High- and Low-Context Learning

Related to these communicative characteristics are orientations toward high-context and low-context learning environments. According to Ibarra (2001), low-context cultures make little use of nonverbal signals, value direct communication with explicit verbal messages, and depersonalize disagreements. High-context cultures rely extensively on nonverbal signals; see communication as an art form in which indirect, implicit, and informal verbal messages are valued; and personalize disagreements (see Figure 2.3). Though

Figure 2.3. Comparisons Between Low-Context and High-Context Cultures

	Low-context	High-context
INTERACTION	Low use of nonverbal signals; direct communication; messages are explicit; disagreement is depersonalized	High use of nonverbal signals; indirect communication; messages are used to engage with others; disagreement is personalized
ASSOCIATION	Personal commitment to people is relatively low; task orientation; success means getting recognized	Personal commitment to people is high; getting things done depends on personal relationships and group process; success means being unobtrusive
TEMPORALITY	Work is done on a schedule; speed and efficiency are valued; promptness is valued; time is a commodity	Needs of people may interfere with schedules; accuracy and completion are more important than speed; time is a process
LEARNING	Analytical thinking is important; learning is oriented to the individual; scientific, theoretical, and philosophical thinking is emphasized; academic style is teacher-oriented	Comprehensive thinking is important; learning is group-oriented; practical thinking is valued; academic style is student-oriented

Source: Adapted from Ibarra, 2001, p. 69–76.

socialization into mainstream and majority culture affects students' orientations toward high-context or low-context learning environments, researchers such as Hall and Hall (1990) and Kochman (1983) suggest that minority cultures, including that of African Americans, tend to be high-context.

INFLUENCES OF HIP-HOP CULTURE ON STUDENT LEARNING

In addition to the more ethnically oriented cultural influences and characteristics described above, another burgeoning cultural influence upon African American learning and achievement is contemporary hip-hop culture. Hip-hop emerged in the New York City boroughs as an alternative source of identity formation and social status for youth in the late 1970s, a time when economic and social disparity left the traditional support pillars of the church, school, and neighborhood—literally and figuratively—crumbling (Rose, 1994).

Initially consisting of four interrelated artistic elements of rapping (i.e., emceeing), deejaying, breakdancing (i.e., bboying/bgirling), and writing graffiti, hip-hop has expanded geographically and culturally to include various urban aesthetics, styles, fashions, linguistic characteristics, and postures. More than just a set of cultural identifiers, hip-hop in different contexts throughout the world is utilized as a tool for education, empowerment, and social activism (e.g., Bynoe, 2004; Ginwright, 2004).

The magnitude of hip-hop's cultural influence upon youth and young adults is much greater than the literal meanings of commercial, mainstream rap music: "[H]ip-hop offers a generational worldview that encompasses the shoes you choose to whether you're inclined to vote or not to how you understand the issue of race" (Wang, 2005, p. 1). Hip-hop is not without controversy among African American intellectual and social leaders, having been described as an empowering and prophetic counter-narrative movement for young African Americans by some (e.g., West, 2005) and labeled as nihilistic and self-destructive by others (e.g., Kilson, 2003; McWhorter, 2003).

Hip-hop does not necessarily replace or negate the cultural influences discussed above; young African Americans who actively participate in and consume cultural facets of hip-hop may demonstrate many of the orientations and styles described above. However, hip-hop now functions as a primary source of stabilization and identity formation for many African American youth and young adults in this post–civil rights era. Dimitriadis (2001) and Perry (2004) suggest that educators must consider it as a burgeoning influence upon learning and achievement that is "consonant, disjunctive, overlapping, [and] contentious" (Lewis, 2002, p. 15) to the more traditional influences and characteristics of African American learners already described.

Social commentators such as Kitwana (2003) argue that African Americans born between the years of 1965 and 1984 (i.e., the hip-hop generation) were surrounded by unique sociopolitical forces in the post–civil rights era according to which they have fashioned a particular set of values, beliefs, and attitudes—all of which students bring with them into learning environments.

Kitwana (2003) cites six major phenomena—many of which continue today—that have significantly contributed to the values, beliefs, and attitudes of the African Americans who now populate high school classrooms and college campuses: (a) popular culture and rap music, (b) globalization, (c) persisting segregation in the midst of so-called democracy and inclusion in America, (d) public policy regarding criminal justice and the policing of youth, (e) media representations of young Blacks, and (f) "the overall shift in the quality of life for young Blacks during the 1980s and 1990s" (pp. 9–20). Lang (2000), Ginwright (2004), and Chang (2005) support the identification of these phenomena by pinpointing factors such as economic isolation, poverty, and the demonization of young Blacks and Latinos as influential sociopolitical forces.

Researchers such as Kitwana (2003) suggest that these sociopolitical phenomena have given the hip-hop generation a distinct view of family, relationships, careers, racial identity, race relations, and politics that differs in part from previous generations. Both Lang (2000) and Kitwana (2003) note that members of the hip-hop generation are more likely to be career-oriented than previous generations of African Americans who, essentially, won the legal rights for the following generation of African Americans to pursue economic prosperity and be career-oriented (instead of rights-oriented). Kitwana notes:

> For many [young African Americans], the American Dream means not just living comfortably but becoming an overnight millionaire while still young. Many of us can't imagine waiting until we are forty, or even thirty-five, for that matter. This desire for wealth is accompanied by a sense of entitlement. That a handful of widely celebrated hip-hop generationers [e.g., professional athletes, entertainers] have achieved the dream makes the possibility real, despite the odds. . . . And this desire to achieve not simply financial security but millionaire status is the driving force of our generation's work ethic. (p. 46)

Lang (2000) echoes these sentiments by highlighting that education is often perceived as a route to a high-salary job among some African American college and university students. He notes that African American campus organizations, such as the Black Student Union, that were originally created for political purposes, in many ways now function as "social cliques and vehicles of professional mobility—something to place on one's resume when applying for a white-collar job" (p. 129). Such academic motivation is not necessarily materialistic or nihilistic in the estimation of students. In a market-driven economy and society, some members of the hip-hop generation equate financial mobility with social equality.

This observed sentiment among young African Americans, however, does not necessarily indicate that the purposes of education and learning revolve only around the moniker of money, power, and respect and are devoid of any social or political motivation in the estimation of hip-hoppers. Lang (2000) notes the perceived connection between hip-hop and politics concisely:

> A number of younger activists have tended to view cultural expression as resistance in and of itself, ignoring the importance of organized, state-directed activity around material conditions. Thus, one hears often references to hip-hop being a social movement in the same vein as Civil Rights and Black Power. Yet hip-hop, like all forms of art and culture, has no fixed political character. (p. 127)

Lang's (2000) observation is correct, since hip-hop lacks some of the clear components of a social movement (e.g., grievance, common goals, communication network, and so forth) compared to previous social movements such as the civil rights movement. However, the systematic drafting of a five-point National Hip Hop Political Agenda (NHHPA) by delegates at the National Hip Hop Political Convention prior to the 2004 presidential election and the recent 2006 convention held in Chicago certainly gives hip-hop and its young African Americans more of a fixed political character than they had in the past.

One of the most notable components of the NHHPA in terms of learning and achievement is its stance on education (National Hip Hop Political Convention, 2004). Relevant positions of the education portion of this agenda include:

- *Primary and Secondary Education*: Equal funding and parity spending in all pubic school districts—urban, suburban, and rural; local control of school districts and local supervision/audit of spending of monies.
- *Curriculum*: Implementation of a curriculum that is socially practical, culturally relevant, comprehensive, developmental, and specific in nature, such as vocational training, based upon engaging students with a variety of learning styles, interests, and skills.
- *Literacy*: Funding and legislation to develop programs geared toward the eradication of illiteracy of all people, including those that have English as a second language.
- *Higher Education*: Free education at all state and federally owned and operated postsecondary institutions, and the direct recruitment and retention of students of color; opposition to all attacks on affirma-

tive action programs at all levels of higher education; demand of roll-back of tuition hikes and the immediate full restoration of all state and federal budget cuts since the beginning of the War on Terror.

Although the above views cannot necessarily be assumed to hold true for all members of the hip-hop generation, it is noteworthy that such stances were drafted and amended by delegates through a systematic process and are now documented. This was a major step toward making coherent and solidifying the collective political views that many young African Americans take with them into learning environments. Such activities as these, which give the hip-hop generation a clearer, more cohesive political identity, have continued in the years following the 2004 presidential election.

In addition to the burgeoning political identity of the hip-hop genera-tion, conventions of race and ethnicity are emerging that begin to challenge those of previous generations:

> This new racial politics is coming into its own with a younger generation social-ized around the dream of an inclusive America. It's enhanced by a youth popu-lar culture, hip-hop, which prides itself on mass cross-cultural appeal, and it insists that the old racial politics is too limited for engaging or defining America today. The old definitions no longer universally apply. (Kitwana, 2006, p. 137)

The old racial politics and definitions to which Kitwana (2006) refers are rigid constructions of race, ethnicity, and cultural ownership—the kind from which many accusations of cultural thievery are posited (e.g., Elvis and rock-and-roll) Hip-Hop is frequently perceived as a participatory culture, one that operates upon notions of civic (rather than primordial) membership and chal-lenges the older notion that Black culture is only available to individuals who are phenotypically Black (Harrison, 2003; Kitwana, 2006). Polar opinions exist on this often-volatile issue such as, on one end, the view that hip-hop tran-scends race (e.g., Temple of Hip Hop) and, on the other end, that hip-hop is a form of expression revolving solely around the experiences of African Ameri-cans (Bynoe, 2002). However, the more common sentiment among hip-hoppers seems to be that there is room for multiple races and ethnicities within the Black cultural domain of hip-hop. One could say that race and ethnicity have never been as socially constructed as they are in hip-hop.

Hip-hop, now integrated into the fabric of American culture, is both a cause and effect of these shifting and more open constructions of ethnicity among young adults. Also not to be overlooked as influences are the prolif-eration of African American images and culture in American media, the in-stitutionalization of civil rights culture, and a declining sense of White privilege among Generation Xers (Kitwana, 2006). These cultural factors, along with hip-hop, challenge the degree to which the conventions of race and ethnicity from previous generations have been adopted by students who presently (and will continue to) populate college campuses.

CHARACTERISTICS OF HIP-HOP ACCULTURATED LEARNERS

As noted above, the exact manners in which hip-hop culture and traditional African American culture conflate to implicate learning and achievement for African American college students are speculative. The role of hip-hop culture as an animating force in the lives of young African Americans is not in question. However, exactly how hip-hop plays out in learning environments (e.g., orientations, motivations, and learning-style preferences) has not yet received the same attention that the orientations, motivations, and learning-style preferences of previous generations of African Americans have. This section suggests some tentative ways in which hip-hop may influence learning, achievement, and the environment in which they take place for African Americans in formal educational settings, such as higher education.

The tendency for many hip-hop generationers to be career-oriented suggests that students may benefit from learning and achievement framed in terms of professional aspirations. This does not mean that African American students are not intrinsically motivated or do not enjoy learning for learning's sake (Cokley, 2003). However, extrinsic motivation is consistent with characteristics of field-dependent learners (as discussed earlier) who tend to be externally motivated. The liberally applied political characterization of cultural participation and education for many hip-hoppers is also notable. The view of culture and education as "political" held by members of the hip-hop generation on college campuses necessitates further exploration.

Many scholars and cultural observers have noted an apparent generational divide among the civil rights generation and the hip-hop generation that is comparable to the generational divide among many White Americans during the Vietnam War (Kitwana, 2003). Some scholars have gone as far as to argue that the ideology and images of the civil rights generation, such as the speeches of Dr. Martin Luther King Jr. and acts of civil disobedience by other civil rights leaders, have little influence on the current generation of young African Americans compared to the empowering messages of hip-hop.

Kelley (2004) criticizes civil rights leadership (e.g., Al Sharpton, Jesse Jackson, and Louis Farrakhan) as suffering from a messiah complex and having demanded only moderate and nonthreatening societal changes. Although such accusations may be startling to some, the demands of the NHHPA (e.g., free public education from kindergarten through doctorate, eradication of all mandatory minimum sentences, and reparations for indigenous peoples) are anything but moderate. Though commonalities exist among the undergirding ideals of civil rights and hip-hop (Alridge, 2005), these similarities are often overlooked in favor of the apparent contrasts between these two generations and their ideals and manifestations.

Perceived and real differences among these two generations have possible implications upon African American learning and achievement. Educational environments in which solidarity has most commonly characterized relations among older and younger generations of African Americans may be challenged. Instead of existing as the natural learning climate, deliberate effort might be necessary to instill common ground among different generations in light of the declining sense of relevance toward (older) cultural institutions (e.g., civil rights), as has been clearly played out in popular culture through films such as *Barbershop* (2002) and critics such as Todd Boyd.

The apparent shifts from conventions of race and ethnicity among the hip-hop generation also have possible effects on learning environments. Most pointedly, the notion that members of the hip-hop generation do not consider race and ethnicity in such fixed manners as previous generations did suggests that young African Americans (among other groups of students) enter college campuses with assumptions about race and ethnicity that differ from those of the people who are attempting to educate them. Clearly, cross-generational and intercultural dialogue is necessary to understand how collective (and individual) views of these constructs are formed, and how students and educators can build conceptual bridges between these differences.

CONCLUSION

African American Culture

Culturally responsive educators agree that culture, the stabilizing systems of constructed meanings that students bring with them into educational environments, implicates learning, achievement, and everything that takes place in the name of education (Gay, 2000; Hale-Benson, 1986; Ibarra, 2001). Educational research into the learning-style preferences, orientations, and characteristics of African American learners suggests that students with strong ethnic identities (and lower degrees of majority culture contact) are often successful in learning environments and pedagogical styles that match their preferences and orientations. As suggested in the first half of this chapter, the characteristics of African American learners with high ethnic identities have received a moderate amount of scholarly attention. The African American cultural orientation toward learning for many of these students includes the following:

- *Holistic*: An environment characterized by harmony, cooperation, affect, socialization, community; relational and creative learning relevant to one's own experiences.

- *Field-dependent*: Learning from a global perspective; emphasizes the social, dialogical aspect of learning; caring relationships not limited to the classroom context.
- *High-context*: Reliance on nonverbal, indirect, implicit, and informal communication; high personal, relational commitment; social time orientation; importance of comprehensive thinking.

Hip-Hop Culture

One of the more pressing issues that challenges the continuing relevance of the existing literature is the role of hip-hop as a cultural influence upon current African American students and, subsequently, upon learning and achievement. That is, how do the emerging values and beliefs about economic mobility, race, politics, social justice, and other issues collectively espoused within the stabilizing set of constructed meanings called hip-hop influence learning and achievement? Below is a list of some of the themes that are emerging in response to this question:

- Students are extrinsically motivated by professional and economic aspirations.
- Students operate upon a construction of race and ethnicity that differs from that of previous generations.
- Social equality takes on new meanings to younger generations of African Americans influenced by hip-hop.
- Different generational perspectives exist regarding the value of traditional African American culture.

Closing the achievement gap in higher education entails considering both African American and hip-hop cultural influences upon Black college students. Regardless of the materialistic, nihilistic, or misogynistic overtones of much of commercialized hip-hop music, educators on college campuses must seek to understand the meanings that students derive from and ascribe to hip-hop in order to remain culturally relevant.

DISCUSSION TOPICS

1. Consider the "traditional" characteristics of African American learners discussed in the first half of this chapter. To what degree do you see these characteristics being manifested among African Americans students today?
2. What specific challenges do majority-White institutional environments

pose to African American learners who consistently exhibit the learning preferences described in the first half of this chapter?

3. What ideological similarities and differences appear to exist among members of the hip-hop and civil rights generations? In what ways is hip-hop an extension of the civil rights movement?
4. How might educators explore the ways in which African American students' identification with and participation in hip-hop implicate learning, achievement, and the educational environment?

REFERENCES

Alridge, D. P. (2005). From civil rights to hip-hop: Toward a nexus of ideas. *Journal of African American History*, 90(2), 226–252.

Baker, H. A., Jr. (1995). *Black studies, rap, and the academy* (New Ed.). Chicago: University of Chicago Press.

Bennett, C. I. (2006). *Comprehensive multicultural education: Theory and practice* (6th ed.). Boston: Allyn & Bacon.

Boyd, T. (2003). *The new H.N.I.C.: The death of civil rights and the reign of hip-hop*. New York: New York University Press.

Boykin, A. W. (1985). The triple quandary and the schooling of Afro-American children. In E. Neisser (Ed.), *The school achievement of minority children: New perspectives* (pp. 57–92). Hillsdale, NJ: Erlbaum.

Bynoe, Y. (2002). Getting real about global hip-hop. *Georgetown Journal of International Affairs*, 3(1), 77–84.

Bynoe, Y. (2004). *Stand and deliver: Political activism, leadership, and hip hop culture*. Brooklyn, NY: Soft Skull Press.

Chang, J. (2005). *Can't stop won't stop: A history of the hip hop generation*. New York: St. Martin's Press.

Cokley, K. O. (2003). What do we know about the motivation of African American students? Challenging the "anti-intellectual" myth. *Harvard Educational Review*, 73(4), 524–558.

Delpit, L. (1996). *Other people's children: Cultural conflict in the classroom*. New York: New Press.

Dimitriadis, G. (2001). *Performing identity/performing culture: Hip hop as text, pedagogy, and lived practice* (Intersections in communications and culture, volume 1). New York: Peter Lang Publishing.

Fordham, S., & Ogbu, J. U. (1986). Black students' school success: Coping with the "burden of acting white." *The Urban Review*, 8(3), 176–206.

Frisby, C. L. (1993). One giant step backward: Myths of black cultural learning styles. *School Psychology Review*, 22(3), 535–557.

Gadzella, B. M., Masten, W. G., & Huang, J. (1999). Differences between African American and Caucasian students on critical thinking and learning style. *College Student Journal*, 33(4), 538–542.

Gallien, L. B., Jr., & Peterson, M. S. (2004). *Instructing and mentoring the African*

American college student: Strategies for success in higher education. Boston: Allyn & Bacon.

Gay, G. (2000). *Culturally responsive teaching: Theory, research, and practice*. New York: Teachers College Press.

Ginwright, S. A. (2004). *Black in school: Afrocentric reform, urban youth, and the promise of hip-hop culture*. New York: Teachers College Press.

Hale-Benson, J. E. (1986). *Black children: Their roots, culture, and learning styles* (Rev. ed.). Baltimore: The Johns Hopkins University Press.

Hall, E. T., & Hall, M. R. (1990). *Understanding cultural differences*. New York: Intercultural Press.

Harrison, A. K. (2003). "Every emcee's a fan, every fan's an emcee": Authenticity, identity and power within Bay Area underground hip-hop. Unpublished doctoral dissertation, Syracuse University, Syracuse, NY. (Digital Dissertations Document No. AAT 3113240).

Hernandez, H. (2000). *Multicultural education: A teacher's guide to linking context, process, and content* (2nd ed.). Englewood Cliffs, NJ: Prentice Hall.

Hilliard, A. G., III. (1998). *SBA: The reawakening of the African mind* (Rev. ed.). Gainesville, FL: Makare Publishing.

Hilliard, A. G., III. (2001). "Race," identity, hegemony, and education: What do we need to know? In W. H. Watkins, J. H. Lewis, & V. Chou (Eds.), *Race and education: The role of history and society in educating African American students* (pp. 7–33). Boston: Allyn & Bacon.

Ibarra, R. A. (2001). *Beyond affirmative action: Reframing the context of higher education*. Madison, WI: University of Wisconsin Press.

Irvine, J. J. (1990). *Black students and school failure: Policies, practices, and prescriptions (Contributions in Afro-American and African studies)*. Westport, CT: Greenwood Press.

Karenga, M. (2003). *Kawaida theory: An African communitarian philosophy*. Los Angeles: University of Sankore Press.

Kelley, N. (2004). *The head Negro in charge syndrome: The dead end of Black politics*. New York: Nation Books.

Kilson, M. (2003, July 17). The pretense of hip-hop black leadership. *The Black Commentator, 50*. Retrieved November 29, 2006, from http://www.blackcommentator .com /50/50_ kilson.html

Kitwana, B. (2003). *The hip-hop generation: Young Blacks and the crisis of African American culture* (Reprint ed.). New York: Basic Civitas Books.

Kitwana, B. (2006). *Why white kids love hip-hop: Wankstas, wiggers, wannabes, and the new reality of race in America* (Reprint ed.). New York: Perseus Books Group.

Kochman, T. (1983). *Black and white styles in conflict* (Reprint ed.). Chicago: University of Chicago Press.

Ladner, J. A. (2000). *The ties that bind: Timeless values for African American families*. New York: Wiley.

Ladson-Billings, G. (2001). The power of pedagogy: Does teaching matter? In W. H. Watkins, J. H. Lewis, & V. Chou (Eds.), *Race and education: The role of history and society in educating African American students* (pp. 73–88). Boston: Allyn & Bacon.

Lang, C. (2000). The new global and urban order: Legacies for the "Hip-Hop Generation." *Race & Society, 3,* 111–142.

Lee, C. D. (2001). Comment: Unpacking culture, teaching, and learning: A response to "the power of pedagogy." In W. H. Watkins, J. H. Lewis, & V. Chou (Eds.), *Race and education: The role of history and society in educating African American students* (pp. 80–99). Boston: Allyn & Bacon.

Lewis, J. (2002). Defining culture. In J. Lewis (Ed.), *Cultural studies: The basics* (pp. 3–38). Thousand Oaks, CA: Sage.

McCarthy, C. (1998). *The uses of culture: Education and the limits of ethnic affiliation.* New York: Routledge.

McWhorter, J. H. (2003, Summer). How hip-hop holds Blacks back. *City Journal.* Retrieved November 29, 2006, from http://www.city-journal.org/html/13_3_how_hip_hop.html

Murrell, P. C. (2002). *African-centered pedagogy: Developing schools of achievement for African American children.* Albany, NY: State University of New York.

National hip hop political convention. (2004). *National hip hop political convention agenda.* Retrieved November 29, 2006, from http://www.Hiphopconvention.org/issues/agenda.cfm

Paris, P. J. (1995). *The spirituality of African peoples: The search for a common moral discourse.* Minneapolis: Augsburg Fortress Publishers.

Pasteur, A. B., & Toldson, I. L. (1982). *Roots of soul: The psychology of black expressiveness.* New York: Doubleday.

Perry, I. (2004). *Prophets of the hood: Politics and poetics in hip-hop.* Durham, NC: Duke University Press.

Perry, T., Steele, C. M., & Hilliard, A. G., III. (2004). *Young, gifted, and Black: Promoting high achievement among African-American students.* Boston: Beacon Press.

Peterson, M. S. (2004). Strategies for effective oral communication. In L. B. Gallien Jr. & M. S. Peterson (Eds.), *Instructing and mentoring the African American college student: Strategies for success in higher education* (pp. 69–83). Boston: Allyn & Bacon.

Richards, D. (1989). The implications of African-American spirituality. In M. K. Asante & K. Asante-Welsh (Eds.), *African culture: The rhythms of unity* (pp. 207–231). Trenton, NJ: Africa World Press.

Rose, T. (1994). *Black noise: Rap music and black culture in contemporary America.* Hanover, CT: Wesleyan University Press.

Shade, B. (1982). Afro-American cognitive style: A variable in school success. *The Review of Educational Research, 52*(2), 219–244.

Smitherman, G. (1986). *Talkin and testifyin: The language of Black America* (Reprint ed.). Detroit: Wayne State University Press.

Spindler, G., & Spindler, L. (2000). The process of culture and person: Cultural therapy and culturally diverse schools. In G. Spindler (Ed.), *Fifty years of anthropology and education 1950–2000: A Spindler anthology* (pp. 365–388). Mahwah, NJ: LEA.

Thernstrom, A., & Thernstrom, S. (2004). *No excuses: Closing the racial gap in learning* (Reprint ed.). New York: Simon & Schuster.

Wang, O. (2005). *Can't stop won't stop Q + A: An interview of Jeff Chang*. Retrieved November 29, 2006, from http://www.cantstopwontstop.com/qa.cfm

West, C. (2005). *Democracy matters: Winning the fight against imperialism* (Reprint ed.). New York: Penguin Books.

Witkin, H., Moore, C., Goodenough, D., & Cox P. (1977). Field-dependent and field-independent cognitive styles and their educational implications. *The Review of Educational Research, 47*(1), 1–64.

THREE

School Cultural Influences

Louis B. Gallien Jr.

PURPOSE

The purpose of this chapter is to address how school culture, interacting with African American culture and hip-hop subculture, can influence student achievement. Additionally, school culture and African American achievement at predominantly White institutions (PWIs) and historically Black colleges and universities (HBCUs) are contrasted. The chapter concludes with a discussion of cultural responsiveness and pedagogies at a fully integrated university.

BACKGROUND

American higher educational institutions in this relatively new millennium face some of their toughest challenges from a growing multicultural base. As students, professors, and staff populations increase from other countries, ethnicities, and races, the learning environments in collegiate institutions will continue to be challenged to engineer pedagogically relevant learning environments with research-based teaching strategies that are culturally responsive to the minority students who will soon constitute a majority on many college and university campuses (Howell & Tuitt, 2003).

For instance, language barriers continue to be a highly politicized source of conflict and polarization between ethnocentric forces that view English as the "coinage of the realm" and internationalists who view second- and third-language acquisition and proficiency as a signpost to a global future (Villanueva, 1993). These issues are not completely new to higher education in the United States. Complaints against foreign professors and teaching assistants have been common since U.S. graduate schools first began to hire both advanced foreign graduate students and professors to fill positions that require them to teach large introductory undergraduate courses. It was not uncommon from the late 1960s to the present to hear complaints from American students regarding the English-language deficiencies of these instructors, who subsequently suffered from low course evaluations as a result of their "bad English." Although few people will argue with the necessity to teach primarily in one language, the level of proficiency, degree of accent, and annunciation will continue to be debated in the Academy.

Language acquisition and proficiency is just one harbinger of the need to examine the impact of changing cultures on American campuses. One of the more ignored topics is the paucity of pedagogically responsive programs on U.S. campuses. While we often read in journals such as the *Chronicle of Higher Education* and *Change* about innovative programs designed to meet the needs of diverse student populations, we rarely encounter studies that examine in much detail the school climates and culturally responsive academic programs in our higher educational institutions.

MULTICULTURAL CAMPUSES

A multicultural campus represents the intersection of multiple cultures and ethnicities. These cultures consist of the racial and ethnic backgrounds of all members of the campus community (i.e., faculty, staff, and students), popular subcultures (e.g., hip-hop), and the unique culture and saga of the school itself.

Racial and Ethnic Culture

There are many universities and colleges in the United States that form portraitures of the insipid multiculturalism of the 21st century. Older, elite, private liberal arts institutions such as Wellesley and Oberlin are close to becoming majority minority campuses. Larger state institutions like the University of California and other state universities in populous states are also becoming more diverse and are mirroring the diverse populations of their states (USNews.com, 2006). As a result, more college campuses are emblematic of our country's growing multicultural population. These campuses have been wrestling with their deepest cultural differences, as noted by many authors over the last few decades, but fewer scholars really delve into how the learning environments of such campuses are impacted (Gallien & Peterson, 2004).

The average college professor is a White male in his late forties. Most professors are products of American graduate schools that have largely ignored the study of adult teaching and learning. As a result, the professional literature (e.g., Tompkins, 1997) notes that most professors tend to teach the way they were taught—in a lecture-oriented fashion with objective-type assessment measures, little group work (except in large introductory sections), and few student-centered teaching environments. These environments may satisfy upper-middle-class White students who are acculturated to such teaching practices, but they are insufficient for a multicultural student base. The question becomes not only one of how we live with our deepest cultural differences, but also how we effectively instruct our new populations of students.

The Clash of Cultures in the Classroom

As mentioned previously, there are many college campuses whose multicultural base is very diverse, but, ironically, instead of these populations being integrated holistically into the school culture, many of these diverse populations live together in so-called campus ghettos—separated by race, ethnicity, and language. Thus, the goal of living and learning in a seamless multicultural milieu has been a major challenge for schools.

This clash is not restricted to living spaces; it also impacts the classroom. As different cultures come together in the classroom, professors must mediate the various learning-style preferences that are present in the culturally diverse classroom. The larger issue is: What teaching methods do professors have at their disposal to meet such a challenge? Some have argued that it is not the job of the professor to mediate differences, but to faithfully transmit the material and their knowledge of the subject in the manner that he or she sees fit. In other words, it is the student's responsibility to understand the material regardless of the way in which the material is presented.

For culturally responsive teaching to be effective, there must be a partnership in the classroom. Students must take ultimate responsibility for their learning, but professors must also accept responsibility for the effectiveness of the delivery of the curriculum to a diverse audience.

School Culture

School culture, according to Lezotte, Hathaway, Miler, Passalacqua, & Brookover (1980), is a broad concept that includes physical attributes of the school, such as heat, light, and noise; psychological attributes, such as satisfaction, morale, trust, openness, and cooperation; and institutional attributes, such as norms, beliefs, and attitudes.

School climate is regarded by many educators as a subelement of school culture that represents the total environmental quality within the school. It consists of those aspects of the school environment that are consciously perceived by members of the school community, such as sense of community, saga, and ethos. Some educators find it useful to think of school climate as the school's personality. However, school climate is subject to change based on shifting school policies and interpersonal experiences of students with their peers, instructors, and school staff.

Notwithstanding conceptual differences, there is general agreement that schools are complex social environments where students share beliefs, fears, values, and norms (Hofman, Hofman, & Guldemond, 2001) and where students' "cognitive and affective functioning is shaped by the characteristics of their schools and schooling" (Hofman et al., 2001, p. 172). Learning in schools takes place in social contexts both inside and outside the classroom. Accordingly, school culture in general and school climate in particular can influence student achievement, attitudes, and persistence.

Two salient nonacademic factors that influence Black students' poorer academic experience and performance at colleges and universities are weaker general institutional support and perceptions of racial climate and race relations. Research suggests that African American students' perception of campus climate is linked to student-faculty and student-student relationships and, thus, has an influence on educational outcomes, such as course grades (Allen & Haniff, 1991).

Perry, Steele, and Hilliard (2004) suggest that Black students perform worse on tests when they believe they are being judged as members of a stereotyped group rather than as individuals. Researchers (e.g., Blascovich, Spencer, Quinn, & Steele, 2001) investigated this stereotype threat and provided empirical evidence to suggest that this phenomenon can be felt as a physiological arousal that often results in substantial decreases in intellectual performance.

One of the more overlooked aspects of choosing a college for many students (and their parents) is an understanding of the particular culture of the institution and whether or not a student's backgrounds and interests fit that particular school culture. Most students choose their college or university based on cost, location, reputation, and job placement (CollegeBoard.com, 2006). Although all of these factors are important, students do not usually ask admissions officials to describe the culture of the institution they are considering attending and then evaluate the culture in terms of a personal "fit."

It is clear that private liberal arts institutions take more stock of this issue than do large public universities that have mandated in-state admissions percentages. Many state institutions reduce admissions decision-making processes to consideration of only grade point average, test scores, rank in class, and the number of Advanced Placement courses taken. And, though affirmative action is barely alive, we do have institutions that guarantee diversity without the notion of a fit between the race and ethnicity of the student and the particular culture of the institution.

Institutional Fit

Student-institution fit can be examined by looking at student, institutional, and environmental variables and specific themes, such as the social integration of students into university life. Perhaps the most influential attempt to explain student-institution fit in higher education and its impact on student persistence is forwarded by Vincent Tinto (1994). His student integration model can be framed by factors that are drawn from experiences prior to college, individual student characteristics, and factors that are culled from experiences at college (see Figure 3.1).

Experiences before college and student characteristics are input variables that cannot be greatly influenced by schools. However, student experiences subsequent to admission, which Tinto refers to as integration variables—e.g., peer and faculty interactions—are affected by school policies and practices. Tinto (1994) suggests that the more central one's membership is to the mainstream of institutional life, the more likely—all else being equal—one is to persist in college. Tinto also argues that insufficient interaction with peers

Figure 3.1. A Conceptualization of Tinto's Student Integration Model

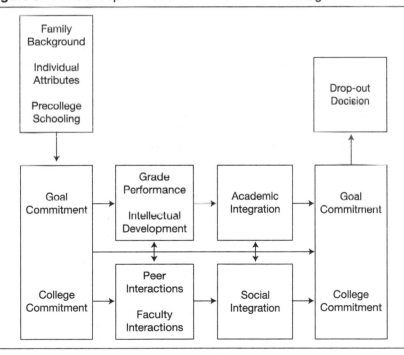

Source: Tinto, 1994.

and faculty and differences with the prevailing value patterns of other students are likely to result in dropouts. In other words, students who feel they do not fit in and have a poor sense of community tend to feel isolated and are at risk of withdrawing. Tinto also maintains that students require academic, social, and personal support from the school. This support, whatever its form, needs to be readily available and connected to other parts of the students' total school experience.

Tinto's model validates the need for schools to assume a proactive role in a student's integration process and underscores the importance of individualization and promoting a positive school climate. Research shows that increasing the national ethnic diversity on a campus, while neglecting to attend to the school climate, can result in difficulties for all students (Hurtado, Milem, Clayton-Pederson, & Allen, 1999).

As we have argued, most college-age students attend public institutions because of lower costs and proximity to their homes; the importance of the campus and classroom climate, together with the culture of the institution, is not among the main reasons students attend their institutions. This can and does cause friction when students encounter a "clash of cultures" along with sharp contrasts between the culture of the institution and their racial and ethnic backgrounds.

For instance, higher education institutions in the Deep South, such as the University of Mississippi, University of Georgia, and University of South Carolina, have deep roots in the history of the Confederacy. Campus symbols such as the Confederate battle flag, Ole' South Weekend, building and sports names that honor Confederate heroes, and other patterns of past institutional identity strongly conflict with most African American groups on campus. However, since these institutions are among the most affordable for African Americans, school administrators faces a difficult situation. How does a university administration change the centuries-old saga and culture of their institution so diversity can be respected and students of color retained without offending alumni donors (e.g., Thornton, 1987) and majority-culture students?

This dilemma has caused many institutions to face their past and make some painful attempts to reconstruct their future. Because of limited options, many students of color have had to attend institutions that are not sensitive to their backgrounds and, at times, are outright hostile. Their education is fraught with difficulties and an eventual "resignation" (or dropout) from an environment that is less than culturally responsive. So, the question remains: How do we create campus and classroom climates that are effective learning environments for our multicultural populations?

The research of Alexander Astin (1985) and the late Ernest Boyer (1987) are helpful as we examine the nature of the campus cultures of many U.S. institutions. Boyer's and Astin's comprehensive understanding of collegiate and university cultures have offered many administrations helpful suggestions for making campus climates responsive to all students.

Boyer (1987) discusses the importance of maintaining a coherent college mission. A clear mission that is shared by all constituencies can induce a higher level of fit, retention, and loyalty among all students. Berea College (founded in 1855) in Kentucky and Berry College (founded in 1901) in Georgia are two liberal arts institutions that have done this. These institutions were founded by a man (John Fee) and a woman (Martha Berry) who believed in the symbolic education of the heart, head, and hands.

Both institutions were founded on deeply religious and spiritual principles to serve students from disadvantaged backgrounds. Moreover, both institutions believe strongly in the value of physical labor; a majority of their student populations work on their respective campuses. Each institution sponsors numerous ecumenical service projects, chapels, and extracurricular programs for people of faith. As a result, these two colleges attract students who are either animated by these particular school cultures or who are highly aware of their distinctive cultures and choose the institution based on either their enthusiastic or tacit agreement with their principles and historic sagas (Clark, 1992).

The culture and mission of these schools also inform and filter the hiring of new faculty members. During their interview process, candidates are made aware of the school's mission and vision and are asked directly if they can support them. Faculty members who seek out such institutions have a higher satisfaction rate than do professors who are just looking for employment or advancement. A similar situation is true for their student populations (Bowen & Schuster, 1986).

Mission-driven institutions usually produce a clientele that is equally motivated toward a career that can be akin to a "calling." Other mission-driven institutions are found among the ranks of women's colleges (e.g., Wellesley, Smith, Spelman, Mills, and so forth), HBCUs (e.g., Morehouse, Fisk, Hampton, Howard, and so on), evangelical institutions (such as Wheaton, Taylor, Westmont, and Gordon), and colleges with counterculture sagas that do not attempt to market their institution to everyone (such as, Oberlin, Grinnell, Reed, and Bard).

Small liberal arts institutions are not the only colleges that have built up reputations as mission-driven institutions. The University of Virginia (founded by Thomas Jefferson in 1801), one of the first public universities in the United States, instituted an Office of African-American Affairs in 1976, long before most institutions with which it competes for Black students. In 1988, the university hired African American Dr. Rick Turner as a dean. Turner had recently graduated from Stanford University and had completed his dissertation on the retention rates of Black students at PWIs, which became his life work. In large part due to his efforts, the University of Virginia has an amazing 87% graduation rate among its African American student population—one of the highest in the United States among public institutions.

Dean Turner has worked diligently at engendering a welcoming environment for African American students that systematically orients students to the school culture while encouraging and sustaining programs generated for the edification of the ongoing identity of Black students as African Americans (see Turner, 2004). Thus, with clear priorities, objectives, and institutional support, even southern institutions that were built on racist legacies can advance the educational objectives of students of color (Gallien & Peterson, 2004).

HISTORICALLY BLACK COLLEGES AND UNIVERSITIES

As a former professor at a historically Black college, I can attest to the effective acculturation an instructor receives once he or she has arrived on campus. From previous research (Gallien & Peterson, 2004; Rovai & Gallien, 2005), we have established the fact that HBCUs provide culturally sensitive and responsive spaces that promote academic achievement among Black students. Theresa Perry (Perry, Steele, & Hilliard, 2004) positions HBCUs in this manner:

> In historically black segregated schools that were intentionally organized to counter the positional identities of African American students, teachers routinely promoted behaviors and practices that countered the identities of their students and students' parents as members of an oppressed people. . . . [T]hese schools were counter hegemonic communities inasmuch as they were designed to forge the collective identity of African Americans as a literate and achieving people. (pp. 90–91)

Horvat and Lewis (2003) found that Black students act differently with different groups of peers. African American students seem to have a more positive sense of self when they are in the company of other African American students, faculty, and staff, a situation that exists at HBCUs. Horvat and Lewis (2003) conclude that when both the professor and students share common cultural characteristics, there is a cultural understanding consisting of common knowledge, communication, values, traditions, attitudes, and norms that can promote learning (Irvine, 2003). School culture at HBCUs is largely influenced by the following six historical values and traditions:

1. A "lift as you climb" mentality, meaning that one's achievement is built on the dreams, aspirations, and achievement of others. This is highly congruent with traditional African American values that have been researched by Boykin (1985), Hilliard, (1997), Karenga (1980), and a host of other African American scholars and writers.

2. If students did not learn the material, the instructor did not teach it. It is up to instructors to ensure that they have done everything in their power to help their students acquire the requisite knowledge base. Otherwise, the instructor has failed the students. This clear delineation of teaching responsibility for learning has made a profound impact on HBCU classroom climates. When professors widely acknowledge their active role in student learning, achievement patterns will be decidedly higher than in institutions where professors do not hold the same educational commitments.

3. A spirit of collaboration and cooperation reigns in the classroom and among faculty members. As a result, there is an ethos of sharing equally both the load and the honor that comes with such dedication. The level of commitment is best summed up with the oft-repeated aphorism that our causes run deeper than our careers.

4. Positive role models are reenforced by the hiring of African American faculty and the convocations, communities, and special programs that bring back to campus alumni who have achieved special status in their chosen vocations.

5. Since most HBCU faculty members graduated from PWIs, they can effectively advise Black students about the degree of bicultural acquisition that must take place in order for them to be successful in these environments. In fact, one will frequently still hear Black faculty members repeating the same message they heard from their own Black mentors: In order to succeed at PWIs, you must work twice as hard as most other students in your classroom (Fries-Britt & Turner, 2002).

6. Finally, recent research by Douglas Guiffrida (2005) addresses the concept of "othermothering" as being key to understanding the effective mentoring partnership between effective pedagogues and African American students. Because Black students perceive White professors to be limited as realistic role models and to be not as sensitive to their culture, they deliberately seek out Black faculty—the few who are present on campus—for positive mentoring.

There are, however, important models of successful cross-cultural mentoring. Scholar and activist Angela Davis credits her relationship with Herbert Marcuse, the late noted Marxist philosopher at Brandeis, as being critical to her growth as a public intellectual (Davis, 1975). Marian Wright Edelman, the executive director of the Children's Defense Fund, credits American historian Howard Zinn for guiding her through a particularly paternalistic administration at Spelman College in the 1960s. Both women are two of the most important Black activists of the last century (Edelman, 2000).

Since many African American students are concerned about relatives and people within their sphere of influence, there are life situations and occurrences that can lead to a feeling of being overwhelmed, especially if the students do not have visible role models who look like them and have actually encountered similar situations when they were in college.

However, race is only one important indicator for successful mentoring. Care for the total individual could trump race as a critical factor in "other-mothering"; thus, White faculty who have attributes and characteristics similar to those of successful Black academicians, could be effective in mentoring Black students.

SCHOOL CULTURE BARRIERS TO ACHIEVEMENT

Gallien and Peterson (2004) highlight seven barriers on the campuses of many PWIs that retard the academic progress of African American students:

1. campus culture and climate
2. classroom/pedagogical dissonance
3. curricular dissonance
4. patterns of miscommunication between Black students, White peers, and professors
5. lack of knowledge about Black history, culture, and traditions
6. lack of deliberate and systematic mentoring channels that impacts overall retention and graduation rates
7. the double-edged sword of affirmative action

As noted previously, if campus climates and culture are not congruent with the lives of African Americans, then there can be a real problem with Black students' levels of comfortability in ethnocentric environments. Further, if some campus administrations refuse to deal effectively with their racist pasts and assumptions, then their African American percentages of attendance, retention, and graduation will continue to be disproportionately small in relation to their state population of Black people.

If pedagogical methods are not considered carefully by professors, then oft-repeated stories of racial experimentation will continue with abysmal results. For example, instead of confronting assumptions about the course and the instructor before class begins, many professors will make assumptions about their students of color that have little basis in the students' realities. Therefore, they may experiment clumsily *in the classroom* when it comes to discussing issues of race or racism, instead of testing their assumptions about Black students or getting to know them *before* the course actually begins.

The same is true for White students. Instead of assuming that they know about a Black student's background, they need to get to know their Black peers on an individual level and not attempt to group or stereotype them based on the latest TV show, film, or music video, or on the experiences of their own Black friends back home.

When discussing curricular issues years ago with a class, a Black student raised her hand and stated: "All this talk about bringing Black professionals and authors to the campus is fine, but, if it were real change, it would be reflected in the curriculum." This profoundly insightful comment struck to the core of the "canon wars." When Black students do not see themselves represented in their courses—especially courses where their contributions are fairly well known—there is a tendency for them to disengage from the course and the instructor. Similarly, if representations of Black people are "stuck" in the period of slavery or segregation or times when African Americans were relegated to inferior positions, then the impact is the same—disillusionment and disengagement. Therefore, it is incumbent for culturally responsive professors to find avenues for including the achievements and history of Black people in their curriculum, especially in the core curriculum of the first two years of collegiate study.

Since there are so few African American professors, there must be greater efforts applied at cross-cultural mentoring. As has been established, race is just one factor in successful mentoring. If majority professors can replicate the philosophy, mind-set, patterns of communication, and attributes that Black students need to thrive in academic environments, then their mentoring can be critical to their students' future academic and vocational success.

There is also the issue of "Negro exceptionalism" that many Black students must face during their academic training in PWIs. They are either confronted with pernicious stereotypes of Black people (based on people's past experience or convictions) that lead majority-culture students and professors to patronize them in their interpersonal relationships, or they face the "superhuman, you must be better than your race" syndrome that places them on a pedestal, only to await a gigantic crash. Either extreme is racist, and either can complicate and retard Black students' progress toward a degree or vocation (Dickerson, 2004).

The key to avoiding these scenarios is an astute awareness of Black history, culture, and traditions, along with a familiarity with current students from hip-hop culture who come from more diverse ethnic backgrounds. Gone are the days when professors can smugly state that their business is not to know their students, but that it is the business of students to know the material. If we are to set our standards high, we must find ways for all of our students to reach those standards for the good of our country's future. As Marian Wright Edelman originally stated (and as President George W. Bush reiterated in his 2002 education program): We cannot afford to leave one child behind.

CONCLUSION

Because there are clear cultural differences between teaching faculties that are predominantly White and emerging student populations of color, there is an urgent need for administrators to address the gap between the racial assumptions, learning-style preferences, and pedagogies of these groups. If administrators seek greater retention and satisfaction rates among minority groups, they should either begin to address the need for a more effective infrastructure or reenforce the one they already possess for these students. As evidenced in this chapter, there are exemplary programs that can guide such efforts.

Campus climates that engender excessive competition, meritocracy, and individualism need to rethink their priorities. Is it more important to retain an image that isolates people or to invite people to be academically challenged and nurtured at the same time? These are not mutually exclusive goals. If college and university admissions officials are doing their jobs well, then each student they choose for admission to their institution will possess the background necessary to earn a degree. Otherwise, the student should not receive a matriculation offer.

The reason so many highly ranked institutions in the United States ensure diverse student populations is not because of "political correctness," but because they know that engineering a broad student and faculty base will offer every student a better education. When students are seated next to someone who has lived in another country, speaks a different language, or is ethnically and racially different, then the person's experiences actually add to both the curriculum and the professor's expertise. As a result, it is in the majority's best interest to see to it that campuses are diverse and to work hard to retain such a climate.

There is much to learn from historically Black institutions in this context. They consistently raise the self-esteem levels of their students while effectively mentoring them for life in a multicultural country. They offer Black students a safe space for four years while they ponder their future and make critical decisions concerning what kind of person they want to be. Thus, many PWIs can transfer some of these important principles into their institutional milieu.

Finally, the rise of teaching and learning centers across the landscape of American higher education can be used as an effective catalyst for addressing these issues. Most of these centers are charged with improving the learning climates of their respective institutions. They have a particularly important role to play in offering professors research and practice principles that highlight different learning styles and effective pedagogical approaches that have been proven to "work" with minority students. All of this, of course, will not succeed unless administrations are serious about welcoming diverse populations. If they are not, it will show in the admission, retention, and graduation rates of minority populations.

DISCUSSION TOPICS

1. What is the role of administrators, professors, and staff in maintaining or engineering a culturally responsive campus climate?
2. What measures can be taken to ensure that colleges and universities mirror the national racial and ethnic populations across the United States?
3. What can be done to ensure that future professors are more adequately prepared to teach diverse populations effectively?
4. What incentives can administrators offer future professors so that they are motivated to positively impact their multicultural populations?
5. What programs can be instituted that would encourage professors to be effective cross-cultural mentors?
6. How can the scholarship of teaching be more effectively promoted in academe?
7. How can student subcultures, such as hip-hop, be framed in the classroom to motivate or ignite more student interest in academic subjects?

REFERENCES

Allen, W. R., & Haniff, N. Z. (1991). Race, gender, and academic performance in U.S. higher education. In W. R. Allen, E. G. Epps, & N. Z. Haniff (Eds.), *College in black and white: African American students in predominantly white and in historically black public universities* (pp. 95–109). Albany, NY: State University of New York Press.

Astin, A. W. (1985). *Achieving academic excellence.* San Francisco: Jossey-Bass.

Blascovich, J., Spencer, S. J., Quinn, D., & Steele, C. M. (2001). African Americans and high blood pressure: The role of stereotype threat. *Psychological Science, 12*(3), 225–229.

Bowen, H. R., & Schuster, J. H. (1986). *American professors: A national resource imperiled.* New York: Oxford University Press.

Boyer, E. (1987). *College: The undergraduate experience in America* (The Carnegie Foundation for the Advancement of Teaching). New York: HarperCollins.

Boykin, A. (1985). The triple quandry and the schooling of Afro-American children. In U. Neisser (Ed.), *The school achievement of minority children* (pp. 57–92). Thousand Oaks, CA: Sage.

Clark, B. R. (1992). *The distinctive college* (2nd ed.). Chicago: Transaction Publishers.

CollegeBoard.com. (2006). *Tips for finding your college match.* Retrieved November 29, 2006, from http://www.collegeboard.com/student/apply/the-application/52.html

Davis, A. (1975). *Angela Davis: With my mind on freedom.* New York: Bantam Books.

Dickerson, D. (2004). *The end of blackness.* New York: Pantheon Books.

Edelman, M. W. (2000). *Lanterns: A memoir of mentors.* Boston: Harper.

Fries-Britt, S., & Turner, B. (2002). Uneven stories: Successful black collegians at a black and a white campus. *The Review of Higher Education, 25*(3), 315–330.

Gallien, L. B., Jr. (1992). *Lost voices: Reflections on education from an imperiled generation.* New York: ERIC Digest.

Gallien, L. B., Jr., & Peterson, M. S. (2004). *Instructing and mentoring the African American college student: Strategies for success in higher education.* Boston: Allyn & Bacon.

Guiffrida, D. (2005). Othermothering as a framework for understanding African American students' definitions of student-centered faculty. *The Journal of Higher Education, 76*(6), 701–723.

Hilliard, A. G., III. (1997). *The re-awakening of the African mind.* Gainesville, FL: Makare Publishing.

Hofman, R. H., Hofman, W. H., Guldemond, H. (2001). Social context effects on pupils' perceptions of school. *Learning and Instruction, 11*(3), 171–194.

Horvat, E. M., & Lewis, K. S. (2003). Reassessing the burden of "acting white": The importance of peer groups in managing academic success. *Sociology of Education, 76*(4), 265–280.

Howell, A., & Tuitt, F. (2003). *Race and higher education: Rethinking pedagogy in diverse college classrooms.* Cambridge, MA: Harvard Educational Review.

Hurtado, S., Milem, J., Clayton-Pederson, A., & Allen, W. (1999). *Enacting diverse learning environments: Improving the climate for racial/ethnic diversity in higher education.* (ASHE-ERIC Higher Education Report, Vol. 26, No. 8). Washington, DC: George Washington University. (ERIC Document Reproduction Service No. ED430514).

Irvine, J. J. (2003). *Educating teachers for diversity: Seeing with a cultural eye.* New York: Teachers College Press.

Karenga, M. (1980). *Kawaida theory: An introduction.* Inglewood, CA: Kawaida Press.

Lezotte, L. W., Hathaway, D. V., Miler, S. K., Passalacqua, J., & Brookover, W. B. (1980). *School learning climate and student achievement.* Tallahassee, FL: SSTA.

Perry, T., Steele, C. M., & Hilliard, A. G., III. (2004). *Young, gifted and black: Promoting high achievement among African-American students.* Boston: Beacon Press.

Rovai, A. P., & Gallien, L. B., Jr. (2005). Learning and sense of community: A comparative analysis of African American and Caucasian online graduate students. *Journal of Negro Education, 74*(1), 53–62.

Thornton, K. P. (1987). Symbolism at Ole Miss and the crisis of southern identity. *South Atlantic Quarterly, 86*(3), 254–268.

Tinto, V. (1994). *Leaving college: Rethinking the causes and cures of student attrition* (2nd ed.). Chicago: University of Chicago Press.

Tompkins, J. (1997). *A life in school: What the teacher learned.* New York: Addison-Wesley.

Turner, M. R. (2004). Chapter 8—The Office of African American Affairs: A celebration of success. In F. W. Hale, (Ed.), *What makes racial diversity work in higher education: Academic leaders present successful policies and strategies* (pp. 112–122). Sterling, VA: Stylus.

USNews.com (2006). America's best colleges 2006. Campus diversity: National universities. Retrieved November 29, 2006, from http://www.usnews.com/usnews/edu/college/rankings/brief/natudoc/natudoc_campdiv_brief.php

Villanueva, V., Jr. (1993). *Bootstraps: From an American academic of color.* Urbana, IL: National Council of Teachers of English.

FOUR

Diversity and Learning on College Campuses

JoAnn W. Haysbert & D. Nicole Williams

PURPOSE

The previous three chapters discuss the African American achievement gap as a problem with many potential causes. They describe the characteristics of African American learners and explain the influences of hip-hop and school culture on learning. The purpose of this chapter is to provide a foundational discussion of diversity and learning on college campuses, to suggest some important theories that can help inform practice, and to describe a representative sampling of exemplary programs aimed at closing the African American achievement gap in higher education.

BACKGROUND

Diverse campuses include different racial and ethnic groups, school cultures, sagas, traditions, and belief systems. Inclusion is the positive interaction of diverse campus groups and represents the practice of employing institutional and teaching strategies that reach out to embrace the diversity inherent in all learners. Accordingly, inclusion becomes a means by which quality and equitable learning take place in all learners, regardless of individual characteristics such as race and ethnicity. The practice of inclusion should facilitate the appreciation of another person's cultural differences as well as the love of one's own cultural heritage (Simmons, 1998).

African American students continue to battle the challenges discussed in previous chapters, such as negative stereotypes, low expectations, cultural isolation, and low levels of faculty and peer support. These factors contribute to the achievement gap between Blacks and Whites as discussed in previous chapters. To become a successfully inclusive campus, administrators, staff, and faculty members must be committed to the goal of inclusion, and this goal must permeate every element of the university.

Racial identity is not simply being Black, biracial, White, Latino, Asian, or Native American. As noted in Chapter 3, Claude Steele (1997) suggests the presence of deeply embedded "stereotype threats" that connect racial identity to academic ability. Such stereotyping and accompanying prejudicial attitudes and behavior take many forms, including "lower expectations of black students, overly positive reactions to work quality, reducing the quality of communications, and reducing the probability that faculty know students well enough to write references" (Hurtado, Milem, Clayton-Pederson, & Allen, 1999, p. 53). Racial stereotyping influences teachers' expectations of students, students' expectations of other students, and students' expectations of themselves (Steele, 1997). Minority students confront subtle and overt racism and discrimination both in and out of classrooms. Educators must concede that these issues are real barriers for minority students, and they must be addressed openly, honestly, and with a vision toward change.

In the classroom, faculty members must foster deliberate inclusiveness of diverse learners. Gurin, Dey, Gurin, and Hurtado (2003) note that students must be engaged with diverse peers if we expect learning and development to occur. However, such individuals will be reluctant to work together unless cross-cultural interaction is promoted by an authority, such as the instructor, and the status of all groups is equal (Allport, 1954). Teachers encourage inclusion when they assign group projects that require students to work together in and outside of class, which establishes the conditions for success.

Learning-style preference can also influence learning. It is defined as the "complex manner in which, and conditions under which, learners most efficiently and most effectively perceive, process, store, and recall what they are attempting to learn" (James & Gardner, 1995, p. 20). Cronbach and Snow (1981) suggest that students tend to reach higher levels of achievement when they are taught in ways that are compatible with their preferred learning style. Thus, teaching styles need to include diverse methods if they are to reach out to all students.

Culture influences communication and the learning-style preferences of all students. As noted in Chapter 2, the African American cultural orientation suggests that many Black students will perform best in a learning environment that includes:

- harmony, cooperation, affect, socialization, and community
- relational and creative learning relevant to their own experiences
- learning from a global perspective that recognizes the importance of comprehensive thinking versus analytical thinking
- reliance on nonverbal, indirect, implicit, and informal communication

Culture impacts both the teacher's and the students' perceptions and behaviors in the classroom. Inclusive teaching recognizes these differences without labeling the differences as deficiencies. Culturally sensitive teachers respond to the individual learning needs of students and recognize that not all students have the same preferred learning style.

There are several ways to conceptualize learning-style preferences, based on information processing, personality, social interaction, and multidimensional and instructional models. Personality models include field theory, which was discussed in Chapter 2, and identify the global, field-dependent preference of many Blacks and the field-independent, analytical tendency of many Whites. Multidimensional and instructional models address the student's environmental preference for learning and include Howard Gardner's (1999) theory of multiple intelligences. Gardner suggests that there are at least eight modalities (or intelligences) that can be used either singly or in combination to describe one's learning-style preference. (He actually suggests there may be more intelligences, such as existential intelligence, but concludes that the court is out on adding more intelligences to the list.) These intelligences are:

- linguistic (words)
- logical-mathematical (numbers/reasoning)
- spatial (pictures)
- bodily-kinesthetic (body)
- musical (music)
- interpersonal (people)
- intrapersonal (self)
- naturalist (nature)

If a teacher is having difficulty reaching a student in the more traditional linguistic method (e.g., lecture), Gardner's theory suggests that the teacher might also address the topic by drawing from other types of intelligence, e.g., interpersonal (i.e., collaborative discussion) and spatial (i.e., using pictures or video). Similarly, the teacher can also draw from other learning-style models, e.g., using words and pictures from Gardner's theory and using collaborative work favored by field-dependent learners. The benefit of teaching to diverse learning styles is the opening of classrooms to more than one approach to complex intellectual work and learning (e.g., James & Gardner, 1995).

Professors must reassess their teaching styles and philosophies and be open to change in order to better match the diversity of their students. The teaching styles and philosophies of a teacher often reflect the teacher's preferred learning style, as discussed in earlier chapters. Teachers should consider their teaching styles in this light and provide multiple approaches to teaching the same material in order to be inclusive of students from diverse cultural backgrounds who may possess different learning-style preferences. Teachers should obtain the skills needed to translate knowledge into effective instruction and enriched curriculum. If teachers are to increase learning opportunities for all students, they must be knowledgeable about the social and cultural context of teaching and learning (e.g., Banks, Cookson, Gay, Hawley, Irvine, Nieto, Schofield, & Stephan, 2001).

ADULT LEARNING

The concepts of andragogy (e.g., Knowles, 1983, 1990) and self-directed learning (e.g., Knowles, 1983; Merriam & Caffarella, 1998) in large part inform the field of adult learning. According to Malcolm Knowles (1970), to effectively facilitate learning in adults, educators must consider the characteristics of the learner and the context in which learning takes place. He suggests that the adult instructional process should be supportive of the adult learner's needs and requirements. Flannery (1995) writes that adult learning theories must be mindful of the influence of social, historical, and economic factors in adult education, and theories "must become inclusive and give voice to all people and groups, allowing missing voices (women, working-class persons, persons of color) to narrate their diverse stories of how and where they learn, and about their values of learning" (p. 156).

Andragogy

In the past, both children and adults were subjected to largely the same set of instructional methods. Knowles's (1988) andragogy model attempts to distinguish between adult education (i.e., andragogy) and childhood schooling (i.e., pedagogy) by recognizing that the process of education for adults is lifelong and continuous, and that the learning characteristics of adults and children differ. Accordingly, Knowles suggests that the instructor of adult students adopt the role of facilitator, rather than lecturer or dispenser of knowledge. Knowles (1970) notes, "one major function of adult education is to sell the people the idea of continuing to learn" (p. 190). He outlines six characteristics of adult learners that differ from those of children and adolescents (1970, 1989, 1990):

1. the need to know
2. the learner's self-concept
3. the role of the learner's experience
4. readiness to learn
5. orientation to learning
6. motivation to learn

The Need to Know. The first characteristic in which andragogy differs from pedagogy is that adults need to know the process and organization entailed in the learning process to a greater extent than young learners do. They need to know why learning is necessary; the learning must have a purpose that is clearly defined and understood by the adult learner. This can often be accomplished by presenting learning in the context of life, a relevant task, or a significant problem. This context should be relevant to all students in the classroom and should draw from multicultural frames of reference.

The Learner's Self-Concept. Adults have a self-concept of being responsible for their own decisions and for their own lives. Consequently, they tend to be more self-directed in their learning. Through maturation, a person's self-concept moves from dependency toward self-directing. Self-directed learning could be described as a process in which individuals take the initiative, with or without the help of others inside or outside the formal educational setting (Merriam & Caffarella, 1998). Self-direction does not necessarily mean that learning takes place in isolation from others. As a result, being self-directed is compatible with the African American tendency to be field-dependent. The works of Tough (1967) and Brookfield (1984) view self-directed learning as a form of learning that considers the planning, implementation, and evaluation of learning to be the primary responsibility of the learner. Whether this learning takes place independently or in collaboration with others rests with the self-directed learner and his or her learning-style preference.

The Role of the Learner's Experience. Unlike children, adults have a vast reservoir of experiences on which to draw while learning, and many learn best when they are respected as persons and can contribute to the learning process by drawing from their experiences. Knowles (1994) asserts that the methodology of adult education should move away from traditional classroom methods that tend to be teacher-centered in favor of methods that are student-centered and make greater use of the experiences of adult learners.

Readiness to Learn. Adults are ready to learn when they experience a need to know something in order to perform more effectively in their lives. Adults learn best when the topic is relevant to them personally and is of near-term value. Adults are often ready to learn in order to gain a skill or new information that has an application to a current situation, to perform externally imposed social roles, or to be better postured for a desired change of job, promotion, or increased salary.

Orientation to Learning. Many adults enter educational activities with a problem-centered orientation to learning. They learn information in the context that the new information is useful in accomplishing some preexisting goal or objective.

Motivation to Learn. According to Knowles (1994), the final characteristic that distinguishes adult learning from childhood learning is that adults are more responsive to intrinsic motivation than extrinsic motivation. Stipek (1988) describes the following techniques that can promote intrinsic motivation in the classroom:

> Students are intrinsically motivated to work when the threat of negative external evaluation is not salient and when their attention is not focused on extrinsic reasons for completing tasks. They will also feel more competent and proud, and thus more intrinsically interested in tasks, when they can take responsibility for their success. Allowing some student choice enhances intrinsic interest in school tasks, and it teaches self-management skills that are essential for success. . . . (p. 73)

Knowles's (1988) assumptions regarding the characteristics of adult learners have significant implications for the planning, implementation, and evaluation of adult learning activities. However, an inclusive model of multicultural awareness that explicitly integrates multicultural issues into higher education courses is presently lacking. Nonetheless, andragogy as a teaching approach for Black college students is relevant, provided the instructor is aware of and draws from the cultural backgrounds of Black learners discussed in Chapters 2 and 3 and helps students cope with the challenges to learning discussed in Chapters 5 and 7.

Based on the above six characteristics of adult learners, Knowles (1989) developed a seven-step educational program planning model. He uses this planning model to expand his principles of andragogy to include strategies ". . . only up to the point at which the learner has acquired sufficient knowledge of the content to be able to start engaging in self-directed inquiry about it . . ." (Knowles, 1989, p. 113). The seven-step process consists of:

1. creating a climate that is informal, democratic, and conducive to learning
2. involving learners in the planning process
3. involving learners in diagnosing their needs and readiness for learning
4. involving learners in framing their learning objectives
5. designing a plan of activities
6. fleshing out the plan of activities
7. involving learners in evaluating their own individual learning outcomes

Knowles (1988) views instructors as the facilitators of educational planning by suggesting procedures and coordinating the process with the learner.

The learner is considered a mutual partner in each of the steps of diagnosing learner needs, formulating the learning process, designing patterns of learning experiences, and evaluating results.

Tough (1978) observes that adults will invest considerable energy in examining the benefits they will gain from learning and the negative consequences of not learning before they undertake learning something on their own. According to the principles of andragogy, if a learner is provided adequate resources and tools for obtaining information, he or she will enhance the capacity to make responsible judgments regarding his or her level of competency development (Knowles, 1990).

MULTICULTURAL EDUCATION

Culturally relevant teaching rests on three principles: (a) students must experience academic success; (b) students must develop and/or maintain cultural competence; and (c) students must develop a critical consciousness through which they challenge the status quo of the current social order (Ladson-Billings, 1995). The challenge of culturally relevant teaching is to entice students to choose academic excellence. Teachers must therefore channel students' skills and abilities in academically important ways.

Banks and Banks (1995) describe multicultural education as

> a field of study . . . whose major aim is to create equal educational opportunities for students from diverse racial, ethnic, social-class, and cultural groups. One of its important goals is to help all students to acquire the knowledge, attitudes, and skills needed to function effectively in a pluralistic democratic society and to interact, negotiate, and communicate with peoples from diverse groups in order to create a civic and moral community that works for the common good. (p. xi)

This definition is consistent with the fundamental purpose of higher education, which is to prepare responsible young people to assume productive roles in society in order to foster the creation of "human capital" (Bowen, Kurzweil, Tobin, & Picler, 2005). Colleges and universities consider themselves forces for change, but they are constrained by thousands of years of tradition (Tien, 1998). Ibarra (2001) observes that the central conflict regarding campus diversity and institutional change is between culturally different populations and traditional academic values—those that involve the way things are done in academia. Within the traditional framework, schools try to provide higher education to all students, including learners of different races and ethnicities. Before a school can educate diverse learners, however, it must first try to recognize the legitimacy of various cultures and their influences on learning.

Hurtado, Milem, Clayton-Pederson, and Allen (1999) believe the key to creating diverse learning environments lies in developing programs and policies to improve the campus climate for racial and ethnic diversity. Administrators must understand the environment from the perspectives of members from different racial and ethnic backgrounds. It is important to ensure that all students see themselves reflected in the environment around them and to avoid feelings of invisibility or marginality that can undermine students' success (Tatum, Calhoun, Brown, & Ayvazian, 2000). The classroom and extracurricular lives of students are interwoven, and both must provide a comfortable learning community. Diverse learning environments cultivate students who are prepared to meet the demands of a complex, diverse society (Hurtado, Milem, Clayton-Pederson, & Allen, 1999).

Tinto (1994) calls for schools to assume a more active role in integrating new students in the school. Accordingly, many colleges include a "freshman experience" orientation that Koutsoubakis (1999) demonstrates can increase student persistence. These orientations are used to: (a) assist new freshmen in making the transition from high school to college; (b) orient students to the services and culture of the college and its campus; and (c) integrate students into an intellectual community of students and faculty. Additionally, Hashway, Baham, Hashway, and Rogers (2000) provide evidence that completion of remedial programs increases first-year retention rates among academically at-risk students. Positive effects are also reported for students completing a summer transition program (Wolf-Wendel, Tuttle, & Keller-Wolff, 1999).

According to William G. Bowen, the 2004 Thomas Jefferson Foundation Distinguished Lecturer at the University of Virginia, the challenge for PWIs regarding African American students is to move beyond finding effective ways to enroll more Black students toward finding effective ways to educate a diverse population of minority and majority students (Foley, 2006). According to Foley, Bowen cites the large "preparation gap" discussed in Chapter 1 as one reason this goal seems so distant. This preparation gap places many African Americans at an educational disadvantage when they enter college. For example, it is more likely that Blacks graduate from high schools with fewer resources and less effective teaching than those of their White peers. Moreover, fewer Black students (30%) than White students (45%) take advanced mathematics courses in high school (Hoffman, Llagas, & Snyder 2003). Consequently, the "freshman experience" orientation and initial on-campus residences for distance education programs take on added significance for African American students, many of whom are less prepared to compete academically in college than Whites. Such programs should have the dual goal of integrating new students into the school and eradicating the student preparation gap.

As Uri Treisman (1992) has demonstrated, when Black college students have the necessary academic skills, they can perform well in the most demanding collegiate environments. According to a summary report of educational equity and reform between 1990 and 2000 (College Board, 2000; Pelavin & Kane, 1990), low-income and minority students who master algebra and geometry and have expectations to go to college enroll in college at the same rate as their White peers with these same academic experiences. They also succeed at about the same rate.

Educators must set high standards and expectations for African Americans. Students on higher tracks—even those who are less academically able—learn more because they are exposed to broader curricula and better teaching (Mickelson, 2003). Educators must challenge students with innovative instruction. Curricula cannot be diluted for some students, because they all need the same skills to succeed in the job market. Educators must invest the time (e.g., extended or flexible office hours) and resources (e.g., study labs equipped with tutors) to assist students in performing at the same levels as their peers. Professors must identify the barriers and identify the ways and means to compensate for those barriers.

EXEMPLARY PROGRAMS

There are numerous examples of successful higher education programs that seek to close the African American achievement gap and are based on the principles of andragogy, self-directedness, and multicultural education previously discussed. The following seven-model programs represent a diverse cross-section of programs that can be used for inspiration:

- Meyerhoff Scholars Program
- Ronald E. McNair Post-Baccalaureate Achievement Program
- Emerging Scholars' Program
- Multicultural Center
- Faculty-Student Mentoring Program
- Peer Advisor Program
- William R. Harvey Leadership Institute

Meyerhoff Scholars Program

Freeman Hrabowski founded the Meyerhoff Scholars Program at the University of Maryland, Baltimore County. The program was developed in response to the low levels of performance and persistence of well-qualified African American science, engineering, and mathematics students on that campus (Maton, Hrabowski, & Schmitt, 2000). The goals of the program are (Gordon & Bridglall, 2004):

- to increase the number of underrepresented students who can successfully complete a course of study in the technical fields in which they are historically underrepresented, thus preparing these students to pursue terminal degrees in these fields
- to increase the number of minority professionals in these fields and in the university faculty, thus creating role models for minority students of later generations
- to close the achievement gap

To achieve these goals, the program includes the following components:

- Careful selection of students
- Provision of merit financial support to reduce concerns about finances
- A mandatory Summer Bridge Program to acclimate students to the rigors of freshman year
- Peer study groups for academic and social support
- Holding all Meyerhoff students responsible for each other and for community service
- The importance of taking advice
- Meaningful and sustained interaction with faculty and mentors
- The importance of continued family involvement
- The centrality of academic excellence and scholarship
- The significance of rigorously and systematically documenting and evaluating program outcomes (Gordon & Bridglall, 2004, p. 31)

Since 1993, more than 400 graduates have completed the program, and nearly all are pursuing advanced degrees in science, engineering, and mathematics. Hrabowski encourages students to work together in a special "honors" program (Bowen, Kurzweil, Tobin, & Picler, 2005). The premise is that like-minded students who work closely together emit a positive energy that is contagious. Students continually inspire one another to do more and better.

Ronald E. McNair Post-Baccalaureate Achievement Program

This program at more than 100 universities is administered by the U.S. Department of Education and targets first-generation, low-income students, and students from underrepresented groups in graduate studies. The purpose of this program is to increase student chances for success in graduate school and to increase the attainment of Ph.D. degrees by students from underrepresented segments of society. The components of the program include:

- personal and academic counseling and assessment
- interaction with faculty and graduate student mentors
- intensive GRE preparation
- study to increase library and research skills
- attendance at professional meetings
- opportunity to present research findings at regional and national research conferences
- assistance with completing graduate admissions and financial aid applications
- participation in admission workshops
- competition for a summer research internship with a $2,500 stipend (Ronald E. McNair Post-Baccalaureate Achievement Program, 2006)

Emerging Scholars' Program

Philip Uri Treisman (1992) established the Emerging Scholars' Program at the University of California at Berkeley (then known as the Mathematics Workshop) and later at the University of Texas at Austin to improve African American students' grades in calculus. Treisman observed African American students and Chinese American students. He found that African American students were socially and academically isolated. He also found that Chinese American students tended to study and complete homework in collaborative and cooperative work groups (Hurtado, Milem, Clayton-Pederson, & Allen, 1999). When students enter the Emerging Scholars' Program, they agree to participate in 8 hours of tutoring and support services a week. Treisman taught calculus in a manner that encouraged African American students to work together and allow peers to serve as teachers. The Treisman model has been adopted by more than 150 colleges and universities.

Multicultural Center

Lee Jones (2004) identifies the Multicultural Center at Washington State University as an excellent example of a well-planned and well-equipped program that serves the needs of minority students at a predominantly White institution (PWI). The center consists of an administrative office, a division of multicultural recruitment, and four subordinate centers: the African American Student Center, the Asian/Pacific-American Student Center, the Chicano/Latino Student Center, and the Native American Student Center. Each center includes a counselor who can assist and advise students. The center's multicultural recruitment staff travels throughout the state to meet with minority students at high schools and community colleges in order to present information regarding the university and to guide students through the admissions process (Jones, 2004). Additionally, each center is able to offer services in the areas of social support, academic advising, and referral to other campus departments, as well as providing information on scholarships, internships, and academic programs.

Faculty-Student Mentoring Program

The Faculty-Student Mentoring Program, under the Office of African-American Affairs at the University of Virginia, is intended to provide upper- and middle-class African American students with "expanded support for intellectual and personal success" (Turner, 2004, p. 117). According to Turner, there were 112 faculty-student pairs actively participating in this program during the 2001–2002 academic year. The goals of the program are:

- to provide students of color with a structured approach in developing a meaningful relationship with university faculty, administrators, or graduate students
- to help students of color continue to form a more positive identification with the university community
- to motivate and inspire students of color through moral, intellectual, academic, and social support that will contribute to their success through graduation and career development
- to promote cross-cultural understanding in the university community (p. 117)

According to Turner (2004), a survey reveals that 90% of participants would like to continue in the program and 91% would recommend the program to others.

Peer Advisor Program

Rick Turner (2004) also describes the Peer Advisor Program, which has been in existence at the University of Virginia since 1984, also under the Office of African-American Affairs. The program's purpose as to help integrate new students into the school. Program goals are:

- to provide sensitive, personalized support to African American first year and entering transfer students
- to promote academic excellence
- to inform students about the services and resources available at the University of Virginia

- to encourage involvement in university organizations and extracurricular activities
- to foster ownership of and pride in the university
- to increase retention (Turner, 2004, p. 116)

The program provides support to new students as soon as they are admitted to the university with communication that usually begins prior to the start of formal coursework. According to Turner (2004), peer advisors are knowledge resources, encouragers, friends, and role models for the entering students.

William R. Harvey Leadership Institute

Universities need special programs designed to nurture students' gifts. All students are not honors students, but they often excel in other arenas. The William R. Harvey Leadership Institute (2004) for students with leadership potential is located at Hampton University. Its mission is to develop entry-level leaders who have the character and commitment to lead and serve ethically. The program identifies students with an interest in leadership and interacting with people, and a desire to change society and commit to the responsibility of community service. Students admitted to the institute are designated leadership fellows and earn a minor in leadership studies upon the successful completion of the 18-credit-hour program in ethics, leadership, and community service. They also receive a $2,500 stipend each academic year. The program is based on the philosophy that character is the foundation of leadership and that leadership provides an opportunity to influence positive change.

CONCLUSION

The solutions for combating inequities and promoting inclusiveness rely on three essential ingredients (Burgess, 1997; Ibarra, 2001; Richardson, 1989):

- Student access (recruitment, college orientation, and admissions programs)
- Student retention (financial support, academic support or advising, and cultural support programs)
- Diverse staff and faculty (hiring women and minority faculty)

Within this framework, this chapter identifies the following strategies that contribute to inclusiveness:

- Integrate all students in the school using programs such as the freshman experience and initial on-campus residences for distance education programs.

- Employ diverse teaching styles.
- Draw from the principles of andragogy and self-directed learning.
- Foster intrinsic motivation in students.
- Create learning communities that facilitate collaborative work.
- Provide remedial and support programs to close the preparation gap.

PWIs often provide full scholarships to minority students, but have difficulty retaining these students. Financial incentives increase the enrollment of minorities for the short term, but do not address long-term goals or other short-term challenges. Minority students leave PWIs due to personal, social, academic, and financial difficulties; language barriers; low self-esteem; fear and isolation; lack of family support; lack of experience with higher education; racism; discrimination; lack of role models, mentors, and satisfactory peer relationships; faculty indifference and low expectations; and a general tendency for institutions to resist change (Powell, 1998).

School policies and practices reflect the values of those who work within the school (Banks et al., 2001). Minorities are urgently needed in higher education institutions because they help prepare all students to face a culturally diverse world; indeed, minority faculty can be the most instrumental educational resource in White institutions (Trueba, 1998). Diverse students need diverse faculty and administrators as role models as discussed in Chapter 3. The presence of minorities conveys a message of commitment to students. Students need to see minorities in key visible positions throughout the campus—not just in a small designated corner. The solution requires inclusion. Minority students need to feel a sense of belonging.

Teachers must also reach students outside of class. On the first day of class, faculty should make it clear that office hours are not only for problem solving. They also provide the opportunity for students and professors to become personally acquainted and to make connections with each other. Teachers should encourage students to stop by their offices. Many students are uncomfortable or nervous about going to a professor's office. The teacher may suggest meetings with small groups as an alternative.

The students of the hip-hop generation are visual learners who are driven and animated by technology. They have iPods, flat-screen televisions, and electronic games. Teachers must utilize technology and multimedia resources in and outside of the classroom, such as Microsoft PowerPoint, e-mail, podcasting, computer-based simulation, and online journals to be effective facilitators of knowledge for these students. Today, teachers must impart knowledge while being caring professionals that can meet the diverse needs of their students.

The exemplary programs discussed in this chapter, such as the Meyerhoff Scholars Program, draw on many of the principles identified in this chapter to promote the inclusiveness and integration of African Americans on college campuses and in classrooms for the purpose of closing the achievement gap. The following chapters will expand and build on these principles as they address the traditional and virtual classroom learning communities, the assessment and evaluation of student learning, and institutional culture.

DISCUSSION TOPICS

1. What are the common themes that run through the exemplar programs discussed in this chapter, and how can these themes be implemented on other college campuses?
2. What are the major elements of an inclusive model of andragogy that integrates multicultural awareness and issues?
3. Evaluate multicultural education as an instrument of social change.

REFERENCES

Allport, G. (1954). *The nature of prejudice*. Cambridge, MA: Addison-Wesley.

Banks, J. A., & Banks, C. A. M. (Eds). (1995). *Handbook of research on multicultural education*. New York: Macmillan.

Banks, J. A., Cookson, P., Gay, G., Hawley, W. D., Irvine, J. J., Nieto, S., Schofield, J. W., & Stephan, W. G. (2001). Diversity within unity: Essential principles for teaching and learning in a multicultural society. *Phi Delta Kappan, 83*(3), 196.

Betances, S. (2004). Chapter 4—How to become an outstanding educator of Hispanic and African American first generation college students. In F. W. Hale, (Ed.), *What makes racial diversity work in higher education: Academic leaders present successful policies and strategies* (pp. 44–59). Sterling, VA: Stylus.

Bowen, W. G., Kurzweil, M. A., Tobin, E. M., & Picler, S. C. (2005). *Equity and excellence in American higher education*. Charlottesville, VA: University of Virginia Press.

Brookfield, S. D. (1984). *Adult learner, adult education, and the community*. New York: Teachers College Press.

Burgess, N. J. (1997). Tenure and promotion among African American women in the academy: Issues and strategies. In L. Benjamin (Ed.), *Black women in the academy: Promises and perils* (pp. 227–234). Gainesville: University Press of Florida.

College Board. (2000). *Equity 2000: A systemic education reform model. A summary report, 1990–2000*. Retrieved November 29, 2006, from http://www.collegeboard.com/prod_downloads/about/association/equity/EquityHistoricalReport.pdf

Cronbach, L., & Snow, R. (1981). *Aptitudes and instructional methods: A handbook for research on interactions*. New York: Irvington.

Flannery, D. D. (1995). Adult education and the politics of the theoretical text. In B. Kanpol & P. McLaren (Eds.), *Critical multiculturalism: Uncommon voices in a common struggle* (pp. 149–163). Westport, CT: Bergin and Garvey.

Foley, J. (2006, May 23). Race an appropriate admission criterion, guest lecturer says. Charlottesville, VA: *The Cavalier Daily*. Retrieved November 29, 2006, from http://www.cavalierdaily.com/CVArticle_print.asp?ID=19753&pid1151

Gardner, H. (1999). *Intelligence reframed*. New York: Basic Books.

Gordon, E. W., & Bridglall, B. L. (2004). A study of the Meyerhoff Scholars Program. In R. Legler (Ed.), *Perspectives on the gaps: Fostering the academic success of minority and low-income students* (pp. 29–37). Naperville, IL: Learning Point Associates.

Gurin, P. Y., Dey, E. L., Gurin, G., & Hurtado, S., (2003). How does racial/ethnic diversity promote education? *Western Journal of Black Studies, 27*(1), 20–29.

Hashway, R. M., Baham, C., Hashway, S. E., & Rogers, R. M. (2000). Retaining students in college. *Educational Research Quarterly, 23*, 35–59.

Hoffman, K., Llagas, C., & Snyder, T. D. (2003). *Status and trends in the education of blacks* (NCES 2003-034). Washington, DC: U.S. Department of Education Institute of Education Sciences.

Hurtado, S., Milem, J. F., Clayton-Pederson, A .R., & Allen, W. R. (1999). *Enacting diverse learning environments: Improving the climate for racial/ethnic diversity in higher education*. Washington, DC: Office of Educational Research and Improvement. (ERIC Document Reproduction Service No. ED430514).

Ibarra, R. A. (2001). *Beyond affirmative action: Reframing the context of higher education*. Madison, WI: University of Wisconsin Press.

James, W. B., & Gardner, D. L. (1995). Learning styles: Implications for distance learning. *New Directions for Adult and Continuing Education, 67*, 19–32.

Jones, L. (2004). Chapter 9—The development of a multicultural student services office and retention strategy for minority students. In F. W. Hale, (Ed.), *What makes racial diversity work in higher education: Academic leaders present successful policies and strategies* (pp. 124–145). Sterling, VA: Stylus.

Knowles, M. S. (1970). *The modern practice of adult education*. Chicago: Association Press.

Knowles, M. S. (1983). *Self-directed learning: A guide for learners and teachers*. Englewood Cliffs, NJ: Cambridge.

Knowles, M. S. (1988). *The modern practice of adult education: From pedagogy to andragogy* (Rev. ed.). New York: Cambridge Books.

Knowles, M. S. (1989). *The making of an adult educator: An autobiographical journey*. San Francisco: Jossey-Bass.

Knowles, M. S. (1990). *The adult learner: A neglected species (building blocks of human potential)* (4th ed.). Houston: Gulf Publishing Company.

Knowles, M. S. (1994). *History of the adult education movement in the United States* (Rev. ed.). New York: Krieger Publishing Company.

Koutsoubakis, D. (1999). A test of the effectiveness of a one-term freshmen orientation program at the foreign campus of an accredited private American university. *Journal of the First-Year Experience, 11*, 33–58.

Ladson-Billings, G. (1995). But that's just not good teaching! The case for culturally relevant pedagogy. *Theory into Practice, 34*(3), 159–165.

Maton, K. I., Hrabowski, F. A., & Schmitt, C. L. (2000). African American college students excelling in the sciences; College and postcollege outcomes in the Meyerhoff Scholars Program. *Journal of Research in Science Teaching, 37*(7), 629–654.

Merriam, S. B., & Caffarella, R. S. (1998). *Learning in adulthood* (2nd ed.). San Francisco: Jossey-Bass.

Mickelson, R. A. (2003). When are racial disparities in education the result of racial discrimination? A social science perspective. *Teachers College Record, 105*(6), 1048–1178.

Pelavin, S., & Kane, M. (1990). *Changing the odds: Factors increasing access to college*. New York: The College Board.

Powell, M. H. (1998). Campus climate and students of color. In L. A. Valverde & L. A. Castenell (Eds.), *The multicultural campus: Strategies for transforming higher education* (pp. 95–118). Walnut Creek, CA: Altamira Press.

Richardson, R. C., Jr. (1989, January 11). If minority students are to succeed in higher education, every rung of the educational ladder must be in place. *The Chronicle of Higher Education*, A48.

Ronald E. McNair Post-Baccalaureate Achievement Program (2006). Retrieved November 29, 2006, from http://www.ed.gov/programs/triomcnair/index.html

Simmons, H. L. (1998). External agents fostering multiculturalism. In L. A. Valverde & L. A. Castenell (Eds.), *The multicultural campus: Strategies for transforming higher education*. Walnut Creek, CA: Altamira Press.

Steele, C. M. (1997). A threat in the air: How stereotypes shape the intellectual identities and performance of women and African Americans. *American Psychologist, 52*, 613–629.

Stipek, D. J. (1988). *Motivation to learn: From theory to practice*. Englewood Cliffs, New Jersey: Prentice Hall.

Tatum, D. A, Calhoun, R. W., Brown, S. C., & Ayvazian, A. (2000). Implementation strategies creating an environment of achievement. *Liberal Education, 86*, 22.

Tien, C. L. (1998). Challenges and opportunities for leaders of color. In L. A. Valverde & L. A. Castenell (Eds.), *The multicultural campus: Strategies for transforming higher education* (pp. 33–34). Walnut Creek, CA: Altamira Press.

Tinto, V. (1994). *Leaving college: Rethinking the causes and cures of student attrition* (2nd ed.). Chicago: University of Chicago Press.

Tough, A. (1967). *Learning without a teacher*. Toronto, Canada: Institute for Studies in Education.

Tough, A., (1978). Major learning efforts: Recent research and future directions. *Adult Education, 28*(4), 250–263.

Treisman, U. (1992). Studying students studying calculus: A look at the lives of minority mathematics students in college. *College Mathematics Journal, 23*, 362–372.

Trueba, E. T. (1998). Race and ethnicity in academia. In L. A. Valverde & L. A. Castenell (Eds.), *The multicultural campus: Strategies for transforming higher education* (pp. 71–93). Walnut Creek, CA: Altamira Press.

Turner, M. R. (2004). Chapter 8—The Office of African American Affairs: A celebration of success. In F. W. Hale, (Ed.), *What makes racial diversity work in higher education: Academic leaders present successful policies and strategies* (pp. 112–122). Sterling, VA: Stylus.

University of North Carolina at Chapel Hill Center for Teaching and Learning. (1997). *Teaching for inclusion: Diversity in the college classroom* (chap. 4). Available online: http://ctl.unc.edu/tfi4.html

William R. Harvey Leadership Institute. (2004). Leadership Institute home page. Retrieved November 29, 2006, from http://www.hamptonu.edu/academics/leadershipinstitute/index.htm

Wolf-Wendel, L. E., Tuttle, K., & Keller-Wolff, C. M. (1999). Assessment of a freshman summer transition program in an open-admissions institution. *Journal of the First-Year Experience*, *11*, 7–32.

FIVE

Challenges in the Traditional Classroom

Marshalita Sims Peterson

PURPOSE

The previous chapters discussed the African American achievement gap in terms of the influences of African American, hip-hop, and school cultures on learning, and described various theories and exemplary programs that can help close this gap. This chapter adds to the discussion by identifying the specific challenges to African American student achievement in the traditional classroom. The next chapter responds to these challenges by identifying and describing successful classroom strategies.

BACKGROUND

Access to higher education is a vital component for opportunities of inclusion and success in today's society. Individual access to and success in higher education involves several variables that are viewed as pivotal elements linked to economic, political, and social power. The link between academic achievement and societal mobility further supports the significance of the higher education experience, and the facilitation of academic success is central to the idea of a "culture of power" built on human capital. Delpit (1988) describes a culture of power in our society from which African Americans are mostly excluded. She asserts that many African Americans have limited access to quality education, which in turn limits their economic, social, and political opportunities. Deliberate steps to increase access to higher education for African Americans are essential. Equally important is the quality of the college experience once the student has gained access; however, access does not guarantee success and challenges still remain in predominantly White institutional cultures.

Challenges to African American achievement in the traditional, on-campus classroom are described in this book within the context of Patricia

Cross's (1992) model of classifying barriers or challenges to adult learning into institutional, situational, and dispositional categories. According to Cross, institutional challenges consist of practices and procedures that exclude or discourage students from full participation in learning. Situational challenges are those arising from one's situation in life at a given time and include both the social and physical environment surrounding one's life. Finally, dispositional challenges are those related to characteristics, attitudes, and self-perceptions related to the adult as a learner. Although Cross asserts that these challenges are often crucial to the decision to participate or not to participate in educational programs, they remain important as students reconsider their participation at different times during their studies.

The use of Cross's (1992) model is largely consistent with John Ogbu's cultural-ecological theory of school performance (e.g., Ogbu, 1987, 1989; Ogbu & Simons, 1998) described in Chapter 1. Ogbu's theory places importance on system forces and community forces as factors that influence student academic performance. The institutional, situational, and dispositional challenges described in this chapter represent system forces. Black students' interpretation and response to these challenges, particularly regarding the way these challenges influence academic achievement, represent community forces. Ogbu asserted that within the context of systematic discrimination there is room for minority agency. Consequently, he saw a need for systematic study of community forces to complement the study of system forces, although he has been criticized for placing too much emphasis on such forces (e.g., Foster, 2004).

Community forces represent excessive stressors for African American students. Upon experiencing this stress, healthy individuals seek to develop coping strategies to reduce it. These coping strategies are typically either emotion-focused or problem-focused (Bird & Melville, 1994). Emotion-focused coping consists of strategies used to regulate the intense feelings aroused by a stressor. Problem-focused coping, on the other hand, consists of the efforts activated to alter, deflect, or in some way manage the stressor itself through direct action. The outcome of successful coping is resilience, which results in student persistence. Alternatively, the outcomes of less successful coping are lower achievement and, in some cases, student attrition.

Resilience is a dynamic process of positive adaptation and development while an individual simultaneously faces a significant amount of adversity and resultant negative stressors (Luthar, Cicchetti, & Becker, 2000). Resilience is a complex phenomenon. The purpose of this chapter is not to identify strategies to promote resilience. Instead, this chapter focuses on the challenges Black students encounter in education that cause undue stress. Before one can recommend successful strategies, one must first examine the conditions that create such stress. How African American students cope with the discrimination they face while attending a predominantly White institution (PWI) is key to their development, resiliency, and educational outcomes.

INSTITUTIONAL CHALLENGES

Institutional challenges are classic system forces erected by the schools themselves that represent barriers to African Americans in achievement. For example, the wisdom of involving students, particularly African American students, in active, student-centered learning is well established, yet, as discussed in Chapter 3, 70%–90% of professors use the traditional teacher-centered lecture as their primary instructional strategy (Gardiner, 1998). Ibarra (2001) attributes many of the challenges to ethnic minority student success in higher education to academic culture, where the tone is largely set by an upper- and middle-class White culture as discussed in Chapter 3:

> Academic culture has always been the central problem for ethnic minorities in higher education. The difference is that today we must rethink and reframe the operative paradigm to address the real problem, which is academic organizational cultures that prefer to confront, not collaborate. And in no way are the pipeline programs born in the 1960s capable of dealing with the growing problem of high-context, field-sensitive students who are abandoning (or never entering) graduate schools, which are dominated by low-context, field-independent professors. (p. 243)

As noted in Chapter 3, educators need to move away from the notion that, to be successful in higher education, one needs to conform to the system rather than have the system adapt to the needs of diverse students.

Ladson-Billings (1994) believes that successful pedagogues are culturally relevant teachers who encompass knowledge of the cultural distinctiveness and strengths of students. She (2000) also suggests that reliance on teacher-centered, culturally neutral models of pedagogy is highly problematic and largely unsuccessful for Black students. Optimal teaching strategies incorporate a combination of teaching methods to accommodate a variety of diverse learners. This approach maximizes the quality, as well as the depth and breadth, of students' educational experiences.

Moreover, the trend by many schools to over-reward or place over-emphasis on scholarly activities rather than teaching excellence exacerbates this situation. Increasingly, research and grant writing are becoming more and more of a priority in higher education. In recognition of this current reality, Ernest Boyer (1997) recommends the repositioning of teaching as one cornerstone of faculty activity and encourages creativity and diversity within the professoriate in order to bring renewal in teaching excellence to institutions of higher education and, ultimately, to society.

One important facet of the No Child Left Behind Act is the emphasis placed on stronger accountability for results in the K–12 school environment. The progress of the K–12 standards-based accountability movement has set the stage for an extension of this movement into higher education. The

K–12 model links student learning with institutional performance measures. Increased accountability for student learning in colleges and universities is also required. Unless our schools do a better job teaching ethnic and racial minority students, the achievement gap will likely maintain the inequality in our society today and in the immediate future. Stronger accountability models without dilution of academic quality are needed in higher education.

Building an effective learning community requires academic support, social support, and a professional commitment to student success. Support services for African American students facilitate opportunities for increased academic performance and educational attainment. A key component of closing the achievement gap between African American and White students in higher education is academic and social support through equitable programs and services. Such services require the linking of classroom activities, where learning is taking place and where challenges and differences in learning are first noted. Such a conduit can foster support to students who might not otherwise access such services. As noted in Chapter 3, there are good models available for such integration.

SITUATIONAL CHALLENGES

Situational challenges are those barriers that relate to both the social and physical environment surrounding the individual. The racial climate on college/university campuses is a significant situational factor in addressing the achievement gap. Kent (1996) points out that college campuses are reflections of society and face the same problems as society at large. Altbach (1991) reports that racial issues are significant in all aspects of campus life, including admissions, curriculum, sports, social interaction, and residence halls. Fleming (1984) asserts that when Black students matriculate in an atmosphere that is hostile, defensive reactions are aroused that interfere with intellectual performance. This inevitably widens the achievement gap between Black and White students. Moreover, racism is not necessarily overt.

Many individuals often make unconscious assumptions about people based on their race or ethnic group. This phenomenon, which is often called the "stereotype threat," is defined as "the event of a negative stereotype about a group to which one belongs becoming self-relevant, usually as a plausible interpretation for something one is doing, for an experience one is having, or for a situation one is in, that has relevance to one's self-definition" (Steele, 1997, p. 616). In other words, the stereotype threat is being at risk of confirming, as a self-characteristic, a negative stereotype about one's ability-stigmatized ethnic group. Steele (1997) suggests that the threat of confirming an unfavorable stereotype can create undue pressure to perform. This pressure may result in decreased performance or lead to disidentification with the performance domain (i.e., achievement). As a result, according to Steele, one's behavior confirms the very stereotype that one attempts to avoid.

A significant aspect of racial stereotyping is, in many cases, the absence of an identifiable wrongdoer who intends harm. According to Lowe (1999), racial stereotyping is both a conscious and often unconscious behavior that perpetuates the ills of racism. Such racial stereotyping, which is systematic and most often negative in nature, can cause individuals to internalize negative images and actually imitate the behavior and attitudes portrayed by the negative imagery. Lowe suggests that subtle as well as explicit racial discrimination demands our attention.

The interactive nature of learning communities is directly linked to the racial climate on campuses and impacts the higher education experience. The racial climate in a classroom can hinder student contribution to classroom discussions and other activities fostered by intellectual engagement. The resulting sense of isolation and alienation can create a classroom climate for African Americans where social connections are limited or do not exist.

Several studies have been conducted addressing the racial climate in colleges and universities. Rankin and Reason (2005) suggest that lower retention and graduation rates among Black students have been linked to negative racial climates, racial stereotyping, racial isolation and alienation, and low educational expectations. According to Bennett and Okinaka (1990), African American students reported greater feelings of alienation and dissatisfaction at predominately White institutions than their White peers did. These experiences were associated with peers and faculty.

Negative consequences of racial discrimination and racial intolerance in the classroom are far-reaching and a carryover from society at large. Loo and Rolison (1986) conducted a study regarding campus climate and racial intolerance at a public university. They found that minority students are significantly more likely than White students to experience social isolation and discrimination. Continued research on racism and racial tolerance on college campuses revealed that subtle or dysconscious racism is expressed through avoidance and displayed by White students and White faculty members (Biasco, Goodwin, & Vitale, 2001). Biasco et al. (2001) further examined racial discrimination and perceptions for minority and nonminority university students. A racial comparison clearly revealed that a larger percentage of minority students perceived/experienced racial discrimination at the university. Sixty-six percent of Black students report experiencing racial discrimination in contrast to 41% of White students. Additionally, 40% of Black students and 11% of White students indicate experiencing discrimination by professors.

Manifestations of racial bias in the classroom setting, as well as the campus at large, influence academic performance and continue to impact achievement for African American students in higher education. Studies addressing discrimination within the classroom provide relevant information about the academic performance of African American students (Marcus, Mullins, Brackett, Tang, Allen, & Pruett, 2003). Students report that discrimination was more prevalent inside class than outside the classroom setting. Perceptions of racial bias within the classroom setting were between 17% and 32%. Racial bias outside the classroom setting ranged from 7.3% to 17%. Twenty-six percent of students reported having their intellectual ability belittled during class by instructors of a race other than their own.

Chapter 3 suggests that the racial climate in the classroom is often dictated by teacher perceptions. Students who are viewed positively by their professors have advantages in academic interactions. Students who are viewed negatively through preconceptions and biases are disadvantaged and experience exclusion and isolation, which serves as a challenge for African American students in higher education, especially for those without extended support systems.

Researchers find racism to be a stress-provoking factor for African American students (Plummer & Slane, 1996; Steele, 1997), as discussed above. Stress caused by racism and racial stereotyping can have negative impacts on academic achievement and self-esteem. Societal stereotypes can affect intellectual functioning with manifestations of inability, self-threat, unwarranted self-consciousness, and disengagement in academic efforts (Steele, 1997).

Researchers have shown that Black achievement is linked to conditions of schooling and racial vulnerability. Aronson and Inzlicht (2004) refer to "stereotype vulnerability" as a tendency to expect, perceive, and be influenced by negative stereotypes about one's social category. Students who are vulnerable will internalize inaccurate perceptions of themselves (self-knowledge) and demonstrate poorer performance than their actual skill level and ability warrant.

Steele (1992) identifies "stigma" as a culprit in Black underachievement and a devaluation that many Blacks face in schools. Steele also suggests that the impact and connection between stigma, racial devaluation, and academic achievement to Black students has been vastly underrecognized. Racial devaluation is often a very painful process that places students in a position of having to prove themselves constantly rather than taking part in insightful and thought-provoking activities that facilitate intellectual engagement. As a result, the racial climate of the classroom leaves students feeling devalued and defeated, which negatively impacts their academic achievement. This is due to professor perceptions of the intellectual inferiority of African American students. Experiences of stereotyping and racial devaluation can manifest in the classroom and impact achievement, which serves as a challenge for African American students in higher education and contributes to the achievement gap.

"Cultural connections" between students and teachers reflect communication "connections" and provide the framework for exchange of information/

ideas and intellectually engaging conversation. Cultural mismatch or incongruence is a significant aspect relating to the academic achievement of African American students. The cultural mismatch theory (Ford, Harris, Howard, & Tyson, 2000) suggests that when communication between the student and teacher is not culturally congruent, there can be adverse outcomes for students. Communities of discourse are effective in the context of cultural frameworks where established communication is cultivated and broadened to engage all students in the intellectual experience.

Finally, the burdens of conflicting job and family responsibilities and financial concerns represent additional situational factors that can adversely affect achievement. These challenges influence both the decision to enter college as well as academic performance while in college. Job and family responsibilities have a positive motivational effect, but a negative effect on the time that is available for studying. Managing time commitments at home with job responsibilities and schoolwork can create a high level of stress. Moreover, preoccupation with conflicting responsibilities can detract from the time and concentration needed to perform well academically.

The rising costs of higher education make financial concerns particularly important, given the low socioeconomic status of some African Americans. Students with lower incomes, who are, therefore, more in need of a loan, will have to shoulder greater financial and emotional burdens to earn a degree. Moreover, low-income students may find employment necessary to pay for their college expenses. Time spent at a job can adversely impact the amount of time available for coursework and campus activities. Johnson, Duffett, and Ott (2005) emphasize the role of finances in the attitudes of students and their families toward higher education, as well as the students' actual experiences of higher education. They report, "Almost half of the young people who dropped out or who never went at all indicate that financial concerns were to blame" (p. 13). Money also plays a significant role in the choice of schooling. Johnson, Duffett, and Ott (2005) also report: "Nearly 6 in 10 (59% African American and 58% Hispanic) of those who took the college path after high school say that they themselves 'would have chosen a different school' if finances were not something they had to worry about" (p. 15).

DISPOSITIONAL CHALLENGES

Culture frames the "context" for individuals to perceive, interact, and learn about the world. Consequently, cultural or dispositional challenges are attitudinal in nature and pertain to the culturally related values, beliefs, meanings, and behavior that can inhibit participation in a higher education learning environment that does not provide a suitable context for learning.

It is imperative to emphasize that all African American students in higher education are not disposed to approach the learning process in the same manner. Research conducted in areas such as learning-style preferences and communication patterns indicate that specific commonalities and patterns emerge that are related to the culture of African American students. These characteristics are identified and discussed in Chapter 2. Other factors also emerge that can moderate Black student achievement in school, such as family history (e.g., voluntary or involuntary immigrant status as discussed above), gender (e.g., Black women tend to outperform Black men academically), peer group norms (e.g., civil rights or hip-hop generation), and social class (e.g., some studies, such as Orr [2003], have shown that wealth can indirectly help close the achievement gap).

In general, African American culture is a high-context culture that tends to focus on information that surrounds an event, situation, or interaction in order to determine meaning from the context in which it occurs. In contrast, White culture is a low-context culture that tends to filter out conditions surrounding an event or interaction to focus on words and objective facts. Successful African American students learn and formulate coping strategies that include characteristics of both high-context and low-context cultures, while unsuccessful students lack the resilience to cope with the low-context learning environment.

The traditional classroom in higher education presents challenges for many African American students who utilize a preferred style of processing, internalizing, and retrieving information. Students may experience a classroom environment that is incongruent with their learning preferences. This type of incongruence or disconnect presents an educational challenge in academic performance and contributes to the achievement gap. In the case of African American learners, the independent study method itself presents a barrier to some learners. This is because the physical and/or psychological distance between learner and instructor and learner and peers is contrary to the preference of high-context students to learn collaboratively in groups or in close contact with their instructors.

Researchers continue to report that students display higher levels of achievement when there is compatibility with a student's preferred learning style and the teaching style of instructors (Cronbach & Snow, 1981). As discussed in Chapters 2 and 3, the African American dominant learning style includes cooperation, interaction, and professorial affect. The traditional style of the educational environment is more aligned with the analytical and independent style. In contrast, many African American students employ field-dependent, people-oriented, and relational approaches to learning. Clearly, this is a challenge for African American students in higher education. There will continue to be a consistent and widening achievement gap between

African American and White students in higher education as long as student learning-style preferences are inconsistent with the dominant teaching styles of instructors. Continued research indicates that incongruence in teaching and learning styles can adversely affect learning outcomes (e.g. Charkins, O'Toole, & Wetzel, 1985; Gadzella, Stephens, & Baloglu, 2002; Matthews, 1991).

CONCLUSION

Success in higher education serves as an entry point for numerous opportunities in our society and closes the million dollar gap described in Chapter 1 (i.e., the difference in expected lifetime wages between college graduates and nongraduates). College graduation is directly related to job prospects, economic empowerment, social mobility, and political capital. However, success in higher education for African American students requires that they overcome significant challenges.

This chapter presents and discusses challenges to African American college student achievement in the traditional classroom. These challenges are impediments to academic achievement, learning opportunities, and intellectual engagement. Cross's (1992) model is used to classify these challenges into institutional, situational, and dispositional categories.

Institutional challenges are erected by the schools themselves and exclude or discourage certain groups of learners from full participation in learning. Schools need to be sensitive to these challenges and develop policies and strategies to eliminate or minimize their effects on student achievement. These challenges consist of a largely low-context academic culture that provides:

- little congruence with the backgrounds of African Americans,
- a largely "one-size-fits-all" teaching style,
- more emphasis on scholarly activities among faculty members than on teaching excellence and student mentoring,
- poor faculty accountability for learning failures relating to pedagogy, and
- limited availability of educational support services

Situational challenges are those barriers that relate to a person's life context at a particular time and to both the social and physical environment surrounding the individual. These challenges tend to be more difficult for schools to address than institutional challenges, since they often reflect society at large. For example, research shows that factors outside the classroom, e.g., economic and family issues, can have a strong influence on achievement. Nonetheless, the impact of these factors can be reduced through creative planning, professional development, financial aid, and appropriate support programs. These challenges include:

- race-based rejection,
- racial stereotyping,
- conflicting job and family responsibilities, and
- financial concerns

Finally, cultural or dispositional challenges are attitudinal in nature and pertain to the culturally related values, beliefs, meanings, and behavior that inhibit full participation in a higher education learning environment. Student dispositional characteristics become challenges when they do not fit within the school's academic culture, e.g., high-context learners in a low-context learning environment. These challenges can be addressed by schools using a mix of support programs, school policy, and professional development programs. Dispositional challenges confronting Black students in a predominantly White institution include:

- a preference for holistic learning in a largely compartmentalized and analytical learning environment,
- a preference for field dependence in a largely field-independent learning environment, and
- a preference for high-context communication in a largely low-context communication environment

The role of culture and approaches to the teaching and learning process is a key variable in addressing the achievement gap between African American and White students in higher education. Teaching and learning-style mismatches; racial stereotyping; racial prejudice; and feelings of rejection, isolation, and alienation create a fragile and complex experience for the African American student in the traditional classroom. The consistent mismatch of teaching- and learning-style preferences in the traditional college classroom perpetuates a fragmented educational experience for students of color, and results in a continuing struggle to bridge the achievement gap. Moreover, the racial climate in the classroom, which is marred by subtle, as well as overt, discrimination, often places the African American student in precarious and awkward situations with feelings of defenselessness and defeat. Experiences of discrimination can be quite defining with regard to psychosocial and psychological processes involving self-esteem, self-concept, respect, value, and self-definition.

For some African American students, the traditional classroom in higher education presents challenges, which fosters an increased sense of resiliency as they learn to cope. For others, encounters of racial conflict and the effects of stress and anxiety pose challenges that negatively impact academic performance. The sum of these factors highlights the critical nature of academic support for African American students in higher education. The initiation, maintenance, and expansion of support services for African American students underscore efforts in closing the achievement gap in higher education.

Academic intentions must embrace cultural consciousness to truly approximate and actualize closing the achievement gap between African American and White students in higher education. African American students (like all students) should be the beneficiaries of a challenging yet responsive and supportive higher education experience that promotes equity and quality in preparing them for opportunities of inclusion and success in the broader context of society. At present, quality in higher education is largely determined by criteria that do not accurately portray the quality of education provided. The two major indicators of quality—accreditation, which tends to be narrowly focused on compliance to basic standards of operation, and *U.S. News & World Report* rankings, which rely mostly on inputs to the school—are consequently not the best indicators of quality. The focus in determining institutional quality should center on learning outcomes, faculty accountability for these outcomes, and the school's ability to make progress in closing the African American achievement gap.

DISCUSSION TOPICS

1. How can the college community be more responsive to the diversity of students in higher education?
2. What teaching methods do we currently use? Are they successful and effective methods for all students?
3. How does racial stereotyping influence classroom learning?
4. How can academic support programs be improved at your school so that the needs of ethnic minorities are better addressed?
5. What policies need to be changed at your school?
6. Do regional accrediting agencies focus sufficiently on assessing learner outcomes? In particular, should they place greater emphasis on evaluating outputs or student learning, rather than maintaining the traditional focus on inputs, such as resources?

REFERENCES

Altbach, P. O. (1991). The racial dilemma in American higher education. In P. G. Altbach & K. Lomotey (Eds.), *The racial crisis in American higher education* (pp. 3–17). Albany, NY: State University of New York Press.

Aronson, J. A., & Inzlicht, M. (2004). The ups and downs of attributional ambiguity: Stereotype vulnerability and the academic self-knowledge of African American college students. *Psychological Science, 15*(12), 829–836.

Bennett, C., & Okinaka, A. M. (1990). Factors related to persistence among Asians, black, Hispanic, and white undergraduates at a predominantly white university: Comparison between first and fourth year cohorts. *Urban Review, 22*(1), 33–60.

Biasco, F., Goodwin, E. A., & Vitale, K. (2001). College students' attitudes toward racial discrimination. *The College Student Journal, 35*(4), 523–528.

Bird, G. W., & Melville, K. (1994). *Families and intimate relationships.* New York: McGraw-Hill.

Boyer, E. L. (1997). *Scholarship reconsidered: Priorities of the professoriate.* San Francisco: Jossey-Bass.

Charkins, R. J., O'Toole, D. M., & Wetzel, J. N. (1985). Linking teacher and student learning styles with student achievement and attitudes. *Journal of Economic Education, 16*(2), 111–120.

Cronbach, L., & Snow, R. (1981). *Aptitudes and instructional methods: A handbook for research on interactions.* New York: Irvington.

Cross, K. P. (1992). *Adults as learners: Increasing participation and facilitating learning.* San Francisco: Jossey-Bass.

Delpit, L. (1988). The silenced dialogue: Power and pedagogy in educating other people's children. *Harvard Educational Review, 58*(3), 280–298.

Fleming, J. (1984). *Blacks in college: A comparative study of students' success in black and white institutions.* San Francisco: Jossey-Bass.

Ford, D., Harris, J. J., Howard, T., & Tyson, C. A. (2000). Creating culturally responsive classrooms for gifted African American students. *Journal for the Education of the Gifted, 23*(4), 397–427.

Foster, K. M. (2004). Coming to terms: A discussion of John Ogbu's cultural-ecological theory of minority academic achievement. *Intercultural Education, 15*(4), 369–384.

Gadzella, B. M., Stephens, R., & Baloglu, M. (2002). Prediction of educational psychology course grades by age and learning style scores. *College Student Journal, 36*(1), 62–68.

Gardiner, L. F. (1998). Why we must change: The research evidence. *The NEA Higher Education Journal, Spring,* 71–88.

Ibarra, R. A. (2001). *Beyond affirmative action: Reframing the context of higher education.* Madison, WI: University of Wisconsin Press.

Johnson, J., Duffett, A., & Orr, A. (2005). *Life after high school: Young people talk about their hopes and prospects.* New York: Public Agenda.

Kent, N. J. (1996). The new campus racism: What's going on? *Thought & Action, 12*(2), 45–57.

Ladson-Billings, G. (1994). *The dreamkeepers: Successful teachers of African American students.* San Francisco: Jossey-Bass.

Ladson-Billings, G. (2000). Racialized discourses and ethnic epistemologies. In N. Denzin & Y. Lincoln (Eds.), *Handbook of qualitative research* (2nd ed.) (pp. 257–278). Thousand Oaks, CA: Sage.

Loo, C. M., & Rolison, G. (1986). Alienation of ethnic minority students at a predominantly white university. *Journal of Higher Education, 57*(1), 58–77.

Lowe, E. Y. (1999). *Promise and dilemma: Perspectives on racial diversity and higher education*. Princeton, NJ: Princeton University Press.

Luthar, S. S., Cicchetti, D., & Becker, B. (2000). The construct of resilience: A critical evaluation and guidelines for future work. *Child Development, 71*(3), 543–562.

Marcus, A., Mullins, L., Brackett, K., Tang, Z., Allen, A., & Pruett, D. (2003). Perceptions of racism on campus. *College Student Journal, 37*(4), 611–626.

Matthews, D. B. (1991). The effects of learning style on grades of first year college students. *Research in Higher Education, 32*(3), 253–268.

Ogbu, J. U. (1987). Variability in minority school performance: A problem in search of an explanation. *Anthropology and Education Quarterly, 18*(4), 312–334.

Ogbu, J. U. (1989). The individual in collective adaptation: A framework for focusing on academic underperformance and dropping out among involuntary minorities. In L. Weis, E. Farrar, & H. G. Petrie (Eds.), *Dropouts from school: Issues, dilemmas, and solutions* (pp. 181–204). Albany, NY: State University of New York Press.

Ogbu, J. U., & Simons, H. D. (1998). Voluntary and involuntary minorities: A cultural-ecological theory of school performance with some implications for education. *Anthropology and Education Quarterly, 29*(2), 155–188.

Orr, A. J. (2003). Black-white differences in achievement: The importance of wealth. *Sociology of Education, 76*(4), 281–304.

Plummer, D., & Slane, S. (1996). Patterns of coping in racially stressful situations. *Journal of Black Psychology, 22*(3), 302–315.

Rankin, S. R., & Reason, R. D. (2005). Differing perceptions: How students of color and white students perceive campus climate for underrepresented groups. *Journal of College Student Development, 46*(1), 43–61.

Steele, C. M. (1992). Race and the schooling of African Americans. *Atlantic Monthly, April*, 68–78.

Steele, C. M. (1997). A threat in the air: How stereotypes shape the intellectual identities and performance of women and African Americans. *American Psychologist, 52*, 613–629.

SIX

Designing and Teaching Traditional Courses

Nancy E. Rhea & Michael K. Ponton

PURPOSE

The purpose of this chapter is to highlight various roles that the instructor should fulfill in the traditional face-to-face (F2F) environment that will facilitate the development of African American students. Topics discussed will inform both instructional design and delivery. To understand the context of these roles, two critical questions are addressed: What instructional processes are possible in a face-to-face environment as differentiated from an online environment? What are the student characteristics particular to African Americans that must be attended to by these processes?

BACKGROUND

Within the context of structured education (i.e., the formal curriculum), a simple definition of teaching is the design and delivery of courses that make student learning possible. Stated less simply, teaching is the creation of an environment that interacts not only with the student's behaviors but also with the student's cognitive and affective processes—students enter educational settings with values, cognitive and learning styles, belief systems, and communication styles that impact the ways in which they construct knowledge.

Good teaching occurs when interactions maximize the efficiency of learning. Thus, the creation of an optimal educational experience involves not only having a repertoire of instructional strategies from which the instructor can choose, but also an understanding of the nature of these various interactions. Good teaching can and does occur inside or outside the traditionally defined classroom.

Of course, an implicit assumption is that the environment can affect learning. Social cognitive theory (SCT; Bandura, 1986) posits that human functioning is understood by considering the bidirectional interactions among three constituent factors: the person, the environment, and behaviors. The person represents the biological/psychological being; the environment is everything external to the person; and behaviors are the actions of the person.

Bidirectional influences consist of the following elements:

- A person subjectively interprets the environment while the environment provides information that shapes a person's thoughts and feelings (person-environment interaction).
- A person intentionally chooses activities in which to engage while the results of such activities provide feedback that influences future behaviors (person-behavior interaction).
- The environment offers opportunities and impediments to activities while activities can change the objective environment (environment-behavior interaction).

SCT recognizes that the person, environment, and behavior are all necessary interacting components that must be considered to fully understand human performance within any context.

Because SCT asserts that humans are capable of thought-induced intentional action, five inherent capabilities (Bandura, 1986) are recognized to exist within each person:

1. *Symbolization.* Through symbolization, a person is able to create mental models of sensory experiences that provide information that influences future behavior.
2. *Forethought.* Using forethought, symbolized information is used to mentally create future scenarios from which goals and plans are formulated.
3. *Vicarious learning.* Vicarious learning allows a person to learn from the trials and successes of others, thereby avoiding wasted time and resources when first learning desired content or skills.
4. *Self-regulation.* After using forethought to create goals and plans, self-regulatory systems are enlisted to direct efforts that are consistent with chosen paths.
5. *Self-reflection.* Self-reflection provides a person with the means to evaluate previous behaviors and their consequences, thereby influencing cognitive processes that influence future activity.

The sociocognitive perspective suggests that instructors can create environments that affect student behavior and ultimate levels of learning, but that the efficacy of such environments is influenced by the student's cognitive and affective processes. Although statistically accurate generalizations can be made regarding any group, individuals have unique internal characteristics that influence behavior and interpretations of behavioral outcomes. Of course, group acculturation can and does create common beliefs, attitudes, intentions, and behaviors among its members, which add to and interact with individual knowledge and the processes of thinking and acting. Major culture-related influences affecting African American students are discussed in Chapters 2 and 3.

FACE-TO-FACE TEACHING CONSIDERATIONS

Discussions about effective teaching practices are not new. In fact, the literature offers many practical volumes that discuss appropriate teaching strategies (e.g., Davis, 1993; Johnson, 1995; Magnan, 1990; Neff & Weimer, 1989; Pregent, 2000) with considerations to learning and cognitive styles (e.g., Sarasin, 1999; Sternberg, 1997). Many traditional instructional strategies, such as lecturing, discussion, and group activities, can be incorporated in either a face-to-face (F2F) or an online environment.

"Face-to-face" implies just that: a physical, simultaneous presence of the instructor and the student. These characteristics (i.e., physical presence and simultaneity) are the major environmental differences between the F2F classroom and the virtual classroom used in an online environment. Physical presence creates an opportunity for verbal communication and nonverbal cues (e.g., facial expressions, bodily gestures, manner of dress, and room arrangements) while simultaneity provides an opportunity for an immediate and impromptu exchange of ideas and information. This situation contrasts with the virtual classroom used in learning management systems where students are physically separated and communication is mostly asynchronous (i.e., computer-mediated communication occurs with a time delay, thereby allowing participants to respond at their own convenience). As teaching and learning is a communicative transaction between the teacher and learner, physical presence and simultaneity serve as the foundation upon which F2F instruction is defined and differentiated from online instruction.

A second implication of F2F teaching is that, in general, if a student is able to participate in this type of instruction, the student is within the geographic proximity of the instructor. Although exceptions do exist, this general characteristic of traditional education facilitates opportunities for additional F2F educative transactions (i.e., teaching and mentoring) to occur outside of the classroom. Thus, teaching via physical presence and simultaneity of interaction can occur in the instructor's office, in transit between buildings, or in the dining hall.

Student Perspectives

Students bring to the classroom a wealth of knowledge and experiences that profoundly affect their learning. Banks (1998) labels one type of knowledge that they possess "personal/cultural," which refers to "the concepts, expectations, and interpretations that students derive from personal experiences in their homes, families, and community cultures" (pp. 76–77). In terms of African American students, what distinguishing characteristics inform teaching? Many scholars (Bennett, 2006; Cokley, 2003; Hale-Benson, 1986; Kuykendall, 1989; Ogbu, 1995; Shade, 1982) have argued that the differences between African American and White cultures have resulted in disparate learning-style preferences between each group's members. Attributed to many African American students is the field-dependent approach to learning that emphasizes the importance of a student-centered environment involving collaboration; by contrast, the field-independent learning style that favors independence has been attributed often to White students (see Chapter 2 for a discussion of field theory).

According to Flannery (1995), African Americans emphasize "communal values . . . which include: knowledge which is valued, how learning occurs, and communication patterns of working together for the good of community" (pp. 153–154). Pascarella and Terenzini (2005) cite numerous studies that suggest that African American students who attend PWIs experience significantly greater levels of social isolation, alienation, personal dissatisfaction, and overt racism as compared to similar students attending historically Black institutions. Thus, one defining characteristic of the African American student is the enhanced importance of experiencing communal and nurturing patterns of communication in instruction.

Rovai and Gallien (2005) believe that students in a classroom setting "should have feelings of belonging, trust, safety, participation, and support" (p. 54). Students should feel as though they matter to other members of their educational group, that they have responsibilities to the group, and that each member's educational needs will be met via a commitment to shared educational goals. In other words, the learning environment should foster a sense of community.

McMillan and Chavis (1986) describe having a sense of community as "a feeling that members have of belonging, a feeling that members matter to one another and to the group, and a shared faith that members' needs will be met through their commitment to be together" (p. 9). Aspects of community differ across contexts; in other words, they are situationally defined (Rheingold, 2000). Regardless of the specific context in which the community exists, however, the sense of community and feelings of belonging are enhanced through social interaction. Using such social interactions within the context of classroom discourse, thereby fostering a sense of community, is of particular importance in teaching the field-dependent African American learner. Outcalt and Skewes-Cox (2002) support this view and write that "HBCUs (historically Black colleges and universities) succeed in educating their African American students largely because they provide a climate in which African American students feel welcome, supported, and encouraged to take part in the social and academic life of the campus" (p. 345).

The position that being African American suggests certain preferences with regard to learning style or any other characteristic is not rooted in a suggestion that the color of one's skin determines cognitive or affective attributes. However, if the color of one's skin influences the nature of experiences in a social world, then it is those experiences that will shape ultimate modes of thinking and acting.

If a group of similarly colored people have similar experiences, the resultant congruence of beliefs, attitudes, intentions, and behaviors serve to define this people's culture as related to their race. Historically for African Americans, being Black has resulted in not being allowed full participation in the majority Euro-American culture. This form of exclusion has effectuated their being marginalized, less educated, and less well-off economically in a global sense. More specifically, being African American has resulted in the perpetuation of certain African traditions (such as communal values that can be related to field-dependent learning preferences) because the lack of full participation in our general society has limited opportunities for Euro-American acculturation. This is truer of less-affluent African Americans who are unable to move from racially homogeneous communities and interact with other culturally diverse communities.

Strategies for Success

Research and educational practice suggest that the academic and social integration of students leads to higher grade point averages and student persistence (e.g., Maton, Hrabowski, & Schmitt, 2000). To increase African American student learning and reduce the achievement gap in higher education, members of the school community must value diversity and acknowledge that Black students are as capable as their White peers. The racial stereotype that African American students are underprepared can result in low academic achievement for Blacks (e.g., Hummel & Steele, 1996). A climate of high expectations is needed.

Additionally, communication should be used in a manner that attends to the influences of individual and culturally informed beliefs, attitudes, intentions, and behaviors, as discussed in Chapters 2 and 3. Accordingly, the instructors of African American students should fulfill the following four roles: engager, motivator, model, and mentor. Using the sociocognitive framework, Figure 6.1 highlights the environmental position of these four roles as an interacting factor along with the student (i.e., the "person") and the student's behaviors in facilitating academic achievement.

Engager. Learning is an active process that requires students to incorporate new knowledge with knowledge already acquired from previous experiences in order to create something both meaningful and applicable to their own personal lives (Brooks & Brooks, 1999). Chickering and Gamson (1987) assert:

> Learning is not a spectator sport. Students do not learn much just sitting in classes listening to teachers, memorizing prepackaged assignments, and spitting out answers. They must talk about what they are learning, write reflectively about it, relate it to past experiences, and apply it to their daily lives. They must make what they learn part of themselves. (p. 3)

When an instructor engages students, the students become active participants in their learning and think about the content of the course as well as the implications and connections of the content in conjunction with their extant knowledge.

Chapter 2 outlines orientations that research suggests are attributable to African American students. In particular, engaging the holistic, field-dependent African American student requires social interaction and caring relationships to facilitate learning. Thus, communication must exist between

Figure 6.1. A Socio-Cognitive Model Outlining the Factors That Interact to Influence Academic Achievement

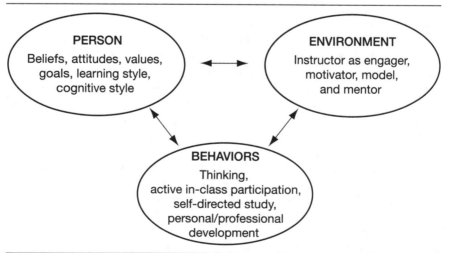

the instructor and student as well as among students in a nonjudgmental environment where individual experience and perspective are valued. To catalyze such an environment requires the instructor to engage African American students by stimulating interaction via thought-provoking questioning. Unfortunately, based upon research of college classroom practices, Weimer (1989) concludes "Quite bluntly, professors ask few questions that require students to think" (p. 69).

There is a range of questions that an instructor can pose. For example, a question can assess recall and comprehension of specific content material, or stimulate a variety of synthetic and evaluative conclusions, none of which is any more correct than the other when respective contexts are considered. In the latter category, questions can be proffered to engage students in the learning process by enabling them to share individual experiences and insights, not just lessons particular to the course, and to facilitate meaningful interaction. This form of questioning is particularly important for the African American students who, as suggested in Chapter 2, learn best when course content is made relevant to the context of their own experiences. Thus, instructors should utilize questions that require divergent thinking where these students can synthesize what they know in order to create, elaborate, and defend possible solutions that are applicable to their own lives. Such questioning in an atmosphere in which personal knowledge is both respected and valued would enhance an instructor's ability to engage African American students.

In addition to serving as a vehicle for thinking and meaningful interaction, questioning also serves another role in the learning experience: It communicates an expectation that students are prepared to respond to the questions posed. When an instructor attentively engages every student during the course of a class meeting, each student knows that he or she may be queried at any time. In addition, the astute instructor who is not willing to terminate the exchange when a student says, "I don't know," but instead is willing to continue probing for a substantive response reinforces not only the expectation that each student must think and prepare adequately for class discussions, but also the recognition that every student has valuable information to contribute.

Although some courses are certainly more content-laden than others (cf. mathematics with history) and discussion may not be the most effective instructional method, nevertheless, to maximize student engagement the instructor should actively seek opportunities to engage students in conversation —to talk *with* students, not just *at* them. Such opportunities may enhance African American students' feelings of being meaningful and active participants in their own learning as well as that of their classmates and even the instructor. As a result, they see themselves as responsible, valued, contributing members of the class group.

When students believe that they are responsible for coming to class prepared, their development as self-directed learners is facilitated. There are many steps toward becoming a self-directed learner, however, and students within a particular class may operate at various levels of self-directedness.

Due to prior educational experiences, African American students may experience low levels of self-directedness; therefore, instructors should anticipate becoming more intricately involved in their students' growth toward autonomy. An instructor may need to elaborate on the concept of "being prepared" for class in that it requires students to regulate their study, both in schedule and adequacy, before class. This involves prioritizing and choosing learning activities over non-learning activities as well as enlisting a multitude of resources to inform discussion. Specifically, the instructor should require students not to limit their pre-class reading to assigned texts but rather to seek out additional books or articles on topics of personal interest that can be related to the course content, thus reinforcing that students have opportunities to make unique and meaningful contributions as valued class members.

Fostering self-directedness in learning is not just a useful pedagogical consideration; it may be the most important educational objective of the curriculum, as it supports lifelong learning. As Bandura (1997) asserts:

> Development of capabilities for self-directedness enables individuals not only to continue their intellectual growth beyond their formal education but to advance the nature and quality of their life pursuits. . . . The rapid pace of technological change and the accelerated growth of knowledge require continual upgrading of competencies if people are to survive and prosper under increasingly competitive conditions. . . . Self-development with age partly determines whether the expanded life span is lived self-fulfillingly or apathetically. These changing realities call for lifelong learners. (p. 227)

When instructors create lifelong learners they are enabling their students to reach great levels of achievement by continued learning and personal development long after graduation. African American students should be empowered to create their own opportunities for success.

Questioning should also be used as an assessment of personal understanding by both the instructor and the student. From the instructor's perspective, questioning affords an opportunity to reveal voids in student knowledge and lack of sophistication in thinking. Unfortunately, a characteristic of many African American college students is poor primary and secondary education. When such inadequacies are identified, the instructors can engage in private talks with individual students to intervene in a manner that is not threatening or embarrassing and offer developmental suggestions. Likewise, similar assessments can be performed by students themselves when the instructor encourages such self-evaluations.

Self-regulation, an important component of self-directed learning, is the personal examination of the adequacy of one's performance, as this feedback provides information that the individual uses as the basis for corrective action. When a student becomes aware of personal deficiencies, he or she can use this self-identified feedback to inform future learning and preparation; however, it is very important that the instructor does not ridicule the student when deficiencies are apparent, as this does not promote the communal, nurturing classroom environment that is so important in engaging the African American student.

Within a multicultural classroom, Allport's (1954) intergroup contact theory suggests that cross-racial communication is more likely to lead to positive outcomes when interactions take place under the following conditions:

- the status of groups is equal
- common goals are pursued
- there is cooperation between groups
- interaction is promoted by an authority (i.e., the instructor)

Thus, in addition to prompting interaction via questioning, the instructor should (a) create an environment that fosters respect between disparate racial/ethnic groups, (b) identify common goals of learning/education, and (c) moderate student discourse and provide assignments that build both cooperation and a valuation of individual perspective and experience. At the institutional level, Chang, Astin, and Kim (2004) suggest that improving the quality of cross-racial interactions requires increasing opportunities for racially diverse students to live and work on campus.

Motivator. Instilling the requirement that African American students be responsible for coming to class prepared is not all that is needed to motivate self-study. If this were the case, each class period could be nothing more than an examination that would motivate student learning through individual study before every class meeting. Therefore, although such expectations of preparation are certainly motivating (i.e., students actually do study for tests), other motivational processes should also be enlisted by the instructor.

A major premise of outcome expectancy theories of motivation is that people engage in activities that they expect will lead to valued outcomes. Bandura (1997) asserts that there are three types of outcomes: personal, social, and self-evaluative:

1. Personal outcomes reside within the individual, such as physical pleasure or pain.
2. Social outcomes are those created by others, such as money, acceptance, or accolades.

3. Self-evaluative outcomes are resultant evaluations based upon a comparison of an individual's actions and behavioral consequences with personal standards of acceptability.

A performance goal (the direct result of behavior) is adopted because an individual believes that attaining the goal will lead to a desirable outcome (an indirect result of behavior); however, expected outcomes do not always occur when the goal is achieved, and sometimes unexpected outcomes occur as well. In order to provide maximum motivation, Bandura indicates that goals should be specific and challenging, with proximal subgoals created that lead to distal goals (i.e., longer-term goals requiring a series of related behaviors and steps).

For example, a young African American male observes the numerous social outcomes (i.e., social rewards) derived from being a professional basketball player, such as fame and fortune. Thus, the young male adopts a distal goal of performance (e.g., practice basketball 4 hours each day for the next 10 years) because of the perceived relationship between accomplishing these goals and his desired outcomes (we write "his" because not everyone is motivated by the same outcomes). Note that a supporting proximal subgoal would be to practice at this level for a single day—the subgoal is not nearly as daunting as the distal 10-year goal and accomplishing this subgoal on a daily basis will lead to the ultimate attainment of the distal goal. For the most part, accomplishing his specific performance goals are within the young male's volitional control; that is, unless there are situational impediments (e.g., he gets the flu) or structural impediments (e.g., he no longer has access to basketball resources) to accomplishing his performance goals, it is within his control to accomplish his goal regarding practice. However, whether or not the attainment of such goals will ultimately lead to his desired outcomes is not within his control—that is, even though the young man accomplishes his practice goals, he still may not secure a lucrative professional basketball contract.

College courses have many performances: for example, reading assigned and unassigned work, writing papers, participating in classroom discussions, and taking tests. For motivation to occur, students must perceive a relationship between successful performances and their desired outcomes. To avoid leaving motivation to chance, however, the instructor should proactively explain to students the relationship between prescribed course performances and individually derived, but perhaps culturally influenced, desired outcomes. This is particularly beneficial for African American students who desire academic work to be personally relevant.

As Chapter 2 suggests, members of the hip-hop generation (i.e., younger African American adults) are more "career-oriented" than older generations of African Americans of the civil rights era who are more "rights-oriented."

This distinction informs motivation by suggesting a different set of desirable outcomes based upon the age of students within the classroom (note that the presence of the nontraditionally aged student in U.S. college classrooms is the result of democratically based policies of access that are not present around the world). Thus, when faced with younger African American students, the instructor should relate successful performances on specific prescribed tasks in terms of knowledge and skills that are important to professional aspirations and resultant outcomes (e.g., monetary success); when faced with older African American students, the relationship should be couched in terms of supporting an egalitarian society where education is the means to participate fully in all aspects of life.

Of course, a better approach for instructors would be to learn about their students individually, including the students' unique aspirations, so that relationships between course tasks and outcomes of individual importance can be made. In a traditional setting, the opportunities for efficient informal communication are greater than in a text-based online environment where communication involves typing and reading. Fortunately for the instructor, similar knowledge and skills are important to many spheres of life, thereby justifying a common curriculum; however, instructors should identify tasks that offer opportunities for students to pursue individual interests and task preferences (e.g., group versus individual work) that legitimately support course objectives. In this manner, the relationship between course performances and individual values becomes more explicit via differentiated instruction, thereby facilitating student motivation and increasing engagement. In addition, allowing students to be responsible for designing course performances and establishing learning goals promotes self-directedness, which, as noted previously, is an important educational objective.

Model. The physical presence afforded by the traditional classroom provides an excellent opportunity for the student to observe the instructor. The instructor's patterns of speech, mannerisms, style of dress, and treatment of others are all within the student's field of observation. In addition, the instructor can serve as a model of someone whose success is predicated upon educational achievement and who manifests qualities such as sociability, sensitivity, discernment, concern, kindness, humility, and fairness.

As a model of behavior, the instructor must be ever vigilant in presenting himself or herself in a manner that is consistent with that of a successful, educated person. In this regard, a student (particularly one from a low socioeconomic background who has had little exposure to educated professionals) is able to observe manners of action appropriate to both business and social arenas that educated persons frequent.

For those who are more civil rights–oriented (i.e., the civil rights generation of African Americans), societal transformations toward egalitarianism require minority citizens to have access to positions of influence, and generally such positions are reserved for those who are educated, represent the best of their constituency in the public eye, and are able to formulate lucid arguments either verbally or in writing. For those who are more career-oriented (i.e., the hip-hop generation), movement up the professional ladder generally involves presenting oneself as a serious individual who has the ability to communicate intelligently and to represent him- or herself and, thus, his or her employer, in a professional manner. Fortunately for the instructor, similar behaviors that are successfully modeled can achieve both objectives.

There are many activities that can lead to similar outcomes; for example, people are employed in a variety of vocations to earn a living. Thus, while motivational considerations such as the correlation between performance goals and desirable outcomes is important, people must choose which activities to pursue based upon what they believe themselves capable of performing (perceived capability is referred to as "self-efficacy"; Bandura, 1997). In the absence of personal experiences, models serve an important role in supplying vicarious information to the student regarding what is possible.

In 2001, 12.9% of all African American postsecondary students were enrolled in historically Black colleges and universities (HBCUs) (National Center for Education Statistics [NCES], 2004a). However, 21.5% of all bachelor's degrees earned by African Americans during the 2001–2002 academic year were awarded at HBCUs (NCES, 2004b). Why is there such a disproportionate amount of degree-granting at HBCUs? Are HBCUs "easier," providing an inferior education and thereby easing the path to a degree?

Based upon a multilevel analysis using hierarchical linear modeling from a national longitudinal data set, Kim (2002) found "no significant difference . . . between HBCUs and HWCUs [historically White colleges and universities] in their ability to influence overall academic ability, writing ability, and math ability" (p. 403). Thus, the disproportionate number of degrees awarded by HBCUs compared to PWIs is not due to an academically easier path. (See Chapter 3 for a discussion and contrast of school cultures at HBCUs and PWIs.)

In addition, Pascarella, Wolniak, Pierson, and Flowers (2004) found "that attending an HBCU substantially increased the net odds that an African American student would plan on obtaining a graduate degree. . . . Such findings reinforce the notion that HBCUs may be particularly potent environments for enhancing the development and aspirations of African American students" (p. 313). The academic success and ambition of African American students who attend HBCUs is due, in part, to the presence of adequate role models that enhance student self-efficacy.

Vicarious experiences can increase efficacy beliefs when models, perceived by observers as being like themselves, engage in successful performances. The resultant notion of "if that person can do it, so can I" encapsulates how a vicarious experience strengthens efficacy beliefs in the absence of authentic mastery experiences. This argument certainly seems to support the importance of the presence of African American instructors for African American students. In 2001, 60.4% of the faculty members at HBCUs were African American, compared to 26.2% who were White (NCES, 2004c). Note that in 1995, 4.9% of the faculty members in all institutions of higher education were African American (NCES, 1999); thus, HBCUs tend to have a disproportionate number of African American faculty when compared to the entire nation.

As discussed in Chapter 3, being African American alone is not sufficient, and may not be necessary, to be deemed an adequate role model by a student. A White instructor who grew up in an underprivileged neighborhood similar to that of a particular African American student may be a better role model for that student than an African American instructor who had the benefits of a privileged life. The important assessment criteria by the student are similarity and empathy. In this regard, instructors should attempt to find and make connections with their students by exposing early-life similarities so that they present an example of what is possible for someone like the student.

For example, in terms of identifying with her female African American mentee, Lincoln, a female White professor, relates that, although she has no experience with the harmful effects of racial bias, she has experience with those of gender bias (Stanley & Lincoln, 2005). When students see that others with backgrounds similar to their own are capable of finishing college and graduate school, they see themselves as capable of similar academic attainments and adopt higher educational aspirations. In presenting legitimate similarities, however, instructors should not state that their backgrounds are "just like" those of the students, as this could be presumptuous and offensive, thereby creating distance. Rather, instructors should just reveal their personal narratives by intentionally highlighting similar experiences (e.g., "my parents never finished high school"), allowing the students to evaluate and juxtapose the information to their own backgrounds.

The positive effects of strong beliefs of personal efficacy have been supported in many spheres of human functioning. As Bandura (1997) asserts:

> [Self-efficacy] beliefs influence the courses of action people choose to pursue, how much effort they put forth in given endeavors, how long they will persevere in the face of obstacles and failures, their resilience to adversity, whether their thought patterns are self-hindering or self-aiding, how much stress and depression they experience in coping with taxing environment demands, and the level of accomplishments they realize. (p. 3)

Motivation results from outcome expectancies, a positive relationship between performance goals and desirable outcomes, and beliefs of personal efficacy. Therefore, to maximize student motivation to engage in academic work, the instructor needs to serve as an authentic (i.e., similar to the student) role model, thereby offering vicarious information to build a strong sense of student self-efficacy. The instructor should attempt to explicitly reveal personal beginnings that are similar to those of the student so that the student believes in the possibility of a similar transformation facilitated by a successful college experience.

Mentor. The effectiveness of modeling rests with the recognition that the instructor was similar to the student in the past; effective mentoring, however, is based upon the instructor being different from the student in the present. This essential difference is knowledge that the instructor, not the student, possesses that is useful to the student's personal or professional development. In a mentoring process, this knowledge is shared with the student to help guide appropriate thought and action.

As addressed earlier, manners of behavior and speech can be modeled; however, why one acts in a certain way, what one says in a certain situation, or even how one thinks about a certain issue is knowledge and affect that are mentored. Mentoring involves the sharing of insights based upon personal experiences; that is, mentoring is teaching issues outside the course content that are equally important to the student's eventual success. If the African American achievement gap is to be closed, not only the gap that exists in higher education but also that which exists in society, instructors must believe themselves responsible for sharing information that may greatly influence the student's success after graduation. They must therefore view themselves as agents of cultural change. Although the curriculum is certainly designed and taught for this purpose (i.e., to facilitate a graduate's success), it represents a foundation of content knowledge focused on academic matters.

Unlike classroom teaching, mentoring involves attending to issues that are not documented on syllabi and in the formal curriculum; therefore, mentors are those who are willing to teach lessons that extend beyond their professional contract and course descriptions for the purpose of a better future. In writing about their cross-race mentoring relationship, Stanley and Lincoln (2005) describe a rewarding mentoring experience as one "characterized by trust, honesty, a willingness to learn about self and others, and the ability to share power and privilege," and they describe good mentors as those willing to learn about their "protégés' strengths and weaknesses, nurture their autonomy, treat them as individuals, capitalize on their skills, and create opportunities for challenge and growth" (p. 46). The personal aspect of mentoring supports the nurturing environment that is important to the African American student.

As suggested above, being able to teach in the traditional classroom suggests a degree of geographic proximity between instructor and student.

Instructors who mentor students should take advantage of fortuitous occasions and also create additional opportunities to share personal insights that are directed at guiding students to personal achievement—mentoring can occur anywhere. Because students always outnumber instructors, instructors must attempt to mentor several students at once, perhaps by making use of extemporaneous discussions within the classroom or by getting involved in extracurricular activities that provide access to student groups. Mentoring supports the creation of a welcoming, supportive, and encouraging climate that Outcalt and Skewes-Cox (2002) suggest is the foundation of HBCU successes with African American students.

By engaging students, the instructor helps students become thinkers; through the instructor's motivation, students assume responsibility for their own learning; and by modeling the instructor, students see the product of being educated. The probability of each student's success is greatly increased when he or she becomes an educated, self-directed thinker. This goal, however, represents individual achievement. Although closing the African American achievement gap may occur one person at a time, closing the opportunity gap requires systematic changes that affect large groups of African Americans. Consequently, mentored lessons should focus not only on skills and knowledge, but also on civic responsibilities. Thus, an important lesson in mentoring students is that individual success should be used to spawn opportunities for others with the intent to break down artificially contrived obstructions to success. The goal of using those skills honed in college—self-directed questioning followed by educated reflection—to ameliorate societal defects is an invaluable lesson that must be mentored, since it is usually absent in academic curricula. As West (2005) asserts:

> To engage in [the] Socratic questioning of America is not to trash our country, but rather to tease out those traditions in our history that enable us to wrestle with difficult realities we often deny. The aim of this Socratic questioning is democratic paideia—the cultivation of an active, informed citizenry —in order to preserve and deepen our democratic experiment . . . One of our most crucial tasks now as democrats is to expose and extricate the antidemocratic impulses within our democracy. It is when we confront the challenges of our antidemocratic inclinations as a country that our most profound democratic commitments are born, both on the individual and on the societal level. (pp. 41–42)

Democracy is not used in this context as a form of government but rather as an egalitarian process. Thus, we believe that motivating successful democrats to use personal achievements for the purpose of creating opportunities for social equity should be a goal of those who mentor African Americans. Successful mentees should have the goal of eventually becoming successful mentors.

CONCLUSION

The following strategies for success are recommended to facilitate closing the African American achievement gap in the traditional classroom setting:

- Use a student-centered approach.
- Vary the conditions of learning to address the learning and cognitive preferences of Black students.
- Build on students' prior knowledge and experiences.
- Adopt the roles of engager, motivator, model, and mentor.

To help implement these strategies, instructors must help bridge ethnic, popular, and school cultures by adapting teaching to suit students' backgrounds. Successful programs for African American students such as the Faculty-Student Mentoring Program and the Peer Advisor Program at the University of Virginia (see Chapter 4) attend to many of the practices supported by this chapter.

The extent to which the roles of engager, motivator, model, and mentor are attended depends upon the motivation of instructors to be teachers and guides for their students; that is, instructors must believe that these roles are important, that they are capable of fulfilling these roles, and that it is their responsibility to do so. However, institutions also have a responsibility in this process.

It is an unfortunate reality that in a majority of universities, professorial standing is heavily determined by a productive research agenda rather than evidence of outstanding teaching. Ponton (1999) argued that this transformed emphasis from teaching to research in American higher education was based upon the development of graduate education from German ideology, emerging post–World War II federal funding that supported university research, and the academic freedom that affords professorial self-direction in both teaching and research.

To reverse this historical movement and maximize the learning opportunities presented in the classroom, universities must provide institutional incentives that reward good teaching. As Chang (2002) argues, the greatest value associated with diversity on campuses will occur when transformation on an institutional level is catalyzed rather than mere accommodation that preserves extant practices.

While it is an optimistic sign that faculty-student interactions are on the rise across all institutions, these gains are the greatest at liberal arts colleges and are below average at both public and private universities (Astin, Keup, & Lindholm, 2002), the latter being where we would argue that the institutional value of research productivity for tenure and promotion is the greatest. Thus, universities must continue to invoke transformative processes that motivate faculty members to be excellent teachers.

Closing the achievement gap is not authentically addressed if White student achievement is decreased rather than African American achievement increased. However, often what is good for African American students is also effective for other groups. Instructional strategies should take a holistic approach in offering methods that enable all participants to achieve with institutional incentives contingent upon measurable results for each participating racial/ethnic group. It is imperative that the classroom environment is constructed to foster positive, enabling feelings for all its participants so that achievement gaps and resultant opportunity gaps are closed forever.

DISCUSSION TOPICS

1. What can an instructor do to engage students in or out of the traditional classroom?
2. Are there any other desirable outcomes that characterize African American students? What course performances could be incorporated that are related to these outcomes?
3. Who are other important models on the college campus? Why are they important? What institutional processes can increase student access to these models?
4. Who are other important mentors on the college campus? Why are they important? What institutional processes can increase student access to these mentors?

REFERENCES

Allport, G. (1954). *The nature of prejudice.* Cambridge, MA: Addison-Wesley.

Astin, A. W., Keup, J. R., & Lindholm, J. A. (2002). A decade of changes in undergraduate education: A national study of system "transformation." *Review of Higher Education, 25*(2), 141–162.

Bandura, A. (1986). *Social foundations of thought and action: A social cognitive theory.* Englewood Cliffs, NJ: Prentice Hall.

Bandura, A. (1997). *Self-efficacy: The exercise of control.* New York: W. H. Freeman.

Banks, J. A. (1998). Multicultural education: Development, dimensions, and challenges. In M. J. Bennett (Ed.), *Basic concepts of intercultural communication* (pp. 69–84). Yarmouth, ME: Intercultural Press.

Bennett, C. I. (2006). *Comprehensive multicultural education: Theory and practice* (6th ed.). Boston: Allyn & Bacon.

Brooks, J. G., & Brooks, M. G. (1999). *In search of understanding: The case for constructivist classrooms.* Alexandria, VA: Association for Supervision and Curriculum Development.

Chang, M. J. (2002). Preservation or transformation: Where's the real educational discourse on diversity? *Review of Higher Education, 25*(2), 125–140.

Chang, M. J., Astin, A. W., & Kim, D. (2004). Cross-racial interaction among under-graduates: Some causes and consequences. *Research in Higher Education, 45*(5), 527–551.

Chickering, A., & Gamson, Z. (1987). Seven principles for good practice in under-graduate education. *AAHE Bulletin, 39*(7), 3–7.

Cokley, K. O. (2003). What do we know about the motivation of African American students? Challenging the "Anti-Intellectual" myth. *Harvard Educational Review, 73*(4), 524–558.

Davis, J. R. (1993). *Better teaching, more learning: Strategies for success in post-secondary settings.* Phoenix, AZ: American Council on Education/Oryx Press.

Flannery, D. D. (1995). Adult education and the politics of the theoretical text. In B. Kanpol & P. McLaren (Eds.), *Critical multiculturalism: Uncommon voices in a common struggle* (pp. 149–163). Westport, CT: Bergin and Garvey.

Hale-Benson, J. (1986). *Black children: Their roots, culture and learning styles* (Rev. ed.). Baltimore, MD: Johns Hopkins University Press.

Hummel, M., & Steele, C. (1996). The learning community: A program to address issues of academic achievement and retention. *Journal of Intergroup Relations, 2*, 28–32.

Johnson, G. R. (1995). *First steps to excellence in college teaching* (3rd ed.). Madison, WI: Atwood Publications.

Kim, M. M. (2002). Historically black vs. white institutions: Academic development among black students. *Review of Higher Education, 25*(4), 385–407.

Kuykendall, C. (1989). *Improving Black student achievement by enhancing students' self-image.* Chevy Chase, MD: The Mid-Atlantic Equity Center.

Magnan, R. (Ed.). (1990). *147 Practical tips for teaching professors.* Madison, WI: Atwood.

Maton, K. I., Hrabowski, F. A., & Schmitt, C. L. (2000). African American college students excelling in the sciences: College and postcollege outcomes in the Meyerhoff Scholars Program. *Journal of Research in Science Teaching, 37*(7), 629–654.

McMillan, D. W., & Chavis, D. M. (1986). Sense of community: A definition and theory. *Journal of Community Psychology, 14*, 6–23.

National Center for Education Statistics. (1999). *Table 231. Full-time instructional faculty in institutions of higher education, by race/ethnicity, academic rank, and sex: Fall 2005.* Retrieved November 29, 2006, from http://nces.ed.gov/programs/digest/d99/d99t231.asp

National Center for Education Statistics. (2004a). *Table 1. Fall enrollment in historically Black colleges and universities (HBCUs), by sex and attendance status of student, and type and control of institution: 2001.* Retrieved November 29, 2006, from http://nces.ed.gov/pubs2004/hbcu/Section7.asp

National Center for Education Statistics. (2004b). *Table 2. Degrees conferred by historically Black colleges and universities (HBCUs) by degree: 2001–02.* Retrieved November 29, 2006, from http://nces.ed.gov/pubs2004/hbcu/Section7.asp

National Center for Education Statistics. (2004c). *Table A-42. Employees in degree granting historically Black colleges and universities, by race/ethnicity, sex, primary occupation, control, and type of institution: Fall 2001.* Retrieved November 29, 2006, from http://nces.ed.gov/pubs2004/hbcu/data/A-42.xls

Neff, R. A., & Weimer, M. (Eds.). (1989). *Classroom communication: Collected readings for effective discussion and questioning.* Madison, WI: Magna.

Ogbu, J. U. (1995). Understanding cultural diversity and learning. In J. A. Banks & C. A. McGee-Banks (Eds.), *Handbook of research on multicultural education* (pp. 582–593). San Francisco: Jossey-Bass.

Outcalt, C. L., & Skewes-Cox, T. E. (2002). Involvement, interaction, and satisfaction: The human environment at HBCUs. *The Review of Higher Education,* 25(3), 331–347.

Pascarella, E. T., & Terenzini, P. T. (2005). *How college affects students* (2nd Rev ed.). San Francisco: Jossey-Bass.

Pascarella, E. T., Wolniak, G. C., Pierson, C. T., & Flowers, L. A. (2004). The role of race in the development of plans for a graduate degree. *The Review of Higher Education,* 27(3), 299–320.

Ponton, M. K. (1999). *The reduced emphasis of teaching undergraduates: A historical perspective.* Washington, DC: The George Washington University ERIC Clearinghouse on Higher Education. (ERIC Document Reproduction Service No. ED422787).

Pregent, R. (2000). *Charting your course: How to prepare to teach more effectively.* Madison, WI: Atwood.

Rheingold, H. (2000). *The virtual community: Homesteading the electronic frontier.* Reading, MA: Addison-Wesley.

Rovai, A. P., & Gallien, L. B., Jr. (2005). Learning and sense of community: A comparative analysis of African American and Caucasian online graduate students. *Journal of Negro Education,* 74(1), 53–62.

Sarasin, L. C. (1999). *Learning style perspectives: Impact in the classroom.* Madison, WI: Atwood.

Shade, B. (1982). Afro-American cognitive style: A variable in school success. *The Review of Educational Research,* 52(2), 219–244.

Stanley, C. A., & Lincoln, Y. S. (2005). Cross-race faculty mentoring. *Change,* 37(2), 44–50.

Sternberg, R. J. (1997). *Thinking styles.* New York: Cambridge University Press.

Weimer, M. (1989). Research summary: Professors part of the problem? In R. A. Neff & M. Weimer (Eds.), *Classroom communication: Collected readings for effective discussion and questioning* (pp. 67–71). Madison, WI: Magna.

West, C. (2005). *Democracy matters: Winning the fight against imperialism.* New York: Penguin Group.

SEVEN

Challenges in the Virtual Classroom

Alfred P. Rovai

PURPOSE

Online higher education is fueled by the emergence of technology-based delivery of courses and programs at a distance. This chapter examines the challenges to African American students within the context of the information age and the use of technology for distance education. In particular, the institutional, situational, and dispositional challenges related to closing the achievement gap in the virtual classroom are identified and discussed.

BACKGROUND

Davis and Botkin (1994) argue that colleges need to reorient, refocus, and realign themselves to meet the challenges of the information age:

> With the move from an agrarian to an industrial economy, the small rural schoolhouse was supplanted by the big brick schoolhouse. Four decades ago we began to move to another economy but we have yet to develop a new educational paradigm, let alone create the "schoolhouse" of the future, which may be neither school nor house. (p. 23)

Today we appear to be well along the road of creating that new schoolhouse and, as Davis and Botkin predicted, it is not constructed exclusively of bricks and mortar.

Increasingly, technology is being used to deliver courses to students who cannot otherwise attend college because of wide distances from campuses and/or work and family responsibilities. Distance learning is often an attractive option for African American students because they are likely to be employed full-time and may choose the scheduling convenience of programs delivered at a distance rather than traditional programs. Additionally, as discussed in Chapter 2, members of the hip-hip generation are more likely to be concerned with careers and financial prosperity than members of the previous civil rights generation were, and consequently, this goal may lead some to seek formal higher education.

Distance education programs do attract minority students. Lederman (2005) reports that nearly one-third of the distance education students at Capella University and Southern Christian University, two distance education institutions, are members of minority groups. Additionally, he reports that 53% of the undergraduate distance education students at the University of Maryland University College are minorities and one-third of this group are African Americans.

Distance education continues to evolve as different communication technologies and learning management systems, e.g., Blackboard, WebCT, eCollege, and ANGEL, are used to deliver courses, and as a variety of course designs emerge, such as fully online courses and a blend of distance and traditional courses. Although the literature provides numerous definitions of distance education, the definition developed by the Association for Educational Communications and Technology (AECT) has broad appeal and is used in this book. According to the AECT, distance education is "institution-based, formal education where the learning group is separated and where interactive telecommunications systems are used to connect learners, resources, and instructors" (Simonson, Smaldino, Albright, & Zvacek, 2003, p. 28). Within this distance education context, the term *distributed learning* is used to identify an instructional model that allows instructor, students, and content to be located in different locations so that teaching and learning occur independently of time and place. Online learning is a specific type of distributed learning that relies on computers and computer-mediated communication.

Within the context of higher education, distance education is designed to serve disciplined adult learners (Guernsey, 1998). *Disciplined* refers to being self-directed and possessing skills in time management. Social constructivists, such as Lev Vygotsky (2006), assert that students do not learn in isolation from others, and cognitive psychology has established that people naturally learn and work collaboratively in their lives. As a result of research in these areas, one goal of distance education is the creation of learning communities where members feel connected to one another and assist each other in their efforts to learn.

In a distributed learning environment that makes use of the Internet and computer-mediated communication, the virtual classroom is the private online space where learning communities of teachers and students come together to engage in teaching and learning. This environment is much like the classrooms in the small rural schoolhouse and the big brick schoolhouse described by Davis and Botkin (1994).

The institutional, situational, and dispositional challenges to African American achievement in the traditional classroom identified and discussed in Chapter 5 can also adversely influence learning in the virtual classroom, despite the assertion that the Internet erases racial differences and that people are more often judged by their ideas rather than their skin color. Although online anonymity can create strong bonds among socially diverse groups (e.g., Hiltz & Wellman, 1997), online courses are not anonymous. *The Chronicle of Higher Education* reports that many scholars are now realizing that the Internet can also perpetuate racial stereotypes by some users:

> Rather than encourage diversity, however, the absence of visual markers of race has led to a "default whiteness" in cyberspace. . . . In other words, many Internet users assume that all other users they encounter are white, unless they are told otherwise. The problem began to emerge when people who were particularly activist about [their race] realized that in order to really be seen on the Internet, they had to keep saying, I'm black, . . . And then other people say, why are you always talking about race? The initial exhilaration is turning, for some people, into a pretty strong frustration. (Young, 2001, p. A48)

INSTITUTIONAL CHALLENGES

The institutional challenges to traditional higher education achievement discussed in Chapter 5 consist of an academic culture that provides:

- little congruence with the backgrounds of African Americans,
- a largely "one-size-fits-all" teaching style,
- more emphasis on scholarly activities among faculty members than on teaching excellence and student mentoring,
- poor faculty accountability for learning failures, and
- limited availability of educational support services

Additionally, institutional quality control of distributed programs and student support services for distance education students that are inferior to those provided to on-campus students represent institutional challenges for students who are enrolled in distributed learning programs.

Quality Control of Distributed Teaching and Learning

Elements of Quality: The Sloan-C Framework (Moore, 2002) describes online learning effectiveness in terms of good practice (i.e., interaction, timeliness, and support), personalizing instruction, facilitating people networks and a learning community, and designing legacies. Palloff and Pratt (2001) suggest that online teaching necessitates adopting new, more-facilitative practices. They also note that "faculty cannot be expected to know intuitively how to design and deliver an effective online course [because] . . . seasoned faculty have not been exposed to techniques and methods needed to make online work successful" (p. 23). Online instructors must move beyond simply attempting to use the Internet to deliver standard classroom models and instead focus on developing ways to utilize the Internet to develop a richness that enhances education. These views suggest that the instructional delivery mode influences course design and pedagogy.

Most higher-education faculty members, with the exception of those who hold degrees in education, have rarely studied the art and science of teaching and learning, and even those with an educational background have rarely been trained or formally educated in the principles of online course design and pedagogy. Consequently, the quality of online teaching can vary by faculty member and by institution, depending on each professor's training in teaching and skills in explaining concepts using computer-mediated communication, assessing student learning at a distance, and using technology effectively.

The limited skills of some online faculty members in designing and conducting courses at a distance adversely affects educational quality, erodes affiliation, and increases alienation among students. Sims, Dobbs, and Hand (2001) note that rather than creating effective learning environments, many distributed learning courses "have proven ineffective, with learning activities a confused labyrinth of information, links, colleagues, discussions and navigation" (p. 517). Other courses are designed as correspondence courses that substitute e-mail for post office delivery of correspondence and incorporate few of the e-learning good practices identified by *The Sloan-C Framework* (Moore, 2002). Hara and Kling (2000) studied pedagogies of distance learning using a qualitative methodology and report student distress with many instructors' practices in managing the communication of course content with students. Pedagogical issues include students' concern about receiving prompt and clear feedback and the complexity of constructing unambiguous conversations via text-based media.

Another aspect of this challenge is the low level of cultural competence displayed by many online instructors. This term involves "mastering complex awarenesses and sensitivities, various bodies of knowledge, and a set of skills that taken together, underlie effective cross cultural teaching" (Diller & Moule, 2005, p. 5). According to Gay (2000), being culturally responsive goes beyond being respectful, empathetic, or sensitive. It also includes having high expectations for students and ensuring that these expectations are realized. The increasing diversity of students within our colleges and universities demands improved teacher skills in this area. Despite the increasing diversity of students, the corresponding diversity of faculty has not kept pace. The proportion of Black full-time faculty was less than one-half the proportion of

Black students enrolled in colleges and universities in 1999 (Hoffman, Llagas, & Snyder, 2003).

One explanation for the achievement gap is that it is related in part to a lack of fit between traditional school practices, which are derived almost exclusively from traditional Western culture, and the home and popular cultures of diverse students and their families (e.g., Ladson-Billings, 1995), as discussed in Chapter 2.

Quality Control of Student Support Services

Like their on-campus peers, online students also have the need for support services. However, "very little research on distance student services has been conducted" (Schwitzer, Ancis, & Brown, 2001, p. 114). Distance students must be provided with adequate access to services such as student advising and counseling, library services, tutorial services, financial aid services, information technology, and job placement, or they may be made to feel like second-class students. For technology-based e-learning systems, the lack of an effective institutional network of technical assistance is a significant barrier (Berge, Muilenburg, & Haneghan, 2002). As a result of these barriers, academic outcomes, such as student achievement, can suffer.

Student affairs professionals should service distance students just as they do on-campus students. However, Woodward, Love, and Komives (2000) acknowledge that distance education is a topic that is not being fully addressed by student affairs. Blimling and Whitt (1998) note that "because student affairs work has traditionally been campus based, little consideration has been given to how student affairs might confront the issue of distance education" (p. 7). Workman and Stenard (1996) suggest that the feelings of alienation and isolation that many distance learners feel may be mediated by providing student services that clarify regulations, build self-esteem, improve campus identity, create opportunities for interpersonal contacts, and provide access to learning support services. Moreover, the provision of such services will likely increase academic success.

SITUATIONAL CHALLENGES

The following situational challenges to traditional higher education achievement were discussed in Chapter 5:

- race-based rejection
- racial stereotyping
- conflicting job and family responsibilities
- financial concerns

In addition to these challenges, issues such as personal costs, the digital divide, and computer-mediated communication play a part in creating situational challenges for African Americans who are enrolled in distributed programs.

Personal Costs

The personal costs of taking courses at a distance represent another challenge. Distance education students encounter many of the same rising financial costs for education as their on-campus peers. Additionally, the nontraditional nature of many distance students introduces additional challenges. Bean and Metzner (1985) identify age as one of the most common variables in studies of nontraditional student attrition. Older students represent a population of adult learners who often have family and work responsibilities that can interfere with the successful attainment of educational goals. For example, Carr (2000) notes that persistence in distance education programs is often 10–20 percentage points lower than in traditional programs. She also notes significant variation among institutions, with some postsecondary schools reporting course-completion rates of more than 80% and others finding that less than 50% of distance education students finish their courses. For these students, the personal costs may outweigh any financial issues, and educational institutions will continue to see students accessing distance education with significant family and work responsibilities and limited time available for studies (Sikora & Carroll, 2002).

Digital Divide

According to the Center for the Digital Future (2005), 78.6% of Americans were online in 2005, using the Internet an average of 13.3 hours per week. Moreover, in 2005, 66.2% used the Internet at home, suggesting that a divide exists between *those who have more* and *those who have less* along an information technology dimension. Fairlie (2004) reports that 70.4% of Whites and 41.3% of Blacks have computers at home, and that 50.3% of Whites and 29.3% of Blacks have easy access to the Internet in the United States. He concludes that racial differences in education, income, and occupation contribute substantially to this Black/White gap in home computer and Internet access rates. This disparity in Internet usage suggests the existence of a digital divide (e.g., Fairlie, 2004; Katz & Aspden, 1997).

The term *digital divide* can take on several meanings, but at the most basic level, it refers to the division between those who can easily access the Internet and those who cannot. This term is also used to address the disparities in computer ownership and access to high-speed broadband digital services. Most of our knowledge about this divide is based on surveys that suggest it is mostly related to ethnic and minority group affiliation, geographic location, household composition, age, education, and income level (Katz & Aspden, 1997).

Those on the wrong side of the digital divide are denied the option to participate effectively in new high-tech jobs; in technology-enhanced education; and in using technology to access knowledge, to actively create and distribute knowledge, and to access social capital. From an educational perspective, the groups most disenfranchised by the digital divide are the same groups that have been historically disenfranchised by education in general.

Hoffman and Novak (1998) report that at each education level, Whites are more likely to own a home computer than African Americans are. However, this disparity can be largely explained by sociological research that shows Black people with a comparable education earn less than their White counterparts, family sizes are larger, and thus the per capita income is lower. Nonetheless, the result is that more Blacks are on the "wrong side" of the digital divide than their White peers, even after controlling for level of education.

The type of computer access that students experience can impact their attitudes about online learning as well as their academic achievement. If students own a computer, they are likely to find that online learning activities are more convenient and desirable than students who must locate an available computer in public places in order to access the Internet and their virtual classroom. Moreover, students without computers in their homes are often irritated by the additional time required to visit a computer lab (Crotty, 2000). This lack of convenience can contribute to negative reactions regarding online learning. McMahon, Gardner, Gray, and Mulhern (1999) report that computer access accounts for 50% of the variance in student attitudes toward online learning based on the results of a longitudinal study involving more than 800 university students.

Limitations on technology access are particularly acute among African American higher education students, placing them at a disadvantage to compete and qualify for higher-salaried jobs (Dervarics, 2003; National Telecommunications and Information Administration, 1999). Contrary to conventional wisdom, Mossberger, Tolbert, and Stansbury (2003) provide empirical evidence based on a national survey of more than 1,800 respondents that suggests the digital divide is growing larger, not smaller. Farrell (2005) also reports "the so called digital divide is widening between black freshmen and students of other ethnic groups. . . . Only 76.5% of black students reported using a personal computer frequently in 2004, compared with 86.7% of white students" (p. 2). The result for those on the wrong side of this divide, typically the poor and ethnic minorities, can be social estrangement and reduced social support or meaningful social connection with mainstream society. Such individuals can experience alienation and an erosion of social capital, become detached from mainstream groups such as student organizations, and feel a lack of connection to other members of society and to other students. Such erosion of support is particularly harmful to African American students who learn best in harmonious and collaborative learning environments, as discussed in previous chapters.

DiMaggio and Hargittai (2001) suggest that as more individuals use the Internet, it becomes less useful to discuss the digital divide in terms of access only. They claim that researchers also need to examine differences in people's online skills, which they refer to as the second-level digital divide. Such skills are directly related to people's ability to use the medium. Although economic, cultural, and social factors have a greater role to play in narrowing the gap in the first level of the digital divide, educational factors are more important in closing the gap in online skills. When one examines the digital divide in terms of the ability of university students to use computer technology effectively, Farrell (2005) writes that most minority college freshmen at schools such as the University of California at Los Angeles (UCLA) are unequipped to manage the digital workplace. Consequently, regardless of how one examines the digital divide, African Americans appear to be at a disadvantage, and this situation can adversely impact their academic achievement, especially as the use of technology-based education expands.

Computer-Mediated Communication

Computer-mediated communication is a second situational challenge for African Americans who are enrolled in online programs. Effective communication is a foundation upon which the success of classroom learning rests. Without face-to-face (F2F) interaction among teachers and students, effective communication in general and learning in particular can become more difficult. Even the best video links do not allow the same quality of communication as F2F interaction (Bal & Teo, 2001). The result is more formal interactions. Text-based communication, which is the backbone of much of Internet-based e-learning, provides even more communication limitations due to the reduction in nonverbal cues, such as facial expressions and gestures, during the text-based communication process. The result of communication at a distance, particularly among members of an online learning community who may be meeting for the first time online, is often a less accurate representation of the participants and their messages.

Walther (1996) reports that participants in online discussions often fill in the blanks when it comes to forming perceptions of others, a concept he labeled *hyperpersonal interaction*. In such situations, members of an online learning community may develop idealistic or unrealistic images of other students and the instructor by projecting images. For example, if an online communicator believes that he or she is communicating with a person of lower intelligence, perhaps as the result of racial stereotyping, then his or her interpersonal communication is likely to reflect this perception.

Additionally, text-based communication between individuals who are not well acquainted can result in miscommunication. For example, a student may perceive the online communication of his or her instructor as sharp and acrimonious as the instructor attempts to be concise and to the point as a time-management tool. According to Walther (1996), such hyperpersonal interaction may influence perceptions of one's online communication partners and the quality of communication. Such perceptions can negatively influence trust and feelings of connectedness among members of the learning community, particularly in a multicultural context where cultural differences are not understood by all members of the community and where cultural bias exists.

Cross-cultural interactions can also create miscommunication. Because of the global reach of distance education, different cultures within the same country, as well as cross-border cultural differences, must be considered. Labi (2005) reports on quality-assurance guidelines for cross-border higher education by the Organization for Economic Cooperation and Development and the United Nations Educational, Scientific, and Cultural Organization. These guidelines for institutions involved in cross-border higher education include ensuring that their programs take into account the cultural and linguistic sensitivities of the receiving country.

Because communication has both verbal and nonverbal components, some cultural groups show their feelings more readily than other groups; some individuals rely more on nonverbal messages to communicate, which are reduced and subject to misinterpretation in an online environment, as noted above. Such differences can have dire consequences in cross-cultural interactions within any multicultural online learning community and can isolate students who are not fully acculturated in the majority culture.

Cross-cultural differences result in individuals who communicate differently and even understand the same message differently (Ibarra, 2001). Moreover, cyberspace itself has a culture and is not a neutral or value-free platform for communications. The greater the cultural differences between online communicators, the greater the potential for miscommunication.

Anthropologist Edward T. Hall's concept of high- and low-context culture (Hall & Hall, 1990), as discussed in Chapter 2, differentiates communication along a continuum that helps us better understand the powerful effect that culture has on communication. At the low-context end of this continuum, low levels of programmed (i.e., mutually understood) information provide context; therefore, communication requires a large amount of explicit information to convey meaning. At the other end of this continuum is a high-context culture in which high levels of programmed information provide context, which consequently requires a relatively small amount of explicit information to convey meaning. According to Hall and Hall (1990), in high-context communication, the listener is already contextualized and does not need to be given much background information.

Since computer-mediated communication is text-based in asynchronous learning management systems, meaning is mostly carried by the written communication itself. Because of this situation, low-context communication is often presumed in computer-mediated communication, possibly placing those whose cultural background relies on high-context communication at a disadvantage (Morse, 2003). According to Ibarra (2001), low-context cultures make little use of nonverbal signals, value direct communication with explicit verbal messages, and depersonalize disagreements. High-context cultures, on the other hand, rely extensively on nonverbal signals; see communication as an art form in which indirect, implicit, and informal verbal messages are valued; and personalize disagreements.

As discussed in Chapter 2, the White majority culture is a low-context culture while many minority cultures, including that of African Americans, tend to be high-context (e.g., Hall & Hall, 1990; Ibarra, 2001). Each individual is different based on his or her level of acculturation to the mainstream American culture. Basic communication rules that may bring success in an intracultural context may not be sufficient for a successful intercultural interaction, particularly when communicators do not know each other very well and the communication medium contains reduced nonverbal cues.

DISPOSITIONAL CHALLENGES

The following dispositional challenges to traditional higher education achievement were discussed in Chapter 5:

- a preference for holistic learning in a largely compartmentalized and analytical learning environment
- a preference for field dependence in a largely field-independent learning environment
- a preference for high-context communication in a largely low-context communication environment

Additionally, in online programs, anxiety regarding technology, feelings of isolation and alienation, and misalignment between student cognitive style and online teaching style are challenges for some students.

Computer Anxiety

Attitudes about online learning are also influenced by anxiety about using computer technology. Estimates tell us that 25%/58% percent of higher education students feel or have felt some level of computer anxiety (e.g., Ayersman, 1996). Bozionelos (1997) describes computer anxiety as fear, anxiety, and frustration involving computer interactions. A certain amount of tension is good; it can act as a motivator. However, when computer anxiety interferes with one's mental processes and causes a person to avoid computers, then the problem is severe and can have profound implications for students who must use computers in online programs.

Students who own computers generally have less computer anxiety than those who do not because they are more familiar with the technology. According to Ropp's (1999) review of the literature, most research concludes that the less experience people have with computers, the more computer anxiety they are likely to exhibit. Consequently, African American students are more likely to exhibit computer anxiety since, as suggested earlier, they are more likely to be on the wrong side of the digital divide. Research suggests that computer anxiety decreases willingness to use computers and results in poor performance levels (Bronson, 1998). Maintaining and improving the quality of education is critical to our nation's social and economic well-being. Moreover, the effective use of technology by online students is a prerequisite for that success.

Cognitive Style

As pointed out in Chapter 2, many researchers (e.g., Perry, Steele, & Hilliard, 2004) believe that Black students learn more successfully in environments characterized by harmony, cooperation, affect, socialization, and a strong sense of community, and learn less in environments that are highly stratified and competitive. Consequently, many Black students employ people-oriented, relational, and field-dependent approaches to learning rather than the field-independent and analytical style favored in most university environments.

Several studies point to the field-dependent tendencies of African American students and the field-independent tendencies of their White peers (e.g., Shade, 1982), suggesting two learning-style typologies: a Black culture characterized mostly by field-dependent components and high-context communication and a White culture characterized by mostly field-independent components and low-context communication.

Although research regarding the effect of cognitive styles on students' learning outcomes is mixed, there is theoretical and empirical evidence to suggest that misalignment of teaching style with the cognitive style preference of students can create learning challenges. In particular, field-dependent students may be at risk in distributed learning programs where instruction frequently relies on independent activities and requires students to have strong analytical and problem-solving skills. Moreover, "research supports the concept that most teachers teach the way they learn" (Stitt-Gohdes, 2001, p. 136). Since many higher education faculty experienced academic success in learning environments that were teacher-centered and relied heavily on the lecture and learner independence, it is reasonable that their preferred style of teaching would be similar.

Additionally, online instruction is characterized by an open learning environment that allows students to choose what they need from a rich, networked database of information, examples, and exercises (Reiser & Dempsey, 2002). Many researchers argue that some learners can be disoriented and may miss information when they are overloaded by multiple-channel messages in nonlinear hypermedia environments (e.g., Ford & Chen, 2000). Ford and Chen (2000) also found that the levels of field-independency have a significant impact on the ways learners organize and navigate information, prioritize content, and develop metacognitive strategies in distributed learning environments. They report that field-dependent learners tend to be less successful than field-independent learners in activities such as reorganizing and reproducing information, recognizing salient cues, and structuring information. Therefore, field-dependent learners may be less successful in distributed instruction environments than in classroom environments.

A survey conducted by the General Accounting Office (GAO) (General Accounting Office, 2003) provides empirical support for this view. It reports that the percentage of historically Black colleges and universities offering at least one distance education course in the 2002–2003 school year was only 56%. Moreover, approximately half of these schools indicated that a primary reason for the limited number of distance education courses was that they prefer teaching in the classroom. The second major reason cited by these schools for not providing education at a distance was limited resources for technology.

However, some researchers, e.g., Frisby (1993), suggest that the concept of a Black Cultural Learning Style (BCLS) is seriously flawed. Frisby's (1993) review of the literature finds that there is little research to support this concept. He writes, "It is high time that BCLS models be laid to rest. Failure to do so may result in the realization that, instead of making significant steps forward, we have indeed made one giant step backward" (p. 552). Nonetheless, the professional literature is mixed on this topic, and there exists evidence that people do learn differently and that these differences are often the product of their cultural background and upbringing. Dunn and Griggs (1996) caution teachers to emphasize the learning-style strengths of the individual student rather than his or her culture, and to match instruction to individual preferences. It would be wrong to attribute a specific learning-style preference based exclusively on the student's ethnicity.

Feelings of Isolation and Alienation

The physical separation of members of a distributed learning community in the virtual classroom can encroach upon the basic human need for social and intellectual interaction, resulting in feelings of isolation and alienation. This can be particularly troublesome for African American and other students who come from cultural backgrounds that value cooperation, affect, socialization, and community, and who possess a field-dependent cognitive style (see Chapter 2 for a discussion of African American and hip-hop cultural characteristics).

The concept of alienation refers to an absence of social support or meaningful social connection. Within the school context, alienation is often related to feeling unconnected to the teacher, other students, and the school community, resulting in low sense of community. Other school-related factors can also increase feelings of alienation, such as negative student-student relationships, low curriculum relevancy, and lack of control over school policies and activities. The distance learner may also have problems separating "work from home life, experiencing tensions in relations with their family and spouse" (Harrell, 1999, p. 270).

Workman and Stenard (1996) report that distance education students generally consider themselves outsiders, and not members of the school community. They note that one should not assume that these students are content with this status, and they also report research that suggests online students have an interest in having stronger ties with the school community. Consequently, it is possible to view sense of community as a measure of how well students integrate socially into a particular school.

CONCLUSION

Chapter 5 discusses the challenges to African American college student achievement in traditional on-campus programs. The present chapter extends this discussion by addressing the additional challenges outlined below that many Black students face in distributed programs.

Institutional Challenges
- quality control of distributed teaching and learning
- quality control of student support services

Situational Challenges
- personal costs
- digital divide
- computer-mediated communication

Dispositional Challenges
- computer anxiety
- cognitive style
- feelings of isolation and alienation

The challenges discussed in this chapter are not unique to African American students; they apply, in varying degrees, to other minorities as well as to the White majority population. An examination of challenges, such as the digital divide, is necessary to fully inform the use of technology to promote social inclusion. Social inclusion is central to the success of the information society. It relates not only to an adequate share of resources, but also to the determination of both individual and collective quality of life (Stewart, 2000). Even if the poor do not have an equal share of economic resources, they can have better opportunities to participate in society than they do presently. Collective action must be taken to increase social participation.

In pursuit of the goal of providing culturally responsive, fair, and equitable distributed learning environments for everyone, Rowland (2000) calls for a distance education pedagogy that is centered on issues of race, economics, power, and education. This goal responds to Gay's (1994) challenge to educators to promote educational equity by changing educational institutions so that all students have an equal chance to achieve academic success:

> Educators must thoroughly understand how culture shapes learning styles, teaching behaviors, and educational decisions. They must then develop a variety of means to accomplish common learning outcomes that reflect the preferences and styles of a wide variety of groups and individuals. By giving all students more choices about how they will learn—choices that are compatible with their cultural styles—none will be unduly advantaged or disadvantaged at the procedural levels of learning. These choices will lead to closer parallelism (e.g., equity) in opportunities to learn and more comparability in students' achieving the maximum of their own intellectual capabilities (e.g., excellence). (p. 20)

Although desired learning outcomes may be the same for all students, many students require variation in how these outcomes are achieved. Consequently, there is a pressing need for enhancing learners' cross-cultural awareness and considering cross-cultural issues in distributed course design, instruction, and dialogue. Teachers who treat all students the same show their lack of preparation for teaching in culturally pluralistic classrooms (Gallien & Peterson, 2004; Vasquez, 1990). Being treated equally does not mean being treated the same. When all students are treated the same, instructors, although unintentionally so, are dysconsciously racist in their practices (Anderson, 1988; King, 1991).

Promising strategies that colleges and universities can pursue in response to the challenges described above are discussed in other chapters. Some schools are pursuing promising programs toward becoming multicultural, pluralistic, and international. For example, the University of Maine is exploring distance methodologies in English as a Second Language (ESL). Additionally, Brigham Young University used a sociocultural model to design a bilingual/ESL endorsement program that it offers at a distance. This model assists teachers and students in supporting learning by providing assistance during social interaction and discourse about culturally meaningful activities. However, the programs consist entirely of minority students. Programs that consist of mostly White students with an African American enrollment should also pay the same attention to sociocultural issues. Although multicultural initiatives such as these are plentiful, there are no large-scale e-learning efforts that address multicultural issues.

Overall, there is significant resistance to institutional responses to the challenges of multicultural distance education. School culture perpetuates the standards to which all who enter must adjust. Resistance to change is still the single most powerful maxim that can be applied to universities (Ibarra, 2001). In sum, the classroom culture of many mostly White universities in the United States is incongruent with the culture and cognitive style of many African American students who may have been raised and educated in a predominantly Black culture or have had little cultural contacts with Whites. Ibarra (2001) criticizes those educators who view diversity purely in terms of recruitment and retention and do not make an effort to adapt their teaching to account for student diversity. He makes a case for changes in higher education based on the richness found in all cultures, in contrast to perpetuating the one-size-fits-all approach to teaching that is dominant on many university campuses.

DISCUSSION TOPICS

1. The increase in racial, ethnic, and cultural diversity in higher education is also reflected in the virtual classroom. Identify positive and negative social, educational, and technological aspects of this diversity from the institution's perspective.
   - Positive: Opportunities and challenges
   - Negative: Constraints, barriers, and weaknesses
2. Consider the previous discussion topic from the student perspective. How do institution and student perspectives differ? How are they similar?
3. How do student support services differ for students enrolled in on-campus and distance education programs? How are these differences likely to influence student attitudes about the institution?
4. Consider your own cognitive style (i.e., field-dependent or field-independent).

Would a mismatch between your cognitive style and your professor's teaching style influence your learning? If so, how? If not, why not?

5. How can digital equity be achieved for all people and groups regardless of race, ethnicity, or socioeconomic status?

REFERENCES

Anderson, J. A. (1988). Cognitive styles and multicultural populations. *Journal of Teacher Education, 24*(1), 2–9.

Ayersman, D. J. (1996). Effects of computer instruction, learning style, gender, and experience on computer anxiety. *Computers in the School, 12*(4), 15–30.

Bal, J., & Teo, P. K. (2001). Implementing virtual team working: Part 2: A literature review. *Logistics Information Management, 14*, 208–222.

Bean, J. P., & Metzner, B. S. (1985). A conceptual model of nontraditional undergraduate student attrition. *Review of Educational Research, 55*(4), 485–540.

Berge, Z. L., Muilenburg, L. Y., & Haneghan, J. V. (2002). Barriers to distance education and training: Survey results. *Quarterly Review of Distance Education, 3*(4), 409–418.

Blimling, G. S., & Whitt, E. J. (1998). Creating and using principles of good practice for student affairs. *About Campus, 3*(1), 10–15.

Bozionelos, N. (1997). Psychology of computer use. XIV. Cognitive spontaneity as a correlate of computer anxiety and attitudes toward computer use. *Psychological Reports, 80*(2), 395–402.

Bronson, M. J. (1998). The impact of computer anxiety and self-efficacy upon performance. *Journal of Computer Assisted Learning, 11*(3), 223 234.

Carr, S. (2000, February 11). As distance education comes of age, the challenge is keeping the students. *The Chronicle of Higher Education,* A39–A41.

Center for the Digital Future. (2005). *Surveying the digital future.* Los Angeles, CA: USC Annenberg School. Retrieved May 30, 2006, from http://www.digitalcenter .org/pages/current_report.asp?intGlobalId=19

Crotty, T. (2000, April 7). Constructivist theory unites distance learning and teacher education. *DEOSNews, 5*(6). Retrieved November 29, 2006, from http://www .ed.psu.edu/acsde/deos/deosnews/deosnews5 6.asp

Davis, S. M., & Botkin, J. W. (1994). *The monster under the bed: How business is mastering the opportunity of knowledge for profit.* New York: Simon & Schuster.

Dervarics, C. (2003). House moves ahead on digital divide help. *Black Issues in Higher Education, 20*(13), 6.

Diller, J. V., & Moule, J. (2005). *Cultural competence: A primer for educators.* Belmont, CA: Thomas/Wadsworth.

DiMaggio, P., & Hargittai, E. (2001). *From the "digital divide" to "digital inequality": Studying Internet use as penetration increases.* Working Paper Series number 15. Princeton, NJ: Princeton University Center for Arts and Cultural Policy Studies.

Dunn, R., & Griggs, S. (1996). Hispanic-American students and learning style. *ERIC Digest.* Urbana, IL: ERIC Clearinghouse on Elementary and Early Childhood Education. (ERIC Document Reproduction Service No. ED 393607).

Fairlie, R. W. (2004). Race and the digital divide. *Contributions to Economic Analysis & Policy, 3*(1). Retrieved November 29, 2006, from http://cjtc.ucsc.edu/docs/r_digitaldivide9 .pdf

Farrell, E. F. (2005, February 4). Among freshmen, a growing digital divide. *The Chronicle of Higher Education, 51*(22), A32.

Ford, N., & Chen, Y. (2000). Individual differences, hypermedia navigation and learning: An empirical study. *Journal of Educational Multimedia and Hypermedia, 9*(4), 281–311.

Frisby, C. L. (1993). One giant step backward: Myths of black cultural learning styles. *School Psychology Review, 22*(3), 535–557.

Gallien, L. B., Jr., & Peterson, M. S. (2004). *Instructing and mentoring the African American college student: Strategies for success in higher education.* Boston: Allyn & Bacon.

Gay, G. (1994). *A synthesis of scholarship in multicultural education* (Urban Monograph Series). Oak Brook, IL: North Central Regional Educational Laboratory.

Gay, G. (2000). *Culturally responsive teaching: Theory, research, and practice.* New York: Teachers College Press.

General Accounting Office. (2003). *Distance education: More data could improve education's ability to track technology at minority serving institutions* (GAO Report Nr. GAO-03-900). Washington, DC: U.S. Government Printing Office.

Guernsey, L. (1998, March 27). Distance education for the not-so-distant. *The Chronicle of Higher Education, 44,* A29–A30.

Hall, E. T., & Hall, M. R. (1990). *Understanding cultural differences.* New York: Intercultural Press.

Hara, N., & Kling, R. (2000). Students' distress with a Web-based distance education course. *Information, Communication & Society, 3*(4), 557–579.

Harrell, W., Jr. (1999). Language learning at a distance via computer. *International Journal of Instructional Media, 26*(3), 267–282.

Hiltz, S. R., & Wellman, B. (1997). Asynchronous learning networks as a virtual classroom. *Communications of the ACM, 40*(9), 44–49.

Hoffman, D. L., & Novak, T. P. (1998). Bridging the racial divide on the Internet. *Science, 280*(April 17), 390–391.

Hoffman, K., Llagas, C., & Snyder, T. D. (2003). *Status and trends in the education of blacks* (NCES 2003-034). Washington, DC: U.S. Department of Education Institute of Education Sciences.

Ibarra, R. A. (2001). *Beyond affirmative action: Reframing the context of higher education.* Madison, WI: University of Wisconsin Press.

Katz, J., & Aspden, P. (1997). Motivations for and barriers to Internet usage: Results of a national public opinion survey. *Internet Research: Electronic Networking Applications and Policy, 7*(3), 170–188.

King, J. E. (1991). Dysconcious racism: Ideology, identity, and the mis-education of teachers. *Journal of Negro Education, 60*(2), 133–166.

Labi, A. (2005, December 16). Two agencies announce quality controls. *The Chronicle of Higher Education, 52*(17), A41.

Ladson-Billings, G. (1995). But that's just good teaching! The case for culturally relevant pedagogy. *Theory into Practice, 34*(3), 159–165.

Lederman, D. (2005, April 13). Expanding access via distance ed. *Inside Higher Ed.* Retrieved November 29, 2006, from http://www.insidehighered.com/news/ 2005/04/13/distance

McMahon, J., Gardner, J., Gray, C., & Mulhern, G. (1999). Barriers to computer usage: Staff and student perceptions. *Journal of Computer Assisted Learning, 15*(4), 302–311.

Moore, J. C. (2002). *Elements of quality: The Sloan-C Framework.* Needham, MA: Sloan Consortium.

Morse, K. (2003). Does one size fit all? Exploring asynchronous learning in a multicultural environment. *Journal of Asynchronous Learning Networks, 7*(1), 37–55.

Mossberger, K., Tolbert, C. J., & Stansbury, M. (2003). *Virtual inequality: Beyond the digital divide.* Washington, DC: Georgetown University Press.

National Telecommunications and Information Administration. (1999). *Falling through the Net: Defining the digital divide.* Washington, DC: U.S. Department of Commerce. Retrieved November 29, 2006, from http://www.ntia .doc.gov/ntiahome/fttn99/contents.html

Palloff, R. M., & Pratt, K. (2001). *Lessons from the cyberspace classroom: The realities of online teaching.* San Francisco: Jossey-Bass.

Perry, T., Steele, C. M., & Hilliard, A. G., III. (2004). *Young, gifted, and black: Promoting high achievement among African-American students.* Boston: Beacon Press.

Reiser, R. A., & Dempsey, J. V. (2002). *Trends and issues in instructional design and technology.* Upper Saddle River, NY: Prentice Hall.

Ropp, M. M. (1999). Exploring individual characteristics associated with learning to use computers in preservice teacher preparation. *Journal of Research on Computing in Education, 31*(4), 402–425.

Rowland, M. L. (2000). *African Americans and self-help education: The missing link in adult education* (ERIC Digest No. 222). Columbus, OH: Center on Education and Training for Employment. (ERIC Document Reproduction Service No. ED448290).

Schwitzer, A. M., Ancis, J. R., & Brown, N. (2001). *Promoting student learning and student development at a distance: Student affairs concepts and practices for televised instruction and other forms of distance learning.* Washington, DC: American College Personnel Association.

Shade, B. (1982). Afro-American cognitive style: A variable in school success. *The Review of Educational Research, 52*(2), 219–244.

Sikora, A., & Carroll, C. D. (2002). *A profile of participation in distance education: 1999–2000.* Washington, DC: Office of Education Research and Improvement.

Simonson, M., Smaldino, S. E., Albright, M. J., & Zvacek, S. (2003). *Teaching and learning at a distance: Foundations of distance education.* Upper Saddle River, NJ: Merrill Prentice Hall.

Sims, R., Dobbs, G., & Hand, T. (2001). Proactive evaluation: New perspectives for ensuring quality in online learning applications. In G. Kennedy, M. Keppell, C. McNaught, & T. Petrovic (Eds.), *Meeting at the crossroads* (pp. 509–518). Melbourne, Australia: University of Melbourne.

Stewart, A. (2000). Social inclusion: An introduction. In A. Stewart & P. Askonas (Eds.), *Social inclusion: Possibilities and tensions* (pp. 1–16). London: Macmillan.

Stitt-Gohdes, W. L. (2001). Business education students' preferred learning styles and their teachers' preferred instructional styles: Do they match? *Delta Pi Epsilon Journal, 43*(3), 137–151.

Vasquez, J. A. (1990). Teaching to the distinctive traits of minority students. *The Clearing House, 63*(7), 299–304.

Vygotsky, L. S. (2006). *Mind in society: Development of higher psychological processes* (New Edition). Cambridge, MA: Harvard University Press.

Walther, J. B. (1996). Computer-mediated communication: Impersonal, interpersonal, and hyperpersonal interaction. *Communication Research, 23*(1), 3–43.

Woodward, D. B., Love, P., & Komives, S. R. (2000). *Leadership and management issues for a new century. New Directions for Student Services, No. 92.* San Francisco: Jossey-Bass.

Workman, J., & Stenard, R. (1996). Student services for distance learners. *DEOSNEWS—The Distance Education Online Symposium, 6*(3). Retrieved November 29, 2006, from http://www.ed.psu.edu/acsde/deos/deosnews/deosnews6_3.asp

Young, J. (2001, September 28). Scholars question the image of the Internet as a race-free utopia. *The Chronicle of Higher Education,* A48.

EIGHT

Designing and Teaching Distributed Courses

Richard C. Overbaugh & Robert A. Lucking

PURPOSE

Chapter 5 identifies and discusses the major challenges to African American college learning in the traditional classroom, and Chapter 6 responds with academic strategies for success. The challenges and strategies discussed in these two chapters are also relevant to the virtual classroom. Moreover, Chapter 7 addresses those challenges that are unique to distributed learning. These challenges include various institutional, situational, and dispositional barriers that require attention from school administrators or from the virtual classroom instructor. The purpose of this chapter is to discuss how the distributed learning instructor can attenuate or eliminate the challenges that pose a particular threat to learning in the virtual classroom environment.

Although good classroom instructors who know and understand their students can adjust their instruction through verbal revision and repetition and can regulate the pace based on immediate feedback from students, online instructors do not have the advantage of seeing smiles, nods of understanding, and blank looks, or experiencing unresponsive silence to help them make similar adjustments. Instead, the online instructor becomes a course designer who must be mindful of the unique characteristics of the distributed learning environment and the characteristics of the learners, working to be sensitive to student dynamics through computer-mediated communication. This chapter explores these issues as well as other aspects of teaching online students who come from a variety of cultures.

BACKGROUND

Online courses are now commonplace throughout much of the academic world. Even though some educators may lose sight of the academic challenges that African American learners face in the whirl of technology-based learning, the debate continues regarding the design and delivery of online courses that will attract and meet the needs of various populations, regardless of their learning-style preferences, cognitive styles, racial and ethnic cultures, or prior experiences.

Learning in any environment should never be based on one single design, and the number of complicating variables increases when planning online learning. Learners are not homogeneous and neither are their attitudes about learning and their confidence to succeed; where one student may be self-motivated and persistent regardless of the structure of the course, another may feel discouraged and disengage. Designing courses for distribution requires even more careful attention to aspects of the instructional process that may not be given much conscious thought in traditional face-to-face (F2F) environments.

While most aspects of designing and delivering instruction are common to all methods and modes of delivery, and design considerations are universal, there may be tremendous differences in the amount of effort needed for various components. One of the first considerations that distributed course designers find different from those in F2F instruction is the tremendous amount of time required "up front" to design and develop course components, such as the syllabus, content forms, methods of information presentation such as lecture notes via appropriate media, thought-provoking questions and projects, and assessments. Nothing should be left to be developed after the course commences.

When planning an online course that provides opportunities for students of all cultures to succeed, instructors also find that they are no longer bound by the traditional schedule of class meetings. Instead, online courses may be divided into units or projects spanning however many days are reasonable for completion. Once the course objectives are defined, the chosen pedagogy, student characteristics, and learning environment will shape the units of instruction, including the number of days needed.

Another significant difference between traditional and online instruction is how discourse takes place in online environments where learning relies heavily on active collaboration and cooperation among students using computer-mediated communication. Students are responsible for individual contributions and for recognizing the validity of the perspectives of others, even when—or especially when—those perspectives may be very different because of socioeconomic status, culture, or communication patterns. Techniques to create, motivate, and mediate online discourse are vital to learning regardless of whether the computer-mediated communication medium is synchronous (e.g., chat, phone, or video/audio conferencing) or asynchronous (e.g., discussion board, listserv, blog, or e-mail). Successful communication requires that both learner and instructor reassess their time management by allocating smaller blocks of time every day or two instead of large blocks one or two days weekly. As a manager of constantly evolving learning events, the instructor will need to engage in course-related communications nearly every day in order to shape effectively the instructional dialogue and manifest a presence in the virtual classroom to help overcome any student feelings of isolation or alienation, as discussed in the previous chapter.

Instructors of online classes should also be prepared for the potentially overwhelming demands of managing, reading, and responding to a large number of student file submissions. As an illustration, a single project in which the students read content, engage in a chat with three classmates to discuss four issues related to the content, create a project to show knowledge acquisition, and complete an assessment can result in a large number of files that must be evaluated by the instructor and have feedback provided. In addition, a common instructional strategy for chat groups is to assign a leader to manage the chat, a summarizer to summarize the chat and post it back to the discussion board, and a rubric with which each student assesses the performance of his/her chat mates. While this strategy reflects a rigorous pedagogy, the result is four files for each student, plus an additional two for each group of four students, plus the actual chat transcript if needed for verification, which totals 95 files for a class of 20 students. The time required to manage and to read that many files can quickly spiral out of control and reduce instructor effectiveness.

Finally, media choices for content delivery and collaborative communication range from simple to complex. Virtually every institution that offers distributed instruction has a learning management system (LMS) such as Blackboard, WebCT, or Angel, all of which offer basic tools such as content presentation, chat, discussion boards, digital drop boxes, and a grade book. However, LMSs typically do not include the more advanced or richer communication media that may be capable of helping marginalized students. One example is synchronous video and audio conferencing, such as provided by Horizon Wimba, which can easily enhance the efficacy of courses via seminar-type sessions. Another example is class-broadcast Web logs (blogs) in which students write about their learning, their perspectives on the subject, and the learning process itself. Blogs are more useful than traditional journals because the instructor and fellow students can read one another's entries and thus gain more understanding about beliefs, perspectives, culture, problems, and successes, all of which contribute to students' sense of community. Finally, a class broadcasting arrangement such as Really Simple Syndication

(RSS) makes blog exchange quite easy. Emerging technologies will continue to be refined over time, so these advanced learning tools will find their way into mainstream practice.

However, because these media fall outside many normal institutional offerings, the instructor must take into account availability, levels of support, cross-platform compatibility, minimal computer configurations, and the technical ability and savvy of the students. This is particularly important for African American students, many of whom are unequipped to manage the digital learning environment because of poor computer knowledge, skills, and experiences, which can adversely impact their academic achievement. Therefore, instructors who believe nonmainstream technologies may further enhance the effectiveness of their courses should naturally be concerned with the implementation viability of each tool. To provide a perspective with which to think about these and the myriad other elements that contribute to instructional development, the following Institutional Instructional Parameters (IIP) framework is provided to help instructors make decisions about which tools and techniques are feasible within the overall structure of the educational unit.

INSTITUTIONAL INSTRUCTIONAL PARAMETERS (IIP)

As a way of thinking about providing for all students—and minority students in particular—a prospective online instructor may wish to consider the Institutional Instructional Parameters (IIP) matrix first set forth by Overbaugh and Casiello (2006) before undertaking the complex process of design, implementation, and assessment. The IIP matrix allows for perspective on how existing infrastructure and administrative and programmatic issues potentially factor into the design and development decisions of online courses (see Figure 8.1). The matrix incorporates the Sloan-C five pillars of quality (Moore, 2002), which include the following elements: (a) learning effectiveness; (b) cost effectiveness; (c) access; (d) faculty satisfaction; and (e) student satisfaction. These pillars are logical domains with which to think of different aspects and perspectives of the online educational process. All five pillars have a high degree of interrelatedness and interdependence, and should therefore inform the course design process. The pillars constitute one cross-section—the X axis—of the IIP matrix. The other cross-section—the Y axis—simplifies the entire (higher education) instructional design and delivery process—from the buildings on campus to students' skill sets—into three hierarchically arranged components. The most fundamental concern is campus infrastructure—whether it is bricks and mortar or virtual. The second level includes the academic colleges and their various programs. At level three, the teaching faculty reside.

Figure 8.1. Institutional Instructional Parameters

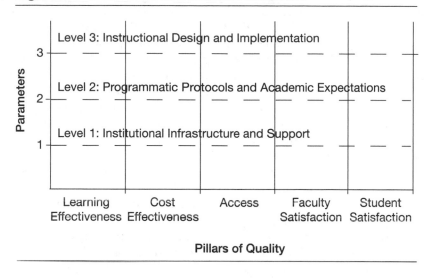

Pillars of Quality

IIP-Level 1: Institutional Infrastructure and Support

The most basic level of concern, IIP-1, refers to the infrastructure, techno-logical facilities, and services of an academic unit. Within the parameters of online education, this is the institutional level at which decisions are made for what technologies should be purchased and supported, and what will be the level of support for the users (students, staff, and faculty). More specifi-cally, the systems and policies at this level are those that directly affect the access pillar—student and faculty access to materials, communication, dis-cussion, help, and so forth. Most of these types of access issues are technical or procedural, with the quality being dependent on resource allocation, and are beyond the control of faculty and students. If access to technology-based communication tools is unavailable and/or unreliable, the potential for quality teaching/learning is minimized and the potential for student feelings of iso-lation and alienation is high. Quality at this level reflects the institution's knowledge of, and commitment to, learners. For example, an institution must be certain that computer labs, help desks, and communication tools are avail-able every day, around the clock.

IIP-Level 2: Programmatic Protocols and Academic Expectations

IIP-2 focuses on the academic beliefs and commitment at the program level regarding the prior knowledge, skills, and attitudes and performance expected of students in order to successfully engage the learning system, methodology, and the instructional materials to complete their programs of study. Likewise, faculty attitudes and commitment to a consistent—or programmatic—set of instructional tools and methodology are equally important.

For example, a programmatic decision and commitment to use a suite of synchronous and asynchronous communications media for student collaboration in a constructivist and student-centered learning environment has implications for students and curricula. When all faculty members choose collaborative instructional strategies, they do not want to spend valuable instructional time teaching students the mechanics of using the enabling communication tools. Therefore, students should be taught how to use the tools at the very beginning of the program of study, or even before (such as the two-week "boot camp" required by the University of Illinois at Urbana-Champaign for new distance education students [Carnevale, 2000]). The training should be done in a meaningful context and to the extent required for students to reach automaticity.

However, knowing how to use a collaborative tool is insufficient. In order to succeed in a collaborative learning environment, students also need to understand and accept that they will have to engage their course(s) on a regular basis each week (The Sloan Consortium, 2005). This is clearly a programmatic expectation—students need to be taught the importance of allocating regular and significant time to enhance their chances for success. Simply providing online resources for students is insufficient; provisions for teaching students to succeed in contemporary learning environments must be included within the curriculum itself. This training in online technologies is particularly important for African American students who are often on the wrong side of the digital divide and consequently lack many of the computer skills and experiences that White students have, as discussed in Chapter 7.

Decisions such as those described above are made primarily by program directors and supported in varying degrees by department heads and administrators. These types of issues are related most strongly to the learning effectiveness and student satisfaction pillars that might imply instructor and student responsibility, but the institution or program is responsible for the identification of common strategies, procedures, and tools that will be used consistently. Programmatic protocols developed at this level significantly influence the way instructors design their courses relative to rigor, pedagogy, mode of delivery, student orientation, and student support/mentoring. Failure to develop a shared vision for distributed courses is a significant barrier to success (Berge & Muilenburg, 2000).

IIP-Level 3: Instructional Design and Implementation

Questions of design and delivery of coursework are carried out by individual faculty members utilizing instructional strategies that may or may not be informed by formal guidance or study. However, the rapid growth of distributed education has caused institutions to rely increasingly on instructional designers, consultants, and advisors to help create pedagogically sound instruction. This assistance runs the gamut from advising individual faculty members on how to improve their teaching strategies to overseeing the development of entire programs.

Providing instruction in distributed environments is inextricably linked to, and dependent upon, the infrastructure, policies, and protocols provided in IIP levels 1 and 2. These issues become particularly important when courses designed to enhance the probability of success for African American students require higher levels of interaction and individual attention. Teaching online requires more time than teaching in a traditional environment (e.g., Shannon & Doube, 2004) as well as a significant change in workload structure (e.g., Thompson, 2004).

To enhance effectiveness, faculty should focus on robust instructional strategies rather than spending time teaching students how to use media delivery tools and solve technical problems (Berge & Muilenburg, 2000). For example, the use of a simple discussion database requires students not only to know how to use the software, but to learn "netiquette" and means for creating effective posts, including copying and pasting text from others' posts when referring to them, and starting appropriate branches and new threads. Students also need to know what their professor expects of them in terms of their interactions and postings. In this regard, a course participation rubric can guide student communication behavior. Clearly, when students are fully prepared to use the discussion board both technically and academically, the instructor is free to focus on teaching and the students on learning.

PRESENTATION OF INSTRUCTIONAL MATERIAL

Three distinct but irrevocably interrelated aspects of content presentation are: the content itself, the media for distribution, and the delivery mode. Obviously, the pedagogy that maximizes the efficacy of knowledge acquisition by students should be the driving force when designing a distributed course (Farrington & Clark, 2000). After determining the overall pedagogical approach, instructors then select appropriate and viable instructional strategies that utilize the necessary media elements to enhance the probability that students, regardless of ethnicity, will meet course goals. However, successful design efforts begin with a careful analysis of the students within the limitations imposed by the teaching/learning environment in order to match the instruction as closely as possible to learner needs (e.g., Dick, Carey, & Carey, 2005). The discussion of the learning implications of African

American and hip-hop cultures presented in Chapter 2 should help guide the instructor in designing courses.

Teaching/Learning Environment

Technology evolution now allows the presentation of instructional content to include text, graphics (including animation), and audio reliably at connection speeds as slow as 56k over dial-up connections. Many argue that requiring laptops or even high-speed Internet connections is an economic burden that cannot be expected of contemporary students, particularly those who may come from lower socioeconomic communities as many African Americans do. Therefore, reliable and consistent access to a 56k dial-up connection should be considered a minimum requirement to pursue distributed education.

Instructional Material Presentation

The challenge to teachers and learners is to reach instructional goals and objectives within the constraints of time, space, and money. The degree to which instruction is structured should reflect the cognitive and learning styles, expectations, and backgrounds of students, as well as the amount of content that needs to be covered, but whatever the instructional strategy, a certain amount of material must be presented to online students. The manner in which content is presented on computer monitor screens should not be random, but should be guided by the subject matter itself and by basic screen design, or message delivery rules. Although significant resources and full textbooks (e.g., Clark & Mayer, 2003) exist on the subject, the following discussion of basic design guidelines will enable online instructors to design effective information presentation.

While African American learners may not process information any differently from other learners, their success is best guaranteed through the application of the most-thoroughly researched practices of instructional design. The simplest method of information distribution is through text or spoken text with appropriate graphics (Clark & Mayer, 2003). In developing course materials, cultural sensitivity should be evaluated within the framework that African American student judgments about the credibility of a source may be influenced by the race of the communicator, the extent to which the message is directly relevant to their cultural identity and experiences, and the extent to which students are highly distrustful of Whites in general.

Text and spoken text are both processed in short-term memory as acoustic information (Pellegrino, Siegel, & Dhawan, 1974, 1976), whereas graphics are visual information, providing an additional channel in which to process the same information in working memory (Baddeley, 1966), thus enhancing meaningful learning by processing both representations and storing the knowledge in dual modes (Mayer & Anderson, 1991; Pavio, 1990). Appropriate graphics are those that represent or extend the same information as the text. In addition, images are more easily remembered than words (Levie, 1987). Given that images can be static (drawings, diagrams, or pictures), or moving (animation or video), instructors should attempt to use whatever form of representation is most appropriate to the content.

Written text should be used when the text and the graphic representation have essentially the same meaning. If the graphic simply serves as a reinforcement of the text, then written text is acceptable as the learner retains control of the pace because of reading speed. Text should always be presented before (or with) the graphic (Bransford & Johnson, 1972). When the graphic is an elaboration or extension of text, the text should be optionally narrated so the learner can focus on the graphic while listening to the description/ directions rather than shifting focus back and forth. Decorative graphics and graphics that are not sensitive to the cultures of the students should be avoided.

Animations become useful when learning tasks are procedural (e.g., drawing blood, operating complex machinery, plate tectonics) or conceptual (e.g., electron flow, spread of disease), where the learner benefits from seeing the steps of the process. Textual information with animations should always be narrated to avoid splitting the learner's attention between the graphic and written text (Moreno & Mayer, 2000).

Video, which may or may not include sound, is also a graphic element and is useful when the subject matter requires in-motion realistic representation. However, even compressed video in a small window requires significant bandwidth (recall that 56k was established as the minimum acceptable connection speed). A 10-frames-per-second (fps) 200 X 300 pixel video window will play using a 56k dial-up connection, but will most likely be degraded beyond usability.

Fidelity refers to the degree of realism represented by a graphic. Instructors should choose the simplest, or lowest-fidelity, elements that will accomplish an instructional goal, because too high a level of realism or detail can become a detriment to learning as a result of the added attention needed for processing (Choi, 1997; Kwinn, 1997). A photograph should never be used when a line drawing is sufficient. Clearly, text and line drawings are inexpensive and easy to produce, whereas video production is time and cost intensive. For example, text and line drawings are sufficient to display a sine wave, but are not sufficient to demonstrate the proper techniques for teaching a student or calming an anxious patient. Animation is likely the best tool to show how a heart attack results from a blockage because video simply cannot show what happens physiologically, and static graphics will not adequately show what happens when an artery becomes blocked.

ONLINE STUDENTS

Although the design issues discussed above are critical components of online instruction, consideration must also be given to the students themselves. Minority populations who feel separated from the mainstream classroom culture and are less inclined to participate in the activities of the traditional classroom (Ogbu, 1991) may actually benefit from the heightened individual attention of interactive online learning. Minority learners are often poorly equipped socioeconomically to become full-time students, or they may simply be disinterested in fulfilling the conventional on-campus role of the more traditional college student (Duderstadt, 1997). Whether carried out by individual instructors or created with the help of a formally trained distance educator, contemporary instructional principles have the potential to meet the needs of minority students through inclusion and engagement at a personal level.

One of the myths surrounding online learning is that students remain encased in a technological cocoon that prevents their race or ethnic heritage from becoming apparent. Although Internet folklore is replete with references to people representing themselves as someone of another gender, race, or age, the realities of online instruction are quite different. In most learning systems, names of students are shown to the entire class. The person named Lakiesha Williams or Maria Louisa Rivera is not likely to be viewed outside racial or ethnic terms by many students; in fact, in an online environment, this is all that fellow students are granted. Neither students nor the instructor can perceive a smiling face, a furrowed brow, or a tall athlete, and as the class progresses, without the instructor's intervention, all of the students' contributions are likely to be viewed through the scrim of the cultural perception of the group.

Acknowledging that race issues surface at the mere presence of both students' surnames and given names, Chester and Gwynne (1998) experimented with the use of aliases within a computer-mediated environment. They reasoned that minority students would be more at ease in expressing themselves and participating in classroom events if their identity were unknown. Through the use of pseudonyms, the researchers hoped that students would establish relationships that might otherwise be unlikely to develop. The researchers questioned whether identity would arise through performance rather than appearance. They speculated that without visual cues to signify student's race, cross-cultural interaction might increase; however, contrary to their expectations, pseudonymity did not appear to provide an answer to complicated questions, and even resulted in some antisocial behavior. The study illustrates, however, that the issue of race does matter in distributed learning environments. Consequently, instructors are encouraged to have students introduce themselves at the beginning of the course and perhaps even create their own home page with digital photographs so that connections can be made between members of the learning community.

ONLINE INTERACTIONS

Because of learners' differences and their lack of proximity to one another and to the instructor, the level of interactivity that learners may experience has become a subject of considerable research. Although recent writers have identified several types of interactivity, the three types defined by Moore (1989) are sufficient to conceptualize the areas of concern for this discussion. The first is learner-to-content interaction, which is normally perceived as the core of most collegiate instruction. The second type is learner-to-instructor interaction, which is regarded as essential by many educators to guide, shape, and mold learner understandings and attitudes, although debate remains as to the requisite frequency and intensity. The third type is learner-to-learner interaction that may take place individually or as part of a group setting; quite often these kinds of interactions take place before or after the defined class time. In online environments, this type of interaction typically takes place in chat rooms and on discussion boards where students are invited or required to interact with one another. Research has documented that achievement, satisfaction, and attitude are all impacted by various dimensions of person-to-person interactions (Jung, Choi, Lim, & Leem, 2002). Accordingly, in the discussion that follows, the greatest portion of the discussion focuses on interpersonal interaction.

Learner-to-Content Interaction

All educational enterprises demand that learners spend a good deal of time interacting with the content. In a collegiate environment, this is usually accomplished through a combination of reading, discussing, reviewing, and completing practice exercises. Although distributed learning is not particularly different in terms of these demands, much has been written about the qualities of good online students. Accordingly, having students respond to a self-assessment may be helpful for them in realizing what weaknesses they may have to remediate in terms of the demands of online learning arrangements. Buchanan (1999), for example, suggests that students respond to a beginning-of-course survey that asks them to rate themselves relative to: (a) working independently, (b) sacrificing personal time, (c) being a self-starter, (d) managing time, (e) having strong study skills, (f) moving beyond being a consumer of direct lecture, (g) divulging personal information and thoughts, and (h) being computer savvy. By responding to such items, students may indirectly realize the necessity for their own commitment to the learning enterprise.

Student levels of previous experience both with distance learning technology and with the content appear to have an impact on distance learners' comfort. Brown (2001) emphasizes that it takes students time to get accustomed to the demands of the world of distance learning, and calls the process a "triple whammy" in which learners face daunting technology, content, and the demands of collaborative, self-directed learning. Brown discovered that students in distance learning environments can be described as devoting energy to community building, course content, teaching methods used, and technology employed. However, the order of priorities is often reversed between veteran distant learners and novices.

Learner-to-Instructor Interaction

Instructors' skills and suitability for online teaching and the patience required as students adjust to a virtual classroom are important (Berger, 1999). By understanding the ways in which faculty make direct contributions to students' learning, instructors can broaden their range of skills in this environment, especially as they relate to what is known as virtual immediacy. Immediacy refers to communication behaviors that reduce social and psychological distance between people (Mehrabian, 1980), and it involves both nonverbal and verbal behaviors. In a traditional classroom, eye contact, smiling, open body postures, and moving around the classroom are all signals of social warming and regard for students. Largely denied these behaviors, distance educators must find other ways of reflecting a positive "classroom demeanor." For example, instructors can use personal examples, provide inviting feedback, and address students by name. Many instructors have found it useful to post autobiographical information or photos of their families, hobbies, or pets as a means of making their personal information available to students. Arbaugh (2001) found that such immediacy behaviors to reduce social distance were positive predictors of student learning and course satisfaction.

If African American students can be made to feel comfortable in a traditional learning environment, there is little to suggest that a given instructor should need to sacrifice any of this comfort level in a distance environment. Faculty who are particularly effective at projecting their unique personalities through these forms of electronic communication may be at a distinct advantage. Brown (2001), in fact, argues that this form of communication and shared space for students involves a three-step process: (a) making friends, (b) gaining community conferment or acceptance, and (c) establishing camaraderie. By using this method of conceptualizing teaching, instructors are able to model behaviors that show sensitivity to diverse human needs, guiding all students through ever greater levels of interpersonal bonding and affiliation. Key to this kind of communication is a measure of authenticity that arises from genuine regard for other humans, and it has been found to be of importance within distributed teaching.

To move students through thoughtful and active discourse, online instructors must engage students through thought-provoking questions about the material being studied. Since the assumption inherent in the literature on online teaching is that interaction is key, the traditional guidance offered to faculty is that they generate demanding questions and then set students to work in finding answers in some collective fashion. For example, Parker (1999) suggests that after demanding questions are posed,

> hypotheses should be discussed and finally teams of students should be assigned to explore electronically a range of possible solutions. The teams can work in chat rooms, through email, or even using telephone communication. In the early weeks of a distance class, forced interaction is usually required. This can take place by linking a portion of the final grade to the length and occurrence of electronic interaction. (p. 16)

Many instructors have found this approach of rewarding participation to be important; however, more research is needed regarding the best sequence of questions.

Since the general counsel is to ask complex questions, instructors may be tempted to post a list of the most esoteric queries they can muster, but this tactic simply leaves most students overwhelmed. Certainly it places marginalized, less confident students at a disadvantage. Accordingly, instructors need a way of structuring the sequence of questions that allows students to become engaged and make increasingly more complex cognitive connections to arrive at a richer understanding of the material. An entire body of literature exists relative to the importance of "scaffolding" in learning—tools or strategies for learning to help students develop understandings beyond their immediate grasp, and Azevedo and Hadwin (2005) suggest that good questioning is a form of scaffolding.

Clustering several questions around one concept, showing a progression of complexity from fact-finding to interpretation and analysis, often accomplishes this, and it allows for students of all abilities to become participants. Those students who struggle with the content can achieve a degree of involvement by responding to more factually oriented questions, and those students who are more facile in the subject can begin to weave connections in their answers that will be useful to the entire class.

Another way to involve all students in the development of meaningful discourse is shaping. Instructors can post questions that are hierarchically arranged around key concepts that guide students toward increasingly more challenging views of the subject. This approach does not ignore the facts upon which greater assumptions rest. Therefore, the instructor's task becomes one of monitoring how students respond, encouraging those who show that they are on the right track, and redirecting those who are not. The instructor must then ask clarifying questions of those students who do not give sufficient detail of their assertions (Lewis, 2002).

Learner-to-Learner Interaction

Many instructors will have difficulty determining just how much student involvement is appropriate, but the literature on learning at a distance emphasizes that learner-to-learner interaction is vital in many disciplines. These interactions not only serve for learning content but also lessen the psychological distance (Comeaux, 1995) and increase students' learning satisfaction (Picciano, 2002). Students should be engaged in participation to the highest degree possible, and content assignments are critical for moving students toward active or collaborative roles. Rovai (2003) reports the results of research suggesting that grading strategies influence online discussions, and discussions are related to students' sense of community. In particular, he reports significantly more discussions per student per week and higher levels of a sense of community in online courses where discussions are a graded course component. Adult students expect to earn credit for engaging in an activity that requires the expenditure of time and effort. Without motivation to engage in discussions, they are less likely to take the time to contribute to discussions.

In a comprehensive review of distance teaching tools and techniques, Belanger & Jordan (2000) conclude that the bulk of research evidence reveals that faculty members who make a shift toward a more learner-centered instructional approach are more successful distance education instructors; the major finding has been that student-centered teaching approaches have been significantly linked to academic achievement and student satisfaction.

A word of warning is in order, however, to protect students from premature exposure to threaded discussions. Considerable attention has been paid by researchers to the fact that asynchronous communication involves multiple threads of interaction occurring simultaneously that can result in student overload and a concomitant reduction in learning. Multiple permutations of dialogue can be overwhelming to students who are unaccustomed to these environments, and minority students who may be feeling uncertain of their place may feel that their coping skills are exhausted.

SENSE OF COMMUNITY

Only when students have become accustomed to all forms of interaction do instructor and students alike come to see themselves as a cohesive whole and to believe that they share a common goal, often called sense of community, which is described by Rovai (2002):

> Members of such classroom communities have feelings of belonging and trust. They believe that they matter to one another and to the group, that they have duties and obligations to each other and to the school, and they possess a shared faith that members' educational needs will be met through their commitment to shared goals. (p. 42)

Promoting such classroom dynamics appears to be daunting, but the core belief expressed here is that students should have an investment in their learning. Verduin and Clark (1991) suggest that distributed instruction can be as effective as traditional teaching as long as (a) the methods of instruction and technology are appropriate to the situation, (b) there is student-student interaction, and (c) there is timely instructor-to-student feedback. Rovai (2002) found that an increased sense of community is possible, and that it is associated with a greater sense of well-being and improved attitudes toward the classroom experience.

A somewhat different way of conceptualizing events in a distributed learning environment from that outlined in Moore's (1989) three forms of interaction is that suggested by Garrison, Anderson, and Archer (2000). These researchers analyzed and classified postings from online class discussions in terms of indicators of cognitive presence, social presence, and teaching presence. Once again, however, the amount of social presence dictates the degree to which people are viewed as "real persons," and this concept relates both to students' perception of the instructor and of the other students. A large amount of presence indicates a kind of illusion of direct communication that occurs when students do not perceive the communication medium, resulting in greater student satisfaction (Gunawardena & Zittle, 1997) and increased academic achievement (Christophel, 1990).

CONCLUSION

All good instructors pride themselves on providing the very best instruction possible, and online teaching is likely no different. The following instructor strategies for success in the traditional classroom discussed in Chapter 6 also apply to the virtual classroom:

- Use a student-centered approach.
- Vary the conditions of learning to address the learning and cognitive preferences of Black students.
- Build on students' prior knowledge and experiences.
- Adopt the roles of engager, motivator, model, and mentor.

However, providing the type of instruction most likely to contribute to the success of African American students in a distributed environment demands that instructors shift some of their focus to aspects of the teaching and learning process that are different from traditional instruction. Attention must be spread judiciously among content presentation, forms of delivery, and interaction as made manifest by the distance that separates participants. While the technologies and learning environment require a reformulation in the ways of conceptualizing the act of teaching, the learning experience remains deeply human, requiring a reaching out of one mind to another.

Mentoring students in distance education is arguably more important than doing so in a traditional on-campus environment because of the additional demands of learning at a distance. Mentoring is less involved in acquiring subject matter expertise and more involved in "providing guidance on becoming a scholar, expressing support for the learner, advocating for learner success and persistence, and mutually establishing roles and relationships" (Stein & Glazer, 2003, p. 21). In a virtual classroom, Stein and Glazer (2003) contend that the mentoring "relationship develops out of negotiation between the learner and mentor with regard to the types of actions required . . . and the action performed becomes negotiated around the needs and academic sophistication of the adult learner" (pp. 21–22).

As discussed in this chapter, distributed learning requires a deliberate and well-planned strategy to be effective (e.g., Chickering & Gamson, 1991; Moore, 2002) and to help close the African American achievement gap. Such a strategy should include the following elements:

- training faculty members in designing and teaching at a distance and in multicultural education prior to assuming teaching duties as part of a comprehensive distributed learning quality-control program
- using a comprehensive planning model to design distributed courses, such as the IIP Model described in this chapter
- specifying minimum student hardware and software requirements to pursue an online program
- respecting the diverse talents of students and their ways of learning, such as:
  - allowing students to choose project topics
  - incorporating diverse views into courses
  - allowing students to participate in assorted types of assignments (e.g., independent work and collaborative work)
  - giving students a choice in their assignments
- sponsoring a student "boot camp" prior to the start of a distributed learning program to help integrate students into the school by addressing issues such as students meeting staff and faculty in order to promote a sense of school community and institutional fit, student

counseling, school support service for distance students, use of technology, and course and program expectations such as the importance of student interaction and time management

- helping students connect their learning experience to their cultural experiences outside the classroom
- promoting student interaction by providing clear guidelines for student participation and by grading online course participation
- providing timely and meaningful feedback
- keeping students interested and motivated

DISCUSSION TOPICS

1. What are some obvious and not-so-obvious manifestations of race in distributed learning environments? Does the presence of race always influence classroom dynamics in some fashion?
2. What are the institution's responsibilities to marginalized students? To what extent should institutions address race-specific concerns?
3. In what ways are programs responsible for addressing the unique needs of minority students?
4. How much and what type of faculty training in course design should be provided by the institution or an affiliate? Should such training be mandatory?
5. What are some emerging communication and collaboration technologies that may become useful in the online environment? What component of the teaching and learning process can be enhanced by an as-yet-to-be-developed technological tool?
6. What are student responsibilities in distributed learning environments? How and to what extent is each evaluated? Should all types of student responsibilities contribute to course grades?
7. What are the various means of establishing instructor presence? How does one distinguish between idle banter and purposeful social-unit building? Can one be too chatty? If so, how?
8. How does one achieve faculty authenticity online and promote that same level of authenticity among students? How does one promote academic expression on the part of novice learners?
9. How does one promote social and academic cohesion? Should this dimension be assessed as part of the normal instructor evaluation process?
10. How does an instructor encourage student diligence without resorting to cajoling?
11. What are the online teaching demands for different academic areas? Does the academic discipline dictate which teaching approach may be selected? What are some examples?

12. Give some examples of assignments and techniques for achieving active student involvement. What separates purposeful work from busywork?

REFERENCES

Arbaugh, J. B. (2001). How instructor immediacy behaviors affect student satisfaction and learning in Web-based courses. *Business Communication Quarterly*, 4(64), 42–54.

Azevedo, R., & Hadwin, A. F. (2005). Scaffolding self-regulated learning and metacognition—Implications for the design of computer-based scaffolds. *Instructional Science*, 33(5–6), 367–379.

Baddeley, A. D. (1966). Short term memory for word sequences as a function of acoustic, semantic, and formal similarity. *Quarterly Journal of Experimental Psychology*, 18, 362–365.

Belanger, F., & Jordan, D. H. (2000). *Evaluation and implementation of distance learning: Technologies, tools, and techniques.* Hershey, PA: Idea Group.

Berge, Z. L., & Muilenburg, L. Y. (2000). Barriers to distance education as perceived by managers and administrators: Results of a survey. In M. Clay (Ed.), *Distance learning administration annual 2000.* Retrieved November 29, 2006, from http://www.emoderators.com/barriers/man_admin.shtml

Berger, N. S. (1999). Pioneering experiences in distance learning: Lessons learned. *Journal of Management Education*, 23(6), 684–690.

Bransford, J. D., & Johnson, M. K. (1972). Contextual prerequisites for understanding: Some investigations of comprehension and recall. *Journal of Verbal Learning and Verbal Behavior*, 11(6), 717–726.

Brown, R. (2001). The process of community-building in distance learning classes. *Journal of Asynchronous Learning Networks*, 5(2), 18–35.

Buchanan, E. (1999) Assessment measures: Pre-tests for successful distance teaching and learning? *Online Journal of Distance Learning Administration*, 2(4). Retrieved November 29, 2006, from http://www.westga.edu/~distance/buchanan24.html

Carnevale, D. (2000, October 27). Social bonds found to be crucial in online education. *The Chronicle of Higher Education*, 47(9), A48.

Chester, A., & Gwynne, G. (1998). Online teaching: Encouraging collaboration through anonymity. *Journal of Computer Mediated Communication*, 4(2). Retrieved November 29, 2006, from http://jcmc.indiana.edu/vol4/issue2/chester.html

Chickering, A. W., & Gamson, Z. F. (Eds). (1991). *Applying the seven principles for good practice in undergraduate education* (New directions for teaching and learning, No. 47). San Francisco: Jossey-Bass.

Choi, W. (1997). Designing effective scenarios for computer-based instructional simulations: Classification of essential features. *Educational Technology*, 37(5), 13–21.

Christophel, D. (1990). The relationship among teacher immediacy behaviors, student motivation, and learning. *Communication Education*, 39(4), 323–340.

Clark, R. C., & Mayer, R. E. (2003). *E-learning and the science of instruction*. San Francisco: Wiley.

Comeaux, P. (1995). The impact of an interactive distance learning network on classroom communication. *Communication Education, 44*(4), 353–361.

Dick, W., Carey, L., & Carey J. O. (2005). The systematic design of instruction. Boston: Allyn & Bacon.

Duderstadt, J. J. (1997). Transforming the university to serve the digital age. *Cause/Effect, 20*(4), 21–32.

Farrington, J., & Clark, R. E. (2000). Snake oil, science, and performance products. *Performance Improvement Quarterly, 39*(10), 5–10.

Garrison, D. R., Anderson, T., & Archer, W. (2000). Critical inquiry in a text-based environment: Computer conferencing in higher education. *The Internet and Higher Education, 2*(2–3), 87–105.

Gunawardena, C., & Zittle, F. (1997). Social presence as a predictor of satisfaction within a computer-mediated conferencing environment. *The American Journal of Distance Education, 11*(3), 8–26.

Jung, I., Choi, S., Lim, C., & Leem, J. (2002). Effects of different types of interaction on learning achievement, satisfaction and participation in web-based instruction. *Innovations in Education and Teaching International, 39*, 2–18.

Kwinn, A. (1997). High fidelity images—How they affect learning. *Journal of Interactive Instruction Development, 10*(2), 12–16.

Levie, W. L. (1987). Research on pictures: A guide to the literature. In D. M. Willows & H. A. Houghton (Eds.), *The psychology of illustration* (pp. 1–27). New York: Springer-Verlag.

Lewis, K. G. (2002). Developing questioning skills. In K. G. Lewis (Ed.), *A sourcebook for UT—Austin Faculty*. Austin, TX: University of Texas Center for Teaching Effectiveness. Retrieved November 29, 2006, from http://www.utexas.edu/academic/cte/sourcebook/questioning.pdf

Mayer, R. E., & Anderson, R. B. (1991). Animations need narrations: An experimental test of a dual-coding hypothesis. *Journal of Educational Psychology, 83*(4), 484–490.

Mehrabian, A. (1980). *Silent messages: Implicit communication of emotions and attitudes* (2nd ed.). Belmont, CA: Wadsworth Publishing Company.

Moore, J. C. (2002). *Elements of quality: The Sloan-C Framework*. Needham, MA: Sloan Consortium.

Moore, M. G. (1989). Editorial: Three types of interaction. *American Journal of Distance Education, 3*(2), 17–24.

Moreno, R., & Mayer, R. E. (2000). A learner-centered approach to multimedia explanations: Deriving instructional design principles from cognitive theory. *Interactive Multimedia Electronic Journal of Computer-Enhanced Learning, 2*(2). Retrieved November 29, 2006, from http://imej.wfu.edu/articles/2000/2/05/index.asp

Ogbu, J. (1991). Immigrant and involuntary minorities in comparative perspective. In M. A. Gibson & J. U. Ogbu (Eds.), *Minority status and schooling: A comparative study of immigrant and involuntary minorities* (pp. 3–33). New York: Garland.

Overbaugh, R. C., & Casiello, A. R. (2006, February). *A framework for the evaluation, design, implementation, and investigation of contemporary teaching and learning.* Paper presented at the annual conference of the Eastern Educational Research Association, Hilton Head, SC.

Parker, A. (1999). Interaction in distance education: The critical conversation. *Educational Technology Review, 12*(Fall/Winter), 13–17.

Pavio, A. (1990). *Mental representations: A dual coding approach.* New York: Oxford University Press.

Pellegrino, J. W., Siegel, A. W., & Dhawan, M. (1974). Short-term retention of pictures and words: Evidence for dual coding systems. *Journal of Experimental Psychology: Human Learning and Memory, 1,* 95–102.

Pellegrino, J. W., Siegel, A. W., & Dhawan, M. (1976). Differential distraction effects in short-term and long-term retention of pictures and words. *Journal of Experimental Psychology: Human Learning and Memory, 2,* 212–218.

Picciano, A. G. (2002). Beyond student perceptions: Issues of interaction, presence, and performance in an online course. *Journal of Asynchronous Learning Networks, 6*(1), 21–27.

Rovai, A. P. (2002). A preliminary look at the structural differences of higher education classroom communities in traditional and ALN courses. *Journal of Asynchronous Learning Networks, 6*(1), 41–56.

Rovai, A. P. (2003). Strategies for grading online discussions: Effects on discussions and classroom community in Internet-based university courses. *Journal of Computing in Higher Education, 15*(1), 89–107.

Shannon, S., & Doube, L. (2004). Valuing and using web supported teaching: A staff development role in closing the gaps. *Australasian Journal of Educational Technology, 20*(1), 114–136.

Sloan Consortium. (2005, November). *Growing by degrees.* Needham, MA: Sloan Consortium.

Stein, D., & Glazer, H. R. (2003). Mentoring the adult learner in academic midlife at a distance education university. *The American Journal of Distance Education, 17*(1), 7–23.

Thompson, M. (2004). Faculty self-study research project: Examining the online workload. *Journal of Asynchronous Learning Networks, 8*(3), 84–88.

Verduin, J. R., & Clark, T. A. (1991). *Distance education: The foundations of effective practice.* San Francisco: Jossey-Bass.

NINE

Assessment for Learning

Joya Anastasia Carter & Alfred P. Rovai

PURPOSE

The goal of education equity is to ensure that all students have an equal opportunity for academic achievement. Historically, the average achievement levels of African American students have been below those of their White counterparts at the elementary, secondary, and postsecondary levels, as discussed in Chapter 1. Research continues to address this persistent achievement gap, and progress is being made. For example, the 2005 Fact Sheet from the White House claims that the reading and math scores for African American 9-year-olds reached their highest levels in the history of the National Assessment of Educational Progress. However, continued efforts are still required.

Previous chapters described promising research-based course design and instructional strategies for closing the achievement gap in traditional and virtual classrooms. The present chapter continues this discussion by addressing how classroom assessment strategies can support this goal. This chapter begins by providing a background on general student assessment theory, and continues by describing specific assessment strategies that can promote education equity within a culturally diverse learning environment.

BACKGROUND

When working toward closing the achievement gap for African American students, it is important to consider how assessments influence pedagogical practice and student learning. There is, however, a measure of uncertainty when dealing with classroom assessments. As Paul Dressel (1976) eloquently observes, "a grade is an inadequate report of an inaccurate judgment by a biased and variable judge of the extent to which a student has achieved an undefined level of mastery of an unknown proportion of an indefinite material" (p. 12). Despite these weaknesses, assessment of learning has an important role to play in the teaching-learning process:

> Assessment is an ongoing process aimed at understanding and improving student learning. It involves making our expectations explicit and public; setting appropriate criteria and high standards for learning quality; systematically gathering, analyzing, and interpreting evidence to determine how well performance matches those expectations and standards; and using the resulting information to document, explain, and improve performance. When it is embedded effectively within larger institutional systems, assessment can help us focus our collective attention, examine our assumptions, and create a shared academic culture dedicated to assuring and improving the quality of higher education. (Angelo, 1995, p. 7)

This description of assessment implies that rather than being something added, assessment is an integral, ongoing aspect of teaching and learning. It is the process of gathering, describing, or quantifying information about learner performance. This process often entails awarding grades and involves a type of assessment that educational practitioners refer to as summative. Summative assessments are also called high-stakes assessments when used for determining promotion, placement, certification, and graduation, or when referring to merit-based rewards. Madaus (1988) defines such assessments as "those whose results are seen—rightly or wrongly—by students, teachers, administrators, parents, or the general public as being used to make important decisions that immediately and directly affect them" (p. 87).

Assessments can also be formative, when their primary aim is to improve teaching and learning, not to provide evidence for grading students. Angelo's (1995) above description of assessment clearly places emphasis on the formative aspects of assessment. Herman, Aschbacher, and Winters (1992) describe two types of formative assessment:

- The first type is meant to determine whether or not students have acquired specific knowledge or skills. This type of assessment should focus on the products or outcomes of student learning.
- The second type is meant to diagnose student strengths and weaknesses. Because we are interested in understanding where the student is going wrong, instructors need to assess the process as well as the product.

One can break down assessment tasks into two broad types: selected response and constructed response. Selected response is the traditional assessment task that requires learners to choose an answer from a given set of response items, often multiple-choice or true-false. These traditional tests usually require that all learners in a class are tested through the same standardized procedures at the same controlled location. Such assessments are not authentic in that they do not resemble "real-life" tasks. However, selected response assessments are usually reliable (i.e., measurements are generally consistent with each other). Selected response assessment tasks do best at assessing lower levels of learning. Accordingly, these assessments can be useful in testing knowledge acquisition and simple recall as part of an overall assessment strategy. However, a sound classroom assessment strategy is not limited to the use of a single assessment type, but rather consists of a system of multiple measurements that include diverse types of assessments.

In student-centered, constructivist learning environments where collaboration, relationships, inquiry, invention, and authentic assessments are valued, overreliance on traditional tests that emphasize factual recall is not consistent with the nature of learning that occurs in these environments (Salomon & Perkins, 1998). Constructivists view traditional assessments as shackling student responses to problems. Their view is that open-ended assessments offer a more accurate view of student learning. Consequently, there is a general move away from traditional, selected response tests and toward performance and constructed response assessments.

Performance assessments are based on observation and evaluation of student-created products, projects, and performances. They require students to perform a task or demonstrate a skill rather than simply select a response. Performance assessments can go well beyond testing the knowledge level of learning by examining understanding, application, analysis, synthesis, and evaluation. In other words, performance assessments are used to assess higher-order thinking skills.

Lee (1998) advocates performance-based assessments over selected response tests, but claims that most tests are designed and later administered from a Eurocentric perspective. Battiste and Henderson (2000) describe such an approach as "cognitive imperialism," which occurs when Eurocentric thinkers automatically assume the superiority of their worldview and ways of learning, and attempt to impose them on others. Consequently, students of color tend to do poorly on tests that are constructed from such a perspective. However, "performance-based assessments have been deemed 'authentic' in the sense that they require students to tackle complex problems that have some real-world currency over an extended period of time" (p. 268). Although they can also be developed from a Eurocentric perspective, performance-based assessments offer the flexibility of allowing students a measure of freedom in their performances. Lee (1998) suggests that once these assessments are designed with the students' background in mind, teachers can expect an increased likelihood that they will see greater student achievement.

Culturally sensitive performance assessments can be instrumental in helping teachers plan future instruction, but the assessments must:

- be linked to and integrated directly with curriculum and instruction, and
- involve tasks that draw on culturally based knowledge and experiences (Lee, 1998, p. 273)

Instructors can employ a variety of performance assessment tasks to understand how students' ideas are evolving and to give feedback on the processes as well as on the products of their thinking. These assessment tasks include case studies, demonstrations, exhibitions, group discussions, interviews, performances, portfolios, presentations, problem-based learning, role playing, student-designed projects, and team projects. Many of these assessment tasks involve collaborative group work. In order to encourage collaboration, students need to be engaged in a contextually based, common activity. Such assessment tasks can result in more meaningful assessments that are better able to measure student learning within authentic contexts that are relevant for the student. Problem-based learning (PBL) is of particular interest in this regard.

PBL is a combined instructional and assessment strategy that facilitates collaboration. Regardless of how PBL is implemented, a learning environment needs to support the following principles if it is to be classified as PBL (Savery & Duffy, 1995):

- Learning is situated in a context that is meaningful to the learner, which leads to greater ability to transfer the learning to other settings. Rather than being told what to do or how to solve a problem, students are able to generate and pursue their own learning.
- Learners construct knowledge through the process of solving problems.
- Learning emphasizes metacognitive skills. Students generate their own strategies for defining the problem and working out a solution. The instructor's role is that of a facilitator who keeps the process moving.
- Learning involves the social construction of knowledge. Students are able to challenge their thoughts, beliefs, perceptions, and existing knowledge by interacting with others.

Portfolio assessments are also of interest in a multicultural student setting. A portfolio is an assortment of student artifacts of learning that represent a variety of performances, allowing the student to provide evidence of learning. Samples of actual work can include essays, reports, videotaped presentations, or a project the student has completed. Reckase (1995) suggests that the portfolio should include:

- student participation in the selection of artifacts through which they learn to value their work
- the criteria for selection
- the criteria for judging merit
- evidence of student self-reflection through which students articulate what they think and feel about their work, their learning environment, and themselves

The portfolio should contain at least one artifact that reflects each educational objective. When a student elects to use more than one artifact to demonstrate fulfillment of an objective, the artifacts should reflect a variety of media or tasks, or perhaps show growth over time.

In contrast to most traditional testing, performance assessments do not have clear-cut right or wrong answers. Rather, there are degrees to which a person is successful or unsuccessful. Thus, one needs to evaluate performance in ways that take those varying degrees of success into consideration. Such a process can be both time-consuming and expensive. Additionally, performance assessments are less reliable than traditional tests—that is, different raters can easily differ on how they assess the same performance, and the same rater can differ on how the same performance is assessed at different times.

To summarize, instructors should measure student progress frequently. Authentic performance tasks, as described above, are most valued in a constructivist, student-centered learning environment. No single assessment task can ascertain whether all educational objectives have been met. A variety of assessment tasks are necessary to provide educators with a well-rounded view of what students know and can do. This diverse, multiple assessment task approach to assessment is the keystone to valid, reliable, and fair information about student achievement. Moreover, performance assessment tasks offer the following advantages in multicultural learning environments:

1. The instruction that accompanies performance-based assessments tends to be iterative (cyclical and repetitive), involving a building process so that there are multiple opportunities for students to acquire information, and ongoing opportunities to have questions addressed by the instructor. This instructional approach is consistent with the oral tradition that is part of the culture of many African American students.
2. Students often have the opportunity to select a context or setting in which to conduct the project that is comfortable and may even be familiar to them. Providing African American students with the opportunity to apply their newly acquired knowledge and skills in a familiar context or setting reduces stress and provides opportunities to interact within a comfortable environment.

3. By working as part of a collaborative small group or team, each student has the opportunity to volunteer to do work and make contributions to the process based upon his or her strengths, and, concomitantly, to work at developing skills in areas of weakness in a less-threatening environment. Such collaborative learning can provide educational environments characterized by harmony, cooperation, affect, socialization, and community in which many African Americans excel.

ASSESSMENT FOR LEARNING

Previous chapters discuss the importance of shifting instruction from a teacher-centered classroom to one that is learner-centered. Examining this instructional shift from an assessment perspective means that the focus of assessment shifts from assessment *of* learning to assessment *for* learning. However, one must keep in mind that assessments of and for learning are both important. Assessment of learning is used for accountability purposes and to determine a student's level of performance or grade. Assessment for learning allows: (a) teachers to check on student learning, (b) students to confirm their own learning, and (c) teachers to revise instruction and students to adjust their study habits.

Assessment for learning is not an easy concept to implement. To increase descriptive feedback to students while reducing judgmental feedback means that the instructor must determine how to comment on the quality of student work and then provide time for students to act on that feedback before being graded. Stiggins (2002) writes that as a result of assessment for learning, students keep learning and remain confident that they can continue to learn at productive levels if they sustain their efforts. In other words, Stiggins suggests that students will not give up in frustration or hopelessness.

Frederiksen and Collins (1989) maintain that one reason gaps in performance exist among groups is because of student differences in familiarity, exposure, and motivation regarding assessment tasks. Such gaps are particularly apparent among Blacks when they are assessed within a White cultural framework and cannot relate to that culture. Moreover, since instructors may be influenced by racial stereotyping and may expect lower achievement on the part of their Black students, their assessment of Black student performance assessments may be biased. Addressing this point, Stiggins (1987) writes, "it is critical that the scoring procedures are designed to assure that performance ratings reflect the examinee's true capabilities and are not a function of the perceptions and biases of the persons evaluating the performance" (p. 33).

Frederiksen and Collins (1989) use the term *transparency* to suggest that students must have a clear understanding of what is required and how they will be assessed. This approach can build greater student appreciation that standards are not arbitrary (Gipps, 1999) as well as promote fairness in the grading process. It also involves students in analyzing their own work, builds ownership of the evaluation process, and "makes it possible to hold students to higher standards because the criteria are clear and reasonable" (Wiggins, 1992, p. 30).

Rubrics

Judicious utilization of rubrics responds to this call for transparency and allows students and teachers to document whatever grade is earned by the student. Therefore, rubrics help shift the focus of assessment from teaching to learning (i.e., from what was taught to what was learned). In turn, students are able to take more responsibility for their own learning, including a greater awareness of their achievement and growth. A typical rubric:

- identifies the educational objectives,
- includes a scale that identifies various levels of performance,
- frequently breaks down an assessment task into dimensions (i.e., components),
- provides students with performance criteria for the various levels of the performance and for each dimension, and
- is given to students at the beginning of learning so they understand what is expected of them

Figure 9.1 is an example of an online course participation rubric that guides online discussions. This rubric divides performance into six dimensions (i.e., quantitative, content, questions, collaboration, tone, and mechanics) and three levels of performance (above average, average, and below average). Although this rubric was developed for online courses, it is easily adaptable for guiding traditional classroom discussions.

Checklists

Another possible scoring format that provides feedback to students is a checklist. Like a rubric, a checklist also contains dimensions of performance and weights that provide the basis for assessing a student's product and/or performance. Rather than describing the dimensions in terms of performance criteria in a narrative format, the dimensions of performance and weights in a checklist are presented simply as a list. Figure 9.2 is an example of such a checklist.

This example shows a checklist that distinguishes between levels of performance using a designated number of points that the student earns on each

Figure 9.1. Online Course Participation Rubric

	Below-Average	Average	Above-Average
QUANTITATIVE	A lurker; tends to access forums on a weekly or less frequent basis; contributions are sporadic	Accesses forums at least once each week; posts one message each week	Accesses forums several times each week; posts two or more messages each week
CONTENT	Postings are superficial; content often includes omissions or errors; recites fact rather than addressing issues	Postings are sometimes long, unclear, and rambling, but rarely are dominated by opinion; arguments are supported by evidence	Postings are concise, clear, insightful, original, and relevant; arguments are well supported
QUESTIONS	Never includes questions that stimulate discussion; rarely responds to questions raised by others	Rarely includes good questions; sometimes responds to questions raised by others	Sometimes includes good questions; frequently responds to questions from others
COLLABORATION	Most comments are student-to-instructor; rarely comments on the work of others	Most comments are student-to-student; supports and encourages other students; evaluates the work of others with constructive comments	
TONE	Postings are empathic rather than aggressive and display such qualities as sociability, sensitivity, concern, and gentleness; self-control is demonstrated by respectfulness, flexibility, temperateness, and discreteness; respect is shown for diversity of views and cultural backgrounds		
MECHANICS	Postings often have numerous errors in spelling and grammar	Postings have few errors in spelling and grammar; messages are well-formatted with appropriate spacing	

Source: Adapted from Rovai, 2000, p. 148, Table 1.

dimension. Some checklists simply ask the evaluator to indicate whether or not the dimension is satisfied. However, even when provided with a certain number of points, the student may remain unclear as to how he or she acquired the points or what he or she needs to do in order to improve performance.

The checklist shown in Figure 9.2 also includes a column titled *Self*. Many teachers use assessments as an opportunity to build the student's capacity for self-reflection, developing intrinsic motivation focused on the quality of their own work. This is an assessment principle that cannot be overemphasized.

Figure 9.2. Grading Checklist

Oral Presentation Checklist			
	Possible	Points Earned	
Key Elements	Points	Self	Professor
Effective attention-getter	10		
Informative overview	5		
Content well-explained	25		
Content well-organized	20		
Effective visuals used to help explain	10		
Effective delivery	25		
Informative closure, links back to attention-grabber	5		
TOTAL	100		

Multicultural Education

The heart of multicultural education is being able to address the reality of diversity in our educational institutions. Without diversity, instruction and assessments are matched to the preferences of the dominant culture. One result is that students from the dominant culture think of themselves as the norm and all others as a deviation from that norm. Additionally, teaching and assessments become biased in favor of members of the dominant culture. Since all people do not learn in the same manner, they should not all be assessed using only one type of assessment.

From his research on assessment contextualized in culture, Estrin (1993) argues that we cannot understand what a student's performance means unless we also understand what that student brings with him or her in terms of language and culture. Once an understanding is achieved, teachers can design their evaluation and instruction around the specific needs and characteristics of their students. One way to do so is by developing culturally relevant assessment tasks.

Culture plays a role in assessment just as it does in instruction. Johnson (1998) explains, "Currently most responsible approaches to assessment recognize the vital importance of both the cultural characteristics and educational experiences of students to the understanding of the ways in which students interact with assessment situations and the meaning of the products obtained from assessments" (p. 181).

Speaking of herself and other advocates for improved educational practices, Johnson (1998) notes, "our goal is to further research focusing on the pedagogical connections that lead to the development and use of assessments that engage the cultural strengths of students—especially black, Hispanic, and the low-income children" (p. 182). This goal is one toward which all educators should strive: to use assessments to guide instruction and therefore meet students' needs.

A student-centered approach to learning is intended to cultivate construction of knowledge that is grounded in meaningful contexts relevant to the student. Multidimensional assessments are based on broader concepts of cognitive style, communication patterns, and the cultural contexts of learning. Chapter 2 identifies the following African American cultural orientations toward learning:

- *Holistic*: Learning environment characterized by harmony, cooperation, affect, socialization, community; relational and creative learning relevant to ones own experiences
- *Field-dependent*: Learning from a global perspective that emphasizes the social, dialogical aspect of learning
- *High-context*: Reliance on nonverbal, indirect, implicit, and informal communication; high personal, relational commitment

Teachers must attend to these cultural orientations. Accomplishment of this goal requires assessments that focus on the processes as well as on the products of learning, and involve students as participants in determining how best they can demonstrate their learning. Consequently, diverse multidimensional assessments are required, such as student journals, peer reviews, research reports, the building of physical models, and performances in forms such as inquiries, plays, debates, and artistic renderings (Shepard, 2000).

Banks, Cookson, Gay, Hawley, Irvine, Nieto, Schofield, and Step (2001) point out that the preferred mode of demonstrating task mastery for some students is writing, while for others it is speaking or performing. Some individuals are motivated by competition and others by cooperation; some prefer to work alone, while others prefer working in groups. Consequently, Banks et al. (2001) suggest that a variety of assessment tasks that are compatible with different learning, performance, work, and presentation styles should be used to determine whether students are mastering the skills they need to function effectively in a multicultural society.

As noted above, for many Black students the African American cultural orientation toward learning emphasizes the social aspects of learning. Moreover, the context of learning must be relevant to their experiences. Such an orientation suggests that emphasis be placed on authentic performance assessments that involve cooperative group work. However, instructors must carefully monitor student participation in ethnically heterogeneous cooperative learning environments. Minority students can be silenced by majority student attitudes and behavior.

When teachers do not consider how students' cultural backgrounds affect their ways of working on a task, they tend to form expectations about how a task will be completed, which may lead to false impressions about student abilities (Garcia & Pearson, 1991). "Because teachers are typically not trained for, or systematic in their use of performance assessment, they may form impressions of students too quickly and use the data they collect from students to maintain those impressions throughout the year" (Meisels, Dorfman, & Steele, 1995, p. 250). Instructors must become knowledgeable both about the subject matter being assessed and about students' cultures and languages in order to use performance assessments fairly in a classroom with students from diverse cultural and language backgrounds (Garcia & Pearson, 1991).

Equity in Group Work

Elizabeth Cohen (1997) developed the theory of complex instruction to treat problems of inequality within heterogeneous cooperative groups. She based her theory on both organization theory and expectation states theory. Within a classroom context, organization theory predicts that uncertain tasks are performed more productively when students work laterally and interact with each other (Perrow, 1967). Expectation states theory predicts that students who possess relatively low status with their peers will interact with classmates less frequently and will learn less than high-status students (Berger, Cohen, & Zelditch, 1966). Cohen (1994) explains:

> Examples of status characteristics are race, social class, sex, reading ability, and attractiveness. Attached to these status characteristics are general expectations for competence. High status individuals are expected to be more competent than low status individuals across a wide range of tasks that are viewed as important. . . . Since in our culture people of color are generally expected to be less competent on intellectual tasks than whites, these racist expectations came into play in [cooperative group activities]. (pp. 33–34)

Cohen (1994) also reports that low-status students engaged in group work "often don't have access to the task . . . and don't talk as much as other students. Often when they do talk, their ideas are ignored by the rest of the group" (pp. 35–36). She concludes that low-status students participate less in inquiry-based discussions than high-status students do, although some can make meaningful contributions.

Since students who participate less in inquiry-based projects score lower on unit tests (Bianchini, 1997), Cohen (1994) suggests that instructors must pay particular attention to unequal participation of students in group work and employ strategies to address status problems based on her theory of complex instruction. Complex instruction (Cohen, 1997) is a classroom management system where instructors delegate authority to students, through norms and roles, to generate student interactions. The instructor intervenes indirectly to equalize students' status in the classroom by raising the status of those students with lower status. The premise is that when status is equalized, all students in the cooperative group will interact equitably and all will learn.

Assigning competence to low-status students means that the teacher publicly recognizes the work they have accomplished. Cohen (1994) suggests that the teacher makes the case to students that everyone in a group assignment needs the others for successful completion of the work, and that no one alone has all the abilities necessary for the assignment but that each student possesses some. Moreover, instructors need to attend to nurturing student attitudes, such as interest in the cooperative project and pride in success. According to Cohen (1994, 1997), such learner-centered classrooms are characterized by:

- varied materials and methods,
- student autonomy,
- individualized tasks in which all students are not doing the same thing,
- varied grouping patterns, and
- less reliance on grading and summative assessments

Distributed Learning Assessments

The assessment principles discussed in this chapter apply to both the traditional and virtual classrooms. However, the unique characteristics of the distance education medium can create challenges to the process of student assessment, particularly when assessments are used for summative purposes. Rovai (2000) points out that identity security and academic honesty for assessments in distributed courses are about the same as they are for a take-home assignment in the traditional classroom. In order to strengthen the validity of online assessments, he suggests postponement of immediate assessment in favor of: (a) a delayed telephone conversation, (b) proctored testing at decentralized locations, and (c) proctored testing at centralized on-campus residencies. Proctored testing is particularly relevant when testing is for high-stakes purposes. Additionally, online services such as Turnitin (http://www.turnitin.com) can be used to help detect plagiarism in submitted papers.

Greater emphasis should be placed on performance assessments in distributed learning environments because of the instructor's reduced control over the conditions in which assessments are conducted. Portfolios represent an excellent choice. Cooperative work is also possible and recommended as part of an overall distance education assessment for learning strategy, but requires additional work on the part of the instructor to provide sufficient scaffolding. The inclination of online instructors to rely exclusively on assessments that involve independent work should be avoided; such a single-minded strategy violates the principle of diverse assessments discussed above. As a minimum, scaffolding should include designation of culturally diverse students to each group and assignment of specific responsibilities to each member of the group.

ASSESSMENT EXAMPLE

Assessment Task Template

An important goal of assessment is to maximize the potential of all students, regardless of race and cultural heritage. This goal ensures that all students have equitable opportunities to learn and achieve at the highest possible levels. Key issues to consider when developing traditional or distributed learning assessment tasks are whether assessment techniques are assessing the full range of higher-order learning outcomes (as opposed to narrow reproduction) and whether there is equity for all students in the opportunities to demonstrate their knowledge. Graded assignments must therefore facilitate assessment for each student, no matter how culturally similar or different the student is from the professor.

A key element to meeting the assessment needs of a diverse student population is a flexible approach. It should be possible to design assessments that allow for a wide variety of tasks to elicit a single response and single tasks that allow for a wide variety of response types, while maintaining standards.

Figure 9.3 is an assignment template that can be used for traditional and distributed learning courses. Embedded within assignments is the recognition that each learner is unique. Where possible, students should be provided the choice of how they demonstrate that they have mastered course competencies.

Sample Assessment Task

The appendix to this chapter is a sample assessment task for a graduate-level educational leadership course that utilizes collaborative learning and role playing in a team project. It supports the social aspects of learning and authentic context preferred by many African Americans. Students who have never participated in collaborative learning groups may need practice in teamwork skills such as tolerant listening, helping one another master content, giving and receiving constructive criticism, and managing disagreements (Fiechtner & Davis, 1991). In the sample assessment task, all group members

Figure 9.3. Assessment Task Template

TITLE

Introduction

Include an introduction that provides students with an informative background that adds interest and motivation, relates the assignment to the real world, and lists the educational objectives from the course syllabus that are assessed by the assignment. Relate the assignment to students' prior knowledge and experience. Many African American students attend best to material that is relevant to their own experiences. Many also prefer externally defined goals and reinforcements.

Task

In a single sentence, summarize what the students must accomplish. A task that reflects a context meaningful to the student should be used.

Resources

List the resources that will be most helpful for students in completing the task, such as the course textbook, handouts, and so forth. Integrate electronic resources via hyperlinks.

Directions

List the procedures and processes that the students should follow in accomplishing the assignment. This section can be large if students require substantial scaffolding, e.g., the assignment uses Problem-Based Learning for the first time. As the academic term progresses, this section can be substantially reduced. Include collaborative group activities where possible. Many African American students prefer sequential organization, structured environments, and relational and dialogical assessment experiences. Under proper conditions, group work encourages peer learning and peer support.

Evaluation

Insert a rubric or checklist so students know what is expected of them and how their work will be graded. Doing this also provides the opportunity for each student to assess his or her own work prior to submitting the assignment for grading.

Conclusion

Provide the opportunity for closure and reflection on the assignment.

---

are assigned the same grade. In such circumstances, Cooper (1990) recommends that the grade should only account for a small part of a student's course grade. Alternatively, students can be assigned individual grades while still maintaining many of the social aspects of the assignment.

CONCLUSION

A key tenet of becoming an effective teacher is developing the ability to instill a deep-seated love for learning in each student. The manner in which teachers approach assessment can help transform merely adequate teachers into highly effective teachers. To be effective within a multicultural learning environment, assessment must be viewed as an integral part of learning and must be perceived by all students as being grounded in authentic (i.e., real world) experience rather than being focused on the recall of abstract knowledge. Authentic assessment has several dimensions and leads to the kinds of skills and processes that underpin a global perspective, including:

- the construction of knowledge rather than reproduction of facts,
- the capacity to understand multiple perspectives, and
- the ability to synthesize knowledge

Assessments that focus on student growth should also be used, such as action-oriented projects, self-assessments, and reflections on the course (Kitano, 1997).

Unless students are required to engage in authentic tasks and address complex real world issues, they will not develop the skills of intercultural competence and global thinking. Becoming explicit about learning outcomes and how assessment tasks relate to these outcomes is a necessary but not sufficient condition for improved cultural responsiveness in teaching. Teachers of students with diverse cultural backgrounds need to open their classrooms to more than one approach to intellectual work. Teaching and learning must become holistic (i.e., engaging all the senses). Holistic learning engages the body, the mind, and the emotions. Performance assessments that engage all these aspects focus on the "big picture" and engage the power of learning. Additionally, educators must acknowledge that people learn both in groups and as individuals, that expectations must be clear, and that sufficient scaffolding must be provided to guide students in completing assessment tasks. Figure 9.3 provides an example of an assessment task that addresses the issue of scaffolding.

It is imperative that we have a clear rationale for assessing students via certain products and performances and for the ways in which we interpret students' performances. We must be vigilant at every step of the way in recognizing potential bias, and looking at a student's behavior and background as well as test performance to justify interpretations of scores and how they are used. Messick (1994) calls this the interplay between evidence and consequences.

Finally, we must be extremely cautious in interpreting inadequate performances by students who are still developing proficiency in English or whose cultures do not match that of the school. A poor performance cannot be assumed to mean that the student has not learned or is incapable of learning what is being assessed.

In summary, this chapter suggests that a classroom assessment strategy characterized by the following principles will promote education equity and help close the African American achievement gap in higher education:

- Assessments should be based on clearly articulated educational objectives.

- Student progress should be monitored frequently, using the concept of assessment for learning.
- Students should receive timely feedback.
- Whenever possible, students should help determine how educational objectives will be assessed.
- A variety of assessment tasks should be used to provide instructors with a well-rounded view of what students know and can do.
- Instructors must become knowledgeable both about the subject matter being assessed and about students' cultures and languages in order to use assessments fairly.
- Instructors must pay particular attention to unequal participation of students in group work and employ strategies to address status problems.
- Assessments should:
    - resemble real life as closely as possible (i.e., be authentic);
    - recognize the vital importance of both the cultural characteristics and educational experiences of students;
    - be mostly performance-based (e.g., portfolio assessments);
    - consist of cooperative group work whenever possible (e.g., PBL);
    - focus on student growth, such as action-oriented projects, self-assessments, and reflections on the course; and
    - include a grading rubric so that students know what is expected, so that grading criteria are transparent, and to promote fair grading by the instructor.

DISCUSSION TOPICS

1. How can teachers publicly recognize the work accomplished by low-status students without appearing to be patronizing?
2. What strategies can teachers use to ensure that everyone in a group assignment needs the others for successful completion of the work?
3. How can the contribution of each student be assessed in group projects?
4. What types of assessment tasks would likely appeal most to White students? To Black students?
5. Evaluate multicultural education as an instrument of change in higher education.
6. What possible links to culture can be used to initiate authentic assessment for a cooperative group of ethnically diverse students?

REFERENCES

Angelo, T. A. (1995). Reassessing (and defining) assessment. *AAHE Bulletin, 48*(3), 7–9.
Banks, J. A., Cookson, P., Gay, G., Hawley, W. D., Irvine, J. J., Nieto, S., Schofield,

J. W., & Step, W. G. (2001). Diversity within unity: Essential principles for teaching and learning in a multicultural society. *Phi Delta Kappan, 83*(3), 196–203.

Battiste, M., & Henderson, J. Y. (2000). *Protecting indigenous knowledge and heritage: A global challenge.* Saskatoon, SK: Purich Publishing.

Berger, J. B., Cohen, B. P., & Zelditch, M., Jr. (1966). Status characteristics and expectation states. In J. Berger & M. Zelditch Jr. (Eds.), *Sociological theories in progress,* Vol. I (pp. 26–46). Boston: Houghton-Mifflin.

Bianchini, J. A. (1997). Where knowledge construction, equity, and context intersect: Student learning of science in small groups. *Journal of Research in Science Teaching, 34*(10), 1039–1065.

Cohen, E. G. (1994). *Designing groupwork: Strategies for the heterogeneous classroom* (2nd ed.). New York: Teachers College Press.

Cohen, E. G. (1997). Understanding status problems: Sources and consequences. In E. G. Cohen & R. A. Lotan (Eds.), *Working for equity in heterogeneous classrooms: Sociological theory in practice* (pp. 61–76). New York: Teachers College Press.

Cooper, J. (1990). Cooperative learning and college teaching: Tips from the trenches. *Teaching Professor, 4*(5), 1–2.

Dressel, P. (1976). Grades: One more tilt at the windmill. In A. W. Chickering (Ed.), *Bulletin* (p. 12). Memphis, TN: Memphis State University, Center for the Study of Higher Education.

Estrin, E. T. (1993). *Alternative assessment: Issues in language, culture, and equity.* San Francisco: Far West Educational Laboratory.

Fact Sheet. (2005, July 14). Ensuring the promise of America reaches all Americans. Washington, DC: The White House, Office of the Press Secretary. Retrieved November 29, 2006, from http://www.whitehouse.gov/news/releases/2005/07/20050714.html

Feichtner, S. B., & Davis, E. A. (1991). Why some groups fail: A survey of students' experiences with learning groups. *The Organizational Behavior Teaching Review, 9*(4), 75–88.

Frederiksen, J. R., & Collins, A. (1989). A systems approach to educational testing. *Educational Researcher, 18*(9), 27–32.

Garcia, G. E., & Pearson, P. D. (1991). The role of assessment in a diverse society. In E. H. Hiebert (Ed.), *Literacy for a diverse society: Perspectives, practices, and policies* (pp. 253–278). New York: Teachers College Press.

Gipps, C. V. (1999). Sociocultural aspects of assessment. *Review of Research in Education, 24*(10), 355–392.

Herman, J. L., Aschbacher, P. R., & Winters, L. (1992). *A practical guide to alternative assessment.* Alexandria, VA: Association for Supervision and Curriculum Development.

Hood, S. (1998). Introduction and overview: Assessment in the context of culture and pedagogy: A collaborative effort, a meaningful goal. *Journal of Negro Education, 67*(3), 184–186.

Johnson, S. T. (Ed.). (1998). Editor's comments: The importance of culture for improving assessment and pedagogy. *Journal of Negro Education, 67*(3), 181–183.

Kitano, M. K. (1997). What a course will look like after multicultural change. In A. Morey & M. K. Kitano (Eds.), *Multicultural course transformation in higher education: A broader truth* (pp. 18–34). Needham Heights, MA: Allyn & Bacon.

Lee, C. D. (1998). Culturally responsive pedagogy and performance-based assessment. *Journal of Negro Education, 7*(3), 268–279.

Madaus, G. F. (1988). The influence of testing on the curriculum. In L. N. Tanner (Ed.), *Critical issues in curriculum: Eighty-seventh yearbook of the National Society for the Study of Education* (pp. 83–121). Chicago: University of Chicago Press.

Meisels, S. J., Dorfman, A., & Steele, D. (1995). Equity and excellence in group-administered and performance-based assessments. In M. T. Nettles & A. L. Nettles (Eds.), *Equity and excellence in educational testing and assessment* (pp. 243–261). Boston: Kluwer Academic Publishers.

Messick, S. (1994). The interplay of evidence and consequences in the validation of performance assessments. *Educational Researcher, 23*(2), 13–23.

Perrow, C. (1967). A framework for the comparative analysis of organizations. *American Sociological Review, 32*(2), 194–208.

Reckase, M. D. (1995). Portfolio assessment: Theoretical estimate of score reliability. *Educational Measurement: Issues and Practice, 14*(1), 12–14.

Rovai, A. P. (2000). Online and traditional assessments: What is the difference? *Internet and Higher Education, 3*(3), 141–151.

Salomon, G., & Perkins, D. (1998). Individual and social aspects of learning. In P. Pearson & A. Iran-Nejad (Eds.), *Review of research in education*: Vol. 23 (pp. 1–24). Washington, DC: American Educational Research Association.

Savery, J. R., & Duffy, T. M. (1995). Problem based learning: An instructional model and its constructivist framework. *Educational Technology, 35*(5), 31–38.

Shepard, L. (2000). The role of assessment in a learning culture. *Educational Researcher, 29*(7), 4–14.

Stiggins, R. J. (1987). Design and development of performance assessments. *Educational Measurement: Issues and Practice, 6*(3), 33–42.

Stiggins, R. J. (2002). Assessment crisis: The absence of assessment for learning. *Phi Delta Kappan, 83*(10), 758–765.

Wiggins, G. (1992). Creating tests worth taking. *Educational Leadership, 49*(8), 26–33.

APPENDIX: A SAMPLE EDUCATIONAL LEADERSHIP ASSESSMENT TASK

Introduction

The situation that will be evaluated in this assignment is depicted in a separately distributed scenario that you must carefully read and analyze. This scenario involves a demonstration by high school students at city hall during a meeting of the city council. About two dozen students from the same public high school protested a recent decision by the city council banning Christmas decorations depicting the birth of Christ from public school property. The mayor directed the police to clear the building of all the students he felt were disrupting the council meeting. Turmoil broke out in the city council chambers; signs were thrown, there was shouting, and several of the students were dragged from the building by police. A few students sustained minor injuries that required medical attention.

This assignment assesses the following course objectives:

1. Evaluate schools regarding educational leadership, communications and conflict management, and human learning and motivational development.
2. Engage in scholarly dialogue about various theories, concepts, principles, and practices of educational leadership, communications and conflict management, and human learning and motivational development.

Task

Analyze the scenario provided separately and reach consensus as a group on each of the following questions:

1. What, if anything, should or could the principal have done to prevent the student demonstration from taking place? Why?
2. What do you discern is the principal's leadership style based on the background provided in the scenario? Why?
3. What are the worldview implications of the major stakeholders, and how do they influence the resolution of the situation?
4. What theory and/or research-based practices in human development and/or motivation could be used to remedy the problem?
5. What conflict resolution techniques do you feel the principal should take to resolve the situation? Why?
6. What changes, if any, would you recommend regarding the principal's leadership style? Why?
7. How should the principal respond to the parents?

The group is to ensure that every member has learned something and that all group members participate equitably in this assignment.

Resources

Scenario (omitted in this example).
Course textbooks.

Directions

You will participate in this group assignment by assuming one of the following roles:

1. *High school principal*—You are a devout Christian. The students involved in the city hall demonstration are all enrolled at your school. You receive numerous phone calls from angry parents complaining about the confrontation. The public, including parents, seem to be attributing the incident to the school's unit on bringing about social change. Evidently, the news was out about a unit being taught at the school that includes the study of both violent and nonviolent means of bringing about social change. Additionally, a few of the parents were suggesting that some teachers may be inciting the students to violent confrontation. Your interest is to develop a strategy that copes with the problem at hand.
2. *High school social studies teacher*—The students involved in the city hall demonstration are all enrolled in your social studies class. The confrontation at city hall followed a unit you taught on how to deal with social issues and strategies for bringing about social change. You discussed several strategies with students, including tactics of confrontation and disruption. Students were told that in some situations, when everything else had failed, radical methods might represent the only viable recourse, and that each individual must make that determination and live with the consequences.
3. *High school PTA president*—You are an atheist and strongly support the decision by the city council banning religious Christmas decorations from public school property. You have been deluged with calls all day from parents who want a special meeting to air their views about the school's unit on social change and to determine whether some teachers are encouraging students to become engaged in violent confrontations.

The instructor will randomly assign roles to each member of the group. Carefully examine the scenario. Initially, work independently to answer each of the seven questions listed in the task section above, based on your assumed role. Next, participate in group meeting(s) led by the school principal in order to reach consensus on answers to the seven questions. Provide one set of responses to each of the seven questions in the form of an essay. Each group will submit one essay. This essay is to adhere to the APA style of writing and formatting. Although there is no established page limit, you need to be concise and adhere to APA writing style where economy of expression and parsimony are valued.

Each student will also complete a brief evaluation on the effectiveness of the group and its members and submit it directly to the instructor. Your evaluation will respond to the following four questions:

1. What were your contributions to the group effort?
2. What were the contributions of the other two members?
3. What action could each member have taken to make the group's work even better?
4. What suggestions can you offer to improve this assignment and future group work?

Check the evaluation checklist below to determine how your work will be evaluated. All students in the group will earn the same grade on this assignment.

Evaluation Checklist

Key Elements	Possible Points
Theory & Practice of Educational Leadership: The essay identifies, discusses, and evaluates the practices of leadership as portrayed in the scenario.	15
Effective Communication and Conflict Resolution: The essay addresses effective communication and draws on specific conflict-resolution principles in a just and responsible fashion that avoids or minimizes harm while respecting the rights of all individuals.	15
Human Learning and Motivational Development: The essay incorporates appropriate elements of human learning and motivational development.	15
Worldview: The essay draws on the relevant worldviews of the various stakeholders in the situation to help inform a conflict-resolution strategy. Students will reflect on the deep-level patterning of worldview that shapes the way people from other cultures interpret experiences.	15
Group Work: Each member of the group is actively and equitably involved in this assignment.	15
Integration & Style: The essay provides a coherent, concise, and logical position that integrates appropriate concepts derived from the professional literature. All questions raised in the task section above are answered clearly by synthesizing multiple sources from the professional literature. The essay cites specific scholarly references and demonstrates a theoretical and practical grasp of the material. It is clear and precise, and demonstrates	25

effective written communication through proper use of grammar, punctuation, syntax, organization, transitions, clarity, and precision of expression.

Total   *100*

Conclusion

After you turn in this assignment, reflect upon the following questions and enter your responses in your course journal:

1. What did you learn during this assignment that you would not have learned by completing this assignment by yourself?
2. How can this assignment help you in your educational profession?

TEN

Organizational Strategies for Success

M. Gail Sanders Derrick & Hope M. Jordan

PURPOSE

Previous chapters described academic strategies for success in the classroom learning environment. The purpose of this chapter is to respond to the non-academic challenges to traditional higher education achievement of African American students. These challenges largely pertain to institutional environmental issues that hinder easy integration of minority students into the school culture. They can also include school policies and procedures that limit the access of Black students to the institution itself, as well as challenges to Black student persistence, such as an unsupportive school culture characterized by cultural divergence, race-based rejection, racial stereotyping, and low minority status.

BACKGROUND

How institutions respond and strategically transform themselves to create a school culture that supports minority student achievement are important components of institutional effectiveness. Consequently, it becomes important for institutions to examine their practices, programs, culture, and climate in ways that support and facilitate an inclusive learning environment.

Much of the research literature focuses on cognitive and academic preparation of minority students in isolation of the cultural context that defines the individual. Cultural norms and expectations are powerful belief mechanisms that may be more influential in life trajectories than pure cognitive ability. It is only through understanding and addressing the influences of culture within the context of learning that institutions can expect to influence the persistence of African American students and, ultimately, improve their graduation rates. We must remember that African Americans' historical access to any formal education has been legally limited. The U.S. Constitution makes no mention of the existence of millions of Blacks or women and, as a result, their histories have been, except for chattel slavery, somewhat conjoined, especially in regard to formal education. In fact, it was illegal in most Southern slave states to formally educate slaves.

The first institutions that admitted free Black people were radical reformatory institutions in the Midwest like Oberlin (in 1833), Knox (in 1845), Grinnell (in 1846), Berea (in 1855) and Wheaton (in 1860), and in New England at abolitionist institutions such as Amherst, Bates, and Middlebury colleges in the antebellum period. Historically Black institutions were largely founded after the Civil War, with the notable exceptions of Lincoln University (founded in 1854), Cheyney State (a teachers college, founded in 1837), and Wilberforce (founded in 1855). These legalized segregation patterns continued long after *Brown v. Board of Education* (1954) and into the federally mandated cross-district busing era (1970s).

At present, educational resegregation is occurring among the lowest-income groups in the United States. We have moved from legal inclusion to both more open access and de facto resegregation across the United States (Gallien & Peterson, 2004). The implications associated with persistence and completion rates also have the potential to improve the quality of life, as discussed in Chapter 1, through long-term social, economic, and political consequences and, thus, have a sustained effect on subsequent generations.

Hiemstra (1991) writes that "a learning environment is all of the physical surroundings, psychological or emotional conditions, and social or cultural influences affecting the growth and development of an adult engaged in an educational enterprise" (p. 8). Thus, a diverse culture, a distinct background, and unique life experiences and circumstances may be both an advantage and an impediment for African American achievement. Institutions and policy makers must address barriers to African American students in the context of culture and heritage, both as individuals and as a collective social group, with specific strategies and processes. By doing so, systems will deliberately and purposefully address the barriers to the success of African American students as they respond to the goal of moving more African Americans into and through higher education. This chapter addresses two components of this goal: (a) increasing Black access to higher education, and (b) maintaining high persistence and graduation rates.

STRATEGIES FOR SUCCESS

Increasing Access

Institutions have seen a decline in the numbers of African Americans on college campuses, despite efforts to attract, admit, and enroll qualified Black students. For example, the University of California Los Angeles reports that it expects only 2% of its 2006–2007 academic year freshman class to be Black (Trounson, 2006), prompting the university to declare the situation a crisis. The declining presence of Blacks on the campus discourages other Blacks from attending, thus making the situation more severe. In California, the problem is "rooted partly in the restrictions placed on the state's public colleges and institutions by the 1996 Proposition 209 that banned consideration of race and gender in admissions and hiring. Other factors include the socioeconomic inequities that undermine elementary and secondary education" (Trounson, 2006, p. A8). Another possible root cause at some schools is an overreliance on numbers, such as Scholastic Aptitude Test (SAT) results or grade point average (GPA), in determining admittance. Trounson (2006) reports that a holistic approach to admissions is needed, where students are evaluated based on the "context of their personal challenges" (p. A8). Finally, high school drop-out rates for Black males are inordinately higher than those of any racial group in the United States. As a result, most Black men do not even apply to higher educational institutions.

Interestingly, research (e.g., Dancer & Gilbert, 2001) provides evidence that historically underrepresented and economically disadvantaged students who earn low scores on SAT tests, and who might not otherwise be admitted, perform at levels comparable to their peers who, on average, score higher on SAT tests when they are supported with careful academic advising and other specialized programs. Research evidence such as this suggests that schools should not rely exclusively on "market forces" to increase college participation, ignoring issues of race, ethnicity, poverty, and the opportunity gap, nor should they rely solely on standardized testing. Instead, schools should offer the broadest possible access in order to move a greater number of historically disadvantaged individuals who have the potential to succeed through higher education.

College entry is also adversely influenced by factors such as lack of meaningful college preparation, tougher high school graduation requirements, the need to pass standardized tests, curricular relevance, school culture that does not support inclusiveness, geographical location, and lack of money or financial support (Harris, 1997). Although these challenges are faced by all potential students, they are particularly relevant to minority students. Moreover, the poor, regardless of ethnicity or race, are the least likely to attend college (e.g., Howell, Williams, & Lindsay, 2003).

One approach used by schools to create greater African American access is the pipeline model proposed by Ibarra (2001). This model focuses on removing barriers and laying new pipelines of access to higher education. Ibarra identifies the following purposes of this model:

- to increase the number of minority students enrolled in higher education

- to offer remedial courses and tutorial support for underprepared minority students
- to assist in meeting the financial, academic, and sociocultural needs of minority students
- to offer academic advice and counseling on issues related to culture (pp. 236–237)

Although new pipelines can be created, significantly greater minority access to higher educations is dependent on strengthening K–12 preparation through challenging curricula and quality instruction. Actions must include strategies to prepare African American students for higher education and to prepare institutions for African American students. However, Shelby Steele (2006), a conservative scholar who opposes affirmative action programs, emphasizes the importance of dealing with people as individuals, and not to count being Black, by itself, as a handicap. He asserts that lower standards signify to Blacks that they do not have what it takes to succeed on their own. He asserts that preferential treatment harms the self-esteem and self-image of Blacks and results in poor grades and student attrition. The stereotype of Black academic failure is therefore reinforced. S. Steele (1991) observes:

> The effect of preferential treatment—the lowering of normal standards to increase black representation—puts blacks at war with an expanding realm of debilitating doubt, so that the doubt itself becomes an unrecognized preoccupation that undermines their ability to perform, especially in integrated situations. (pp. 117–118)

Cole and Barber (2003) report that the "stereotype threat" (previously coined by C. M. Steele [1997]) can manifest itself in high-achieving minorities by racial preferences. They conclude that preferences ensure that minority students as a group are less prepared than their peers and that even minority students who do not need preferences respond to such an environment by worrying about confirming the negative stereotype.

The challenge to colleges and universities that value culturally responsive environments is to create a broader competition for college access that values diversity in learners and puts more emphasis, not less, on the principle of merit. Providing academic support programs for students who did not receive the best K–12 education is one possible strategy that recognizes weaknesses in college preparation but does not lower quality. College programs that provide tutoring and counseling to local high school students who might not otherwise get the support they need is another example.

Many minority students wish to attend college but lack confidence that they will be able to succeed once they arrive. For example, Johnson, Arumi, and Ott (2006) report that the percentages of surveyed Black and White high school students who indicate they will definitely attend college are high (72% and 83% respectively). However, they also note that only 49% of Black students feel they will have the skills needed to succeed in college by the time they graduate from high school, as compared to 68% of White students.

A study of public attitudes on higher education found that 76% of African Americans believe that many qualified people are shut out of higher education, as compared to 51% of the White respondents, and believe that the "essential path to workplace success is closed for a large number of Americans, especially those from low-income and minority families" (Immerwahr, 2004, p. 10). These beliefs are powerful influences on behaviors. This lack of confidence further supports the need for colleges and universities to engage in partnerships with K–12 schools and to implement both academic services and mentoring and support programs that build efficacy in minority students.

Black males in particular attend college in low numbers. At some postsecondary schools, for every two African American females enrolled, there is only one African American male (Cuyjet, 2006). The shift in earning and political power in favor of Black women can adversely affect Black male self-esteem, role perception, and family stability. A strategy is needed to increase African American access to higher education and to rectify the gender imbalance in college attendance.

Michael Cuyjet, acting associate provost for student life and associate professor of education at the University of Louisville, during an interview in *Inside Higher Education* states:

> The two most significant factors hindering enrollment in the first place (as different from the problem of attrition of those who do enroll) could be characterized as under-preparedness and cultural disincentives. Many African American males are provided with less-than-adequate academic preparation due to poor school practices and discriminatory practices such as being tracked into behavior disorder classes in inordinately high proportion to their numbers in the school population. Compounding this broad lack of attention to their academic success, many African American young men fail to consider academic achievement a worthwhile goal and, in fact, often consider college education (and even high school graduation) as not worth the effort or not "cool" among their peers. (Jaschik, 2006, p. 1)

It is encouraging to note that, with the assistance of outside grants and state and federal monies, many higher educational institutions are engineering early intervention programs. Early outreach programs, such as the African American Men of Arizona State University (AAMASU; Jones & Hotep, 2006), are needed to affect the recruitment, persistence, and graduation rates of African American male college students. AAMASU begins in high school and includes collaborations with parents to prepare male students for the realities of college, including addressing the role of culture in the college setting. It also works "to support the process of university entrance, persistence, and graduation" (Jones & Hotep, 2006, p. 304). Additionally, the program includes a college student organization component that provides "holistic programming at the university level to enhance the critical analysis, independent study, and programming skills of ASU African American male participants" (pp. 307–308).

Two additional programs that gained national attention originated at two prestigious Southern institutions, Davidson College and the University of Virginia. Davidson College, founded in 1837, is a top-ranked liberal arts college that developed and implemented the highly successful three-week July Experience program on the school's main campus in North Carolina. It is designed for high-rising high school juniors and seniors and offers educational, social, and creative experiences facilitated by Davidson College professors as a "taste" of an excellent liberal arts postsecondary education. The program includes a scholarship program for minority sutdents with financial need.

At the University of Virginia (UVA), founded in 1801, the Office of African-American Affairs is celebrating over 30 years of existence. This program brings all African American students to campus two weeks before the fall term commences in order to acclimate them to a majority campus with a racially checkered past. UVA leads most research institutions in the United States on the retention and graduation rates of its Black students. As mentioned previously in Chapter 4, this office monitors and supports Black students from matriculation to graduation.

In sum, it is fairly clear that once an institution makes a commitment to support students of color, even though the institution may have once been a hostile environment for Blacks, its rates of satisfaction and graduation rise. The issue of Black access to higher education begins long before a student actually applies for and enters college. The access gap in higher education has its foothold in the standards, expectations, and preparation in the K–12 educational systems. Strategies to consider for expanding African American access to higher education include:

- adopting a holistic approach to admittance that:
  - compensates for life situations that limit or prohibit access
  - reduce the unique obstacles that may face first-generation college students
- making higher education more affordable and accessible for all Americans, reforming the student aid system, increasing college assistance for low-income students, and increasing funding for historically Black colleges and universities (HBCUs).
- designing scholarship programs to recruit additional Black students if African Americans are underrepresented on campus, in particular,

enhancing the recruitment of African American males to counter their low numbers in college

- allowing four-year colleges and universities to offer specific bachelor's degree programs at two-year colleges
- creating remote campuses and learning centers in areas of significant low-income populations
- seeking federal and state aid to offer a college education to prison inmates
- promoting programs delivered by technology at a distance
- developing outreach programs that send a clear message to minority high school students—college is within their reach and financial aid options are available
- engaging in K–16 partnerships that:
  - create and facilitate a going-to-college culture
  - allow colleges of education to partner with underperforming schools to improve student achievement
  - strengthen the preparation of students for a successful college education
  - provide knowledge about and assistance with the college application process

Maintaining High Persistence and Graduation Rates

Ibarra (2001) suggests that once minority students gain access to higher education, institutions must not only provide academic and financial support, but also work toward social and cultural integration of the student into the university. In other words, policy makers and institutions must put more effort into strategies that address how to keep African American students in the education pipeline once they are admitted.

Guiffrida (2006) notes that the need for minority students to maintain cultural bonds and common belief structures to succeed at college is supported through research (e.g., Guiffrida, 2003, 2004; Padilla, Trevino, Gonzalez, & Trevino, 1997). Guiffrida (2006) writes "students perceived their families and members of their home communities as providing essential cultural connections and nourishment that helped them deal with racism, cultural isolation, and other adversities at college" (p. 458). Although African American students may be physically integrated into the school, psychological integration is more difficult, particularly for those attending predominantly White institutions (PWIs). Kuh and Love (2000) make a distinction between integration (students being socialized into the larger dominant culture and abandoning their former culture) and connection (students' subjective sense of relatedness to the dominant culture without losing their own heritage). The assumption is that institutions should seek both strategic and informal ways to capitalize on opportunities for building a sense of community and to recognize that students of diverse cultures need to maintain their cultural identity while navigating the larger institutional environment.

The alignment of shared values and beliefs between the individual and institutional culture and practice is evident in the success and persistence of African American students attending HBCUs. African American students are more successful, experience greater satisfaction, and are more likely to persist to completion in environments that are nurturing in ways that provide social support, reduce racial isolation, and are inclusive and affirming (Laird, Bridges, Holmes, Morelon, & Williams, 2004). This is congruent with the mission and philosophy of HBCUs. HBCUs provide the institutional and personal supports needed both academically and socially and, thus, improve student involvement and engagement. Since engagement has been shown to be predictive of persistence and development for all students in any setting, it becomes critical for institutions to examine the ways and the perceptions of how and why students are or are not engaged on their respective campuses.

Tinto's (1993) student integration model is one of the most widely cited theories of student departure and has been used to explain student attrition from higher education. He argues that a student needs to break away from past traditions and associations in order to achieve integration into the institution's academic and social setting. Guiffrida (2006) asserts that a cultural advancement of Tinto's (1993) theory is clearly needed "in moving Tinto's theory away from an integrationist perspective that emphasizes student adaptation to the majority culture to one that values diversity and encourages colleges and universities to affirm and honor diverse student cultures" (p. 458).

Critics of Tinto's (1993) model have also argued that the failure to recognize cultural variables limits the model's applicability to minority students (Guiffrida, 2006; Kuh & Love, 2000). Tierney (1992) asserts that this cultural separation of tradition and supportive connections may have the opposite effect on minority success and persistence. Research has affirmed that minority students need to:

- retain and nurture connections to their cultural heritage (e.g., Guiffrida, 2003),
- maintain the supportive relationships of family and home community (e.g., Guiffrida, 2004; Rosas & Hamrick, 2002),
- seek opportunities to connect with others with shared cultural heritages (e.g., Guiffrida, 2003, 2004)

Research suggests that maintaining one's cultural heritage becomes an important indicator of college success for African American students at either HBCUs or PWIs. The idea of assimilation into the larger culture while maintaining one's personal foundation requires institutions to acknowledge diversity on the college campus not through admittance but through genuine opportunities for students' leadership and presence. Students who perceive their institutions as inclusive and affirming with high expectations for success gain more from their college experience (Kuh, 2001). High levels of student engagement have been linked to beneficial outcomes for student success, particularly for African American students.

Economics also has an influence on persistence. Race and ethnicity are closely associated with family income, and data indicate a significant gap in persistence between affluent students and low-income and minority students. Tuition at colleges and universities has risen faster than federal and state need-based grants, the primary source of financial support for equalizing financial access across income groups (Heller & Becker, 2003). The data show that the personal issues students face—finances, family background, family obligations, and educational preparation before college—are barriers to college persistence.

In summary, organizational strategies to promote high student persistence and graduation rates include:

- commitment to the goal of increasing African American student success
- development and implementation of an accountability system that assigns responsibility for learning
- ensuring that closing the racial and ethnic achievement gap is a strategic priority of school planning
- providing Black students with opportunities for leadership
- implementation of programs for faculty understanding of the role of culture in learning
- ensuring that school culture reflects a multicultural rather than dominant culture orientation through actions such as:
  - hiring, mentoring, and developing a culturally diverse faculty
  - evaluating the campus climate and programs with the goal of strengthening the overall climate so that African Americans feel that they are listened to, valued, respected, and treated fairly
- strengthening the academic and social integration of Black students in the school through programs such as:
  - the freshman experience
  - initial on-campus residences for distance education programs
  - out-of-class school involvement and leadership participation
- strengthening drop-out prevention programs by actions such as:
  - personalizing the college experience by creating meaningful personal bonds between students and other members of the school community
  - providing professional career counseling

- giving students status and recognition
- increasing self-esteem and school success
- improving self-concepts and academic skills
- improving environmental conditions that in turn improve the quality of cross-racial interactions
- providing counseling services to assist Black students in developing coping mechanisms and resilience in a potentially unfavorable campus environment
- the use of organizational learning to institutionalize a philosophy of intentional cultural pluralism campus-wide that impacts every office
- assistance in meeting the financial, academic, and sociocultural needs of minority students
- support for a continuing research agenda regarding the achievement of Black students in order to:
  - identify best practices at predominantly White and historically Black colleges and universities
  - determine how online technologies are impacting learning processes and how they might improve learning outcomes and close the achievement gap
- building and nurturing a strong sense of school community

CONCLUSION

Higher education institutions must develop policies and strategies for minority success and address the issues of nonacademic barriers, including cultural barriers to learning and persistence, as a component of strategic planning. PWIs and HBCUs are faced with similar issues, although both can gain from the experiences, strategies, and programs that are unique to each. Silva, Cahalan, and Lacireno-Paquet (1998) assert that research in factors in participation "should be seen not as trying to fully explain why people do or do not decide to participate . . . but rather as attempting to increase knowledge about one of the many influences on such decisions" (p. 74). Understanding the complex set of variables related to closing the achievement gap for African American students requires recognition by institutions and program planners in higher education.

The federal government has addressed the role of race, gender, and socioeconomic status with student achievement and has tied federal funding to consistent student gains and academic outcomes for all students in the K–12 setting under the No Child Left Behind Act. The African American achievement gap continues to remain largely unchanged, despite millions of dollars put into state and federal programs, training, and professional development. The achievement gap begins early in education and is not abated by the time students are ready to enter college. Simply getting African American students into the higher education door is not enough; we must find ways to assist all students in their pursuit of higher education.

DISCUSSION TOPICS

1. What is your impression of race and racism in the United States today?
2. What is your impression of race and racism on your campus? How is it similar to racism in society? How is it different?

REFERENCES

Cole, S., & Barber, E. (2003). *Increasing faculty diversity: The occupational choices of high achieving minority students.* Cambridge, MA: Harvard University Press.

Cuyjet, M. J. (Ed.). (2006). *African American men in college.* San Francisco: Jossey-Bass.

Dancer, L. S., & Gilbert, L. A. (2001). *The Longhorn Scholars Program: A snapshot from 1999–2001.* Austin, TX: The University of Texas at Austin, Connexus: Connections in Undergraduate Studies.

Gallien, L. B., Jr., & Peterson, M. P. (2004). *Instructing and mentoring the African American college student: Strategies for success in higher education.* Boston: Allyn & Bacon.

Guiffrida, D. A. (2003). African American student organizations as agents of social integration. *Journal of College Student Development, 44*(3), 304–319.

Guiffrida, D. A. (2004). Friends from home: Asset and liability to African American students attending a predominantly white institution. *NASPA Journal, 24*(3), 693–708.

Guiffrida, D. A. (2006). Toward a cultural advancement of Tinto's theory. *Review of Higher Education, 29*(4), 451–472.

Harris, Z. M. (1997). *Access to higher education. Reconceptualizing access in postsecondary education and its ramifications for data systems report of the Policy Panel on Access.* Washington, DC: National Postsecondary Education Cooperative and American Council on Education.

Heller, D., & Becker, W. E. (2003). *Review of NCES research on financial aid and college participation and omitted variables and sample selection issues in the NCES research on financial aid and college participation.* Washington, DC: Advisory Committee on Student Financial Assistance.

Hiemstra, R. (1991). Aspects of effective learning environments. In R. Heimstra (Ed.), *New directions for student services: Number 50. Creating environments for effective adult learning* (pp. 5–12). San Francisco: Jossey-Bass.

Howell, S., Williams, P., & Lindsay, N. (2003). Thirty-two trends affecting distance education: An informed foundation for strategic planning. *Online Journal of*

Distance Learning Administration, 6(3). Retrieved November 29, 2006, from http://www.westga.edu/~distance/ojdla/fall63/howell63.html

Ibarra, R. A. (2001). *Beyond affirmative action: Reframing the context of higher education.* Madison, WI: University of Wisconsin Press.

Immerwahr, J. (2004). *Public attitudes on higher education, a trend analysis, 1993 to 2003.* Washington, DC: The National Center for Public Policy and Higher Education, and Public Agenda. Retrieved November 29, 2006, from http://www.highereducation.org/reports/pubatt/

Jaschik, S. (2006, April 21). *African-American men in college. Inside higher education.* Retrieved November 29, 2006, from http://insidehighered.com/news/2006/04/21/cuyjet

Johnson, J., Arumi, A. M., & Ott, A. (2006). *Issue No. 2: How black and Hispanic families rate their schools.* New York: Public Agenda, Education Insights.

Jones, A, & Hotep, L. O . (2006). African American Men of Arizona State University (AAMASU). In M. J. Cuyjet (Ed.), *African American men in college* (pp. 300–312). San Francisco: Jossey-Bass.

Kuh, G. D. (2001). Assessing what really matters to student learning: Inside the National Survey of Student Engagement. *Change, 33*(3), 10–17; 66.

Kuh, G. D., & Love, P. G. (2000). A cultural perspective on student departure. In J. M. Braxton (Ed.), *Reworking the student departure puzzle* (pp. 196–213). Nashville, TN: Vanderbilt University Press.

Laird, T. F., Bridges, B. K., Holmes, M.S., Morelon, C. L., & Williams, J. M. (2004, November). *African American and Hispanic student engagement at minority serving and predominantly white institutions.* Paper presented at the Annual Meeting of the Association for the Study of Higher Education, Kansas City, MO.

Padilla, R. V., Trevino, J., Gonzalez, K., & Trevino, J. (1997). Developing local models of minority student success. *Journal of College Student Development, 38*(2), 125–138.

Rosas, M., & Hamrick, F. A. (2002). Postsecondary enrollment and academic decision making: Family influences on women college students of Mexican descent. *Equity and Excellence in Education, 35*(1), 59–69.

Silva, T., Cahalan, M., & Lacireno-Paquet, N. (1998). *Adult education participation decisions and barriers: Review of conceptual frameworks and empirical studies.* Washington, DC: U.S. Department of Education, National Center for Education Statistics.

Steele, C. M. (1997). A threat in the air: How stereotypes shape intellectual identity and performance. *American Psychologist, 52*, 613–629.

Steele, S. (1991). *The content of our character: A new vision of race in America.* New York: HarperCollins.

Steele, S. (2006). *White guilt: How blacks and whites together destroyed the promise of the Civil Rights Era.* New York: HarperCollins.

Tierney, W. G. (1992). An anthropological analysis of student participation in college. *Journal of Higher Education, 63*(6), 603–618.

Tinto, V. (1993). *Leaving college: Rethinking the causes and cures of student attrition.* Chicago: University of Chicago Press.

Trounson, R. (2006, June 11). *Jacki Robinson's alma mater draws few black students.* Minneapolis, MN: Star Tribune, A8.

ELEVEN

Summary and Conclusions

Alfred P. Rovai & Louis B. Gallien Jr.

The African American achievement gap (i.e., the difference in academic performance based on race and ethnicity) has not closed, although progress is being made. The research literature provides substantial evidence of differences between African Americans and Whites along a number of dimensions, ranging from socioeconomic status to academic attainment. This book takes a fresh look at research on closing the achievement gap in both traditional and distributed higher education learning environments, and provides suggestions for school administrators and faculty members regarding promising strategies that can help achieve this goal.

THE AFRICAN AMERICAN ACHIEVEMENT GAP

Higher education unlocks many doors to economic, professional, and social opportunities. Over their lifetimes, college graduates are expected to earn nearly $1 million more than high school graduates (Bowen, Kurzweil, & Tobin, 2005). This million dollar gap affects more Blacks than Whites because of the disproportionate college enrollments based on race and ethnicity. From 2000 to 2002, 45.5% of White high school graduates age 18 to 24 enrolled in college, compared with only 39.9% of African American graduates (Wills, 2005). Black students also remain less likely than White students to finish college.

A report from the National Center for Education Statistics (NCES; Hoffman, Llagas, & Snyder, 2003) shows that Black females made up 63% of the Black enrollment in colleges and universities in 2000, representing a substantial Black gender gap in college enrollment. Moreover, in 2005, Black males at NCAA Division I institutions had a graduation rate of 36%, compared to 46% and 60% for Hispanic and White males, respectively (Cuyjet, 2006).

A variety of explanations have been offered to account for this achievement gap. Spenner, Buchmann, and Landerman (2005) report that significant differences in academic achievement between African American students and Whites emerge as early as the first semester of their first year in college. Most arguments that attempt to explain this gap focus on differences in various forms of human capital and status attainment between Blacks and Whites. Status attainment and human capital perspectives are related to theories of income difference, and posit that low socioeconomic status and low levels of human capital (e.g., lower education and work experience) limit wealth accumulation (e.g., Becker, 1994, 2005). This perspective suggests that students' educational outcomes are a function of their family background, cognitive abilities, quality of prior schooling, and learning-style preferences. However, prior research suggests that status attainment and human capital variables do not fully explain the gap. Depending on the research conducted, at most, these variables are able to explain one-half of the gap in grades and test scores (e.g., Bowen & Bok, 1998).

Deficits in cultural capital also influence students' educational outcomes. Spenner, Buchmann, and Landerman (2005) suggest that factors related to cultural capital have an independent and mediating effect on initial college grades, and may explain part of the achievement gap. However, Ogbu (1991) contends that being a member of a racial minority group does not predict school performance. Rather, it is the terms of the minority group's incorporation into the mainstream society and the group's social position in that society that explain school performance.

Finally, deficits in social capital can also help explain the achievement gap. According to Baron, Field, and Schuller (2001), social capital broadly consists of social networks, social norms, and the value of these networks and norms for achieving mutual goals. Proponents of this concept see social capital as fundamental to social relations among people. Since learning is largely a social endeavor, students with well-developed social capital are likely to possess higher educational outcomes. For example, students use social networks, such as family, peers, professionals, and academic ties, as sources of academic support. Bowen and Bok (1998) suggest that Black students are disadvantaged by racially homophilous peer networks, because the Black distribution of ability, as measured by test scores, is lower on average than the White distribution.

AFRICAN AMERICAN AND HIP-HOP CULTURAL INFLUENCES

Many educators (e.g., Ibarra, 2001) assert that culture impacts learning and achievement, and that changes in higher education are needed based on the richness found in all cultures. "Learning new ways to see and value diversity will be more productive for higher education in the long run than any stop-gap measures now in place" (Ibarra, 2001, p. xi).

African American Cultural Orientation

Much of the educational research into the learning-style preferences, orientations, and characteristics of African American learners concludes that students with strong ethnic identities (and lower degrees of majority culture contact) are often successful with learning environments and pedagogical styles that match their preferences. The African American cultural orientation suggests that many Black students will perform best in a learning environment that is:

- *Holistic*: Characterized by harmony, cooperation, affect, socialization, and community, with relational and creative learning relevant to one's own experiences
- *Field-dependent*: Emphasizes learning from a global perspective and the social, interactive aspects of learning
- *High-context*: Relies on nonverbal, indirect, implicit, and informal communication; high personal, relational commitment; social time orientation; importance of comprehensive thinking versus analytical thinking

Hip-Hop Cultural Orientation

Younger Black adults are also influenced by hip-hop. Below is a list of some of the themes that are emerging in response to research into this popular cultural movement:

- Students are extrinsically motivated by professional and economic aspirations.
- Students operate upon constructions of race and ethnicity that differ from those of previous generations.
- Social equality takes on new meanings to younger generations of African Americans who have been influenced by hip-hop.
- Different generational perspectives exist regarding the value of traditional African American culture.

Closing the achievement gap in higher education entails considering the varying influences of both African American and hip-hop cultural influences upon Black college students. Educators on college campuses must seek to understand the influences of African American culture and the meanings that students derive from and ascribe to hip-hop in order to remain culturally responsive. These influences and meanings contain the essential components of change. Failing to understand this, educators have failed to grasp the essential ideas about learning and closing the African American achievement gap.

SCHOOL CULTURAL INFLUENCES

An examination of school cultures and learning outcomes at both predominantly White and historically Black colleges and universities (HBCUs) reveals the following factors:

- Nonacademic factors that influence Black students' poorer academic experience and performance:
  - weaker general institutional support
  - racial climate, e.g., racial stereotyping and racial tensions
- Academic factors that influence Black students' poorer academic experience and performance:
  - differences between Black and White cultures suggest different approaches to pedagogy that typically are not observed on predominantly White campuses
  - many African American learners see little congruence between their educational experiences in predominantly White schools and their cultural upbringing and beliefs about education, which center on cooperation, collaboration, and cultural relevancy
  - not attending to the use of culturally responsive pedagogies can create greater stress in African American students who enter predominantly White schools.
  - higher education should be based on the richness found in all cultures, in contrast to perpetuating the "one-size-fits-all" approach to teaching that is dominant on many predominantly White campuses
- HBCUs provide a relatively stable and culturally supportive academic foundation for Black students in order to promote student academic success
- Less supportive predominantly White institutions (PWIs) should examine school culture on HBCU campuses and adopt best practices, as appropriate, to strengthen and enrich teaching and school climate on their campuses so that all students have an equal chance to achieve academic success

DIVERSITY AND LEARNING ON COLLEGE CAMPUSES

Closing the African American achievement gap requires the use of research-based interventions and tested pedagogical strategies that can mitigate the institutional, situational, and dispositional challenges many African Americans encounter on college campuses. Achievement of this goal also requires educational practice that:

- filters curriculum content through students' cultural frames of reference to make the content more personally meaningful and easier to master;
- employs teaching strategies that reflect the culture, learning-style preferences, and needs of all students; and
- facilitates students in making choices and engaging in the learning process as they work from their strengths

When colleges and universities fail to take responsibility for the learning of all students, they are reneging on their commitment to teaching and learning. They must recognize that teaching and learning is as valuable to faculty tenure and promotion as scholarly work, such as conducting and publishing research and obtaining and working on grants. Certainly in an era of accountability, effective teaching is required.

Since institutional policies and practices largely reflect the values of those who work within the school (e.g., Banks, Cookson, Gay, Hawley, Irvine, Nieto, Schofield, & Stephan, 2001), the integration of minorities in higher education is urgently needed to influence school culture and to help prepare all students to face a culturally diverse world. Indeed, the presence of minority administrators and faculty can be the single most instrumental way for PWIs to promote multicultural education and help close the achievement gap (e.g., Trueba, 1998). Additionally, Black students need diverse faculty and administrators as role models and mentors. The presence of minorities interspersed throughout all levels of administration and faculty conveys a message of commitment to the students. Students need to see minorities included in key visible positions across campus and not merely in a small element of the institution designated to promote minority interests.

Black students can also benefit from a mostly constructivist approach to teaching that values interactions and collaborative work. This philosophy of teaching creates a more student-centered learning environment that matches the field-dependent preference of many African Americans, while a teaching style based on lectures creates a teacher-centered learning environment. Teachers should employ a variety of teaching styles, including teacher-centered styles as necessary, in order to respond to the learning-style preferences of all students, while also considering the teaching style best suited for the content to be presented.

CHALLENGES IN THE TRADITIONAL CLASSROOM

One should note that all African American students in higher education are not disposed to approach the learning process in the same manner. Research conducted in areas such as learning-style preferences, cognitive styles, and communication patterns suggest that specific commonalities and patterns emerge that are related to the culture of African American students and that are related to the challenges outlined below, when contrasted with academic culture at a PWI. However, other factors also emerge that can moderate Black student achievement and the challenges described below, such as family history, gender, peer group norms, and social class.

Institutional Challenges

Institutional challenges are erected by the schools themselves and exclude or discourage certain groups of learners from full participation in learning. Institutional challenges that adversely affect African Americans in higher education include an academic culture that provides:

- little congruence with the backgrounds of African Americans,
- a largely "one-size-fits-all" teaching style,
- more emphasis on scholarly activities among faculty members than on teaching excellence and student mentoring,
- poor faculty accountability for learning failures, and
- limited availability of educational support services

Situational Challenges

Situational challenges are those barriers that relate to a person's life context at a particular time and to both the social and the physical environment surrounding the individual. African American situational challenges to higher education achievement include:

- race-based rejection,
- racial stereotyping,
- conflicting job and family responsibilities, and
- financial concerns

Dispositional Challenges

Finally, cultural or dispositional challenges are attitudinal in nature and pertain to the culturally related values, beliefs, meanings, and behavior that inhibit full participation in a higher education learning environment. Dispositional challenges confronting Black students include:

- a preference for holistic learning in a largely compartmentalized and analytical learning environment,

- a preference for field-dependence in a largely field-independent learning environment, and
- a preference for high-context communication in a largely low-context communication environment

DESIGNING AND TEACHING TRADITIONAL COURSES

In reponse to the challenges outlined above, the following strategies for success are recommended to facilitate closing the African American achievement gap in the traditional classroom setting:

- Use a student-centered approach.
- Vary the conditions of learning to address the learning and cognitive preferences of Black students.
- Build on students' prior knowledge and experiences.
- Adoption of the roles of engager, motivator, model, and mentor by the instructor.

To help implement these strategies, instructors must help bridge ethnic, hip-hop, and school cultures by transforming pedagogy to respond to students' diverse backgrounds and cultures. Pedagogical transformation does not simply entail adding multicultural content to existing classes. It requires building the capacity for students to shift their frameworks and reasoning within diverse frames of reference. Ethnically diverse perspectives and learning-style preferences must be included in the construction of courses. Schools must also reward diversity efforts to encourage innovation and participation and to overcome simple pedagogical inertia on the part of the faculty.

CHALLENGES IN THE VIRTUAL CLASSROOM

In addition to the challenges faced by Black students in the traditional classroom, there are challenges Black students face in the virtual classroom:

Institutional Challenges

- *Quality control of distributed teaching and learning.* The limited skills of some online faculty members in designing and conducting courses at a distance adversely affects educational quality, erodes affiliation, and increases alienation among students. Moreover, many online instructors display a low level of cultural competence.
- *Quality control of student support services.* Distance students must be provided with adequate access to services such as student advising and counseling, library services, tutorial services, financial aid services,

information technology, and job placement. Otherwise, they can be made to feel like second-class or inferior students.

Situational Challenges

- *Personal costs.* Distance education students tend to be older, have families, and work full-time. The burden of pursuing a college degree while balancing work and family responsibilities is likely to create additional stressors for distance students.
- *Digital divide.* The term *digital divide* can take on several meanings, but at the most basic level it refers to the division between those who can easily access the Internet and those who cannot. From an educational perspective, the groups most disenfranchised by the digital divide are the same groups historically disenfranchised by curricular and pedagogical practices, evaluation and assessment, and other aspects of education.
- *Computer-mediated communication.* Text-based computer-mediated communication, which is the backbone of much of Internet-based e-learning, provides communication limitations based on the reduction of nonverbal cues, such as facial expressions and gestures, during the text-based communication process. These limitations disproportionately affect African American learners because of their tendency to rely on nonverbal, indirect, implicit, and informal communication.

Dispositional Challenges

- *Computer anxiety.* Attitudes about online learning are adversely influenced by anxiety about using computer technology. Students who own computers generally have less computer anxiety because they are more familiar with the technology. In this regard, Black students tend to be on the wrong side of the digital divide.
- *Cognitive style.* Ibarra (2001) contrasts two higher education typologies: an Anglo culture characterized mostly by low-context, field-independent, and focused-detailed components, and ethnic cultures characterized mostly by high-context, field-dependent, and global-holistic components. E-learning courses tend to favor field-independent learners by relying on instructional strategies that emphasize individualized and analytical learning over cooperative and holistic learning.
- *Feelings of isolation and alienation.* The physical separation of members of a distributed learning community can encroach upon the basic human need for social and intellectual interaction in the virtual classroom, resulting in feelings of isolation and alienation. This can be particularly troublesome for African American and other students from cultural backgrounds that value cooperation, affect, socialization, and community.

DESIGNING AND TEACHING
DISTRIBUTED COURSES

Distributed learning requires deliberate and well-planned strategies to be effective and to help close the African American achievement gap. Such strategies should build on the strategies aimed at the traditional classroom identified above and should include the following additional elements:

- training faculty members in designing and teaching at a distance and in multicultural education prior to assuming teaching duties as part of a comprehensive distributed learning quality-control program
- using a comprehensive planning model to design distributed courses, such as the Institutional Instructional Parameters Model described in Chapter 8
- specifying minimum student hardware and software requirements to pursue an online program, e.g., reliable and consistent access to a 56k dial-up Internet connection
- respecting the diverse talents of students and their ways of learning, for example, by:
  - allowing students to choose project topics
  - incorporating diverse views into courses
  - allowing students to participate in assorted types of assignments (e.g., independent work and collaborative work)
  - giving students a choice in their assignments
- sponsoring a student "boot camp" prior to the start of a distributed learning program to help integrate students into the school by addressing issues such as meeting staff and faculty in order to promote a sense of school community and institutional fit, student counseling, school support service for distance students, use of technology, and course and program expectations, such as the importance of student interaction and time management
- helping students connect their learning experience to their cultural experiences outside the classroom
- promoting student interaction by providing clear guidelines for student participation (e.g., see the sample online course participation rubric in Chapter 9) and by grading online course participation
- providing timely and meaningful feedback
- keeping students interested and motivated

ASSESSMENT FOR LEARNING

According to the principles of total quality management, quality in manufacturing is the result of regular inspections or assessments along the production lines, followed by needed adjustments. Quality is not achieved exclusively by end-of-line inspections; by then, it is too late. Similarly, assessments in education are utilized throughout the learning process, followed by needed adjustments in teaching and learning, in order to achieve quality in education.

Rather than assessment *of* learning, the focus of assessment in the multicultural classroom should be on assessment *for* learning, in which both instructors and students seek to assess where students are in their learning so that teaching and learning activities can be shaped by information gained from assessments. Classroom assessment strategy characterized by the following principles will promote education equity and help close the African American achievement gap in higher education:

- Assessments should be based on clearly articulated educational objectives.
- Student progress should be monitored frequently.
- Students should receive timely feedback.
- Whenever possible, students should help determine how educational objectives will be assessed.
- A variety of assessment tasks should be used to provide instructors with a well-rounded view of what students know and can do.
- Instructors must become knowledgeable both about the subject matter being assessed and about students' cultures and languages in order to use assessments fairly.
- Instructors must pay particular attention to unequal participation of students in group work and employ strategies to address status problems.
- Assessments should:
  - resemble real life as closely as possible (i.e., be authentic);
  - recognize the vital importance of both the cultural characteristics and educational experiences of students;
  - be mostly performance-based, e.g., portfolio assessments;
  - consist of cooperative group work whenever possible, e.g., PBL;
  - focus on student growth, such as action-oriented projects, self-assessments, and reflections on the course; and
  - include a grading rubric so that students know what is expected, so that grading criteria are transparent, and to promote fair grading by the instructor

ORGANIZATIONAL STRATEGIES FOR SUCCESS

Strategies for success at the institutional level can be categorized by type as: (a) increasing Black access to higher education, and (b) maintaining high persistence and graduation rates once they are enrolled. Ibarra (2001) identifies three significant factors hindering African American enrollment in higher education: underpreparedness, cultural disincentives, and financial issues. One approach used to increase African American attainment of a higher education is Ibarra's pipeline model. It is based on the view that barriers to higher education access must be removed and new pipelines of access laid. This model includes the following objectives:

- to increase the number of minority students enrolled in higher education
- to offer remedial courses and tutorial support for underprepared minority students
- to assist in meeting the financial, academic, and sociocultural needs of minority students
- to offer academic advice and counseling on issues related to culture (Ibarra, 2001, pp. 236–237)

Once Black students gain access to higher education, strategies to close the achievement gap require attention to institutional attitudes and behaviors, in addition to the classroom learning environment discussed above. Organizational strategies for success are largely nonacademic, and are meant to improve school culture and the integration of all students into the university. For example, research (e.g., Hale, 2004) shows that students on campuses with more cross-racial interactions can benefit from observing more students interacting across racial and ethnic differences and being on a campus that promotes positive race relations. Moreover, such interactions enhance self-confidence, motivation, intellectual and civic development, educational aspirations, cultural awareness, and commitment to racial equity (e.g., Chang, Astin, & Kim, 2004; Gurin, Dey, Hurtado, & Gurin, 2002).

Research also demonstrates that Tinto's (1994) student attrition model is valuable in explaining why some students drop out of college and others do not. Student experiences subsequent to admission, which Tinto refers to as "integration" variables, are affected by school policies and practices. However, Kuh and Love (2000) suggest that integration involves the socialization of students into the dominant culture and the requirement to abandon their former culture. Therefore, for African American students, it may be more appropriate to ensure that school culture reflects a multicultural rather than dominant culture orientation before attempting to integrate students into the institution.

Guiffrida (2005) reports that African American college students perceive their families and members of their home communities as providing essential cultural connections that help them deal with racism, cultural isolation, and other adversities at college. He suggests that cultural connections play a larger role in minority college student persistence than simply facilitating social integration into the university.

CONCLUSION

Continued efforts to close the academic achievement gap are essential if we are to have a society characterized by social equity. In an educational context, the term *social equity* sounds simple enough: It is the concept that everyone deserves an equitable education, regardless of race, religion, gender, or any other discriminating feature. The challenge for educators is how to close the achievement gap by creating the opportunities for a wider participation of all people in higher education and by fostering a fair and inclusive environment that respects the dignity of each member of the school community.

Research suggests that the underachievement of many African Americans in college results from a combination of factors, including negative stereotypes and low expectations, academic and cultural isolation, lack of support from faculty and peers, and persistent racism and discrimination (Bridglall & Gordon, 2004). Much of the discrimination Blacks encounter is institutionalized in our society. Gould (1999) makes the point:

> When the major institutions of society are constructed within the culture and in the interests of one group instead of another, even when the subordinate group is included within those institutions, its performance will be, on average, less proficient than the dominant group. Organizations may systematically favor the culturally constituted performances of one group over the developmentally equivalent, substantively different, performances of another group. (p. 172)

The existence of institutionalized discrimination does not mean that excellent schools cannot be formed. They can and do make a difference, but to do so, school culture—including coursework—must reflect diverse ethnic cultures and promote the interests of all students, not just the students who are members of the majority culture.

Morey and Kitano (1997) call for the transformation of the content and structure of courses to meet the learning needs, learning-style preferences, and life experiences of a diverse student population. Figure 11.1 presents a framework centered on diversity and inclusion for making course changes to better address a multicultural learning community. Four elements of pedagogy —content, instructional strategies, assessment, and classroom dynamics— are summarized across exclusive and transformed educational strategies.

Excellent schools possess an ethos in which academic success and effort are important. The school must do its part to remove or reduce the impact of challenges faced by minority students by providing a strong social support system that values and promotes academic achievement, and by providing academic and socioemotional scaffolding to assist students' understanding of self, diversity, and their talents.

The development of lifelong learners is a well-recognized goal of higher education. Lifelong learners are autonomous learners who exhibit resource-

Figure 11.1. A Paradigm for Multicultural Course Change:
Examining Course Components and Levels of Change

Component	Exclusive	Transformed
CONTENT	Traditional Eurocentric perspectives; confirms traditional perspectives or supports racial stereotypes	Reconceptualizes content through a shift in paradigm or standard; presents content through a nondominant perspective
INSTRUCTIONAL STRATEGIES	Instructor is expert, source of understanding, dispenser of all knowledge; emphasis is on knowledge reproduction, independent study and competition	Instructor is collaborator, tutor, facilitator, encourager, and community builder; methods center on student experience, engagement, and knowledge construction, such as analyzing concepts against personal experience, issues-oriented approaches, collaborative learning, and building critical thinking and metacognitive skills
ASSESSMENT	Primarily selected response and papers reflecting independent work	Diverse constructed response methods; authentic knowledge application, portfolios, cooperative projects, performances, self-assessments, and reflection; student choice
CLASSROOM DYNAMICS	Teacher-centered, direct instruction, didactic, individual work; focus is exclusively on content; avoidance of social issues in classroom; no attempt to monitor student participation	Learner-centered, Socratic, authentic, individual, and group work; processing of social issues in the classroom; challenging of biased views and sharing of diverse perspectives; equity in participation

Sources: Adapted from Kitano, 1997, p. 24, and Rovai, 2004, p. 81.

fulness and initiative in choosing and persisting in learning activities that steer their lives in personally satisfying directions. Although these learning activities can be institutionally controlled, the critical concern for higher education is to develop learners who are armed with the cognitive strategies necessary to diagnose their educational needs and identify and pursue those learning resources that they believe will maximize personal growth. There is nothing antithetical between being a self-directed learner and intentionally choosing to engage in formal programs of instruction or seeking out the assistance of others more knowledgeable. Thus, higher education should recognize that the interdependent learning activities preferred by many African American students are not at odds with fostering lifelong learning tendencies when such activities are pursued as a result of personal agency and empowerment.

One important obstacle to closing the achievement gap is the present attitude of many school administrators and faculty members at PWIs, who are more likely to make stereotypical attributions by associating deficits with Blacks and superior achievement with Whites. Attributions framed by a deficit frame of reference suggest that the African American achievement gap is either self-inflicted or a natural outcome of socioeconomic and educational backgrounds. According to Erickson (1987):

> As the anthropology of education became a distinct field in the mid-1960's, its members were generally appalled by the ethnocentrism of the cultural deficit explanation. It was not literally racist, in the sense of a genetic explanation. Yet it seemed culturally biased. The poor were still being characterized invidiously as not only deprived but depraved. (p. 335)

Administrators and faculty must learn to regard existing racial and ethnic achievement patterns as unnatural. Those who have a deficit frame of reference turn the focus of the achievement gap away from their own attitudes, beliefs, and practices to those of students. They externalize the problem and fail to see how changes within themselves could help close the gap. The focus of their attitudes, beliefs, and practices must move away from deficit-thinking to equity-thinking. Organizational learning is required to bring about changes in the cognitive frames of individuals so that "the knowledge production itself may become the form of mobilization" that induces individuals to make the cognitive shift (Gaventa & Cornwall, 2001, p. 76).

Not only must the cognitive frameworks of school administrators and faculty change, but leadership and faculty ownership are also important factors in any institutional program to close the achievement gap. Additionally, the school's strategic planning system must be used to orchestrate programmatic change, and senior school leadership must actively monitor progress and be proactive on this issue with all stakeholders—administrators, faculty and staff members, and students. As Mickelson (2003) asserts, "school problems are linked to the failure of white-controlled institutions to incorporate non-dominant cultures into school culture, curricula, pedagogy, or structures" (p. 1067).

Regional accreditation agencies should also move away from the present practice of largely allowing institutions to define quality and how they will reach it and toward holding institutions accountable for learning, even if it means redefining the accreditation process to place learning by all students at the center of the process. Moreover, popular media rankings of schools, such as school rankings by *U.S. News & World Report*, are based on the following factors (Morse & Flanigan, 2005):

- peer assessment
- retention rates
- faculty resources
- student selectivity
- financial resources
- graduation rate performance
- alumni giving rate

Only retention rates (weighted 20% in national universities and liberal arts colleges and 25% in master's and comprehensive colleges) and graduation rate performance (weighted 5%, only in national universities and liberal arts colleges) are output variables. Visibly missing as a criterion is student learning achievement.

Swail, Redd, and Perna (2003) provide useful insights into the college retention issue for minority students. They assert that student retention is the result of an interaction between cognitive, social, and institutional factors that impact students positively or negatively. They conclude that an effective retention program requires a strategic alignment of institutional resources for the purposes of retention success. Moreover, effective retention is conscious of the impact of race, class, and culture in the life of the Black student, and actively seeks positive ways to validate and integrate culture into institutional support. Finally, Swail, Redd, and Perna also conclude that effective retention is assessment driven and evaluates programmatic activities for alignment with assessed student needs.

There is no simple formula that ensures student persistence and achievement. Moreover, African Americans are not homogeneous with regard to their learning characteristics. Black adult persistence and achievement is a complicated response to multiple challenges. It is not credible to attribute Black attrition or achievement to any single student, course, or school characteristic. There are numerous internal and external factors that come into play, as well as interactions between factors. Each student is unique and his or her achievement evolves from a highly individualized and complex interaction of both nonacademic and academic factors. A self-evaluation checklist for faculty members is presented in Figure 11.2 to help inform them of practice in a multicultural environment.

Although continued research into the African American achievement gap is still needed, it is time to move away from defining the problem and to start taking action based on what we already know. Research and existing programs —many of which are cited in this book, such as the Meyerhoff Scholars Program and the Ronald E. McNair Post-Baccalaureate Achievement Program— strongly suggest that progress can be made. Ideas alone will not accomplish the goal of closing the achievement gap. Action is required to respond to all the institutional, situational, and dispositional challenges described above and graphically depicted in Figure 11.3. This approach is consistent with that of Erickson (1987), who suggests that one should consider all the possible variances in order to approach students in a culturally respectful and aware manner.

Action on the part of the student is required in order to help counter the potential stream of negative consequences likely to follow multiple encounters with adversity in the college experience. Students need to develop educational and emotional coping skills in areas such as time management, goal setting, and dealing with racial prejudice and racial stereotyping in order to promote resilience in the face of stress and adversity. In particular, drawing strength and pride from their cultural heritage and from their families and members of their home communities to promote cultural resilience is essential. However, the achievement gap cannot completely close without complementary institutional action. This action should take the form of the organizational and academic strategies outlined below. These strategies have two goals: (a) to eliminate the vestiges of discrimination in higher education, and (b) to help Black students cope and develop resilience where discrimination is still present.

Organizational Strategies

Expand African American Access to Higher Education
- Adopt a holistic approach to admittance that:
    - compensates for life situations that limit or prohibit access, and
    - reduces the unique obstacles that may face first-generation college students
- Make higher education more affordable and accessible for all Americans; reform the student aid system and increase college assistance for low-income students; increase funding for HBCUs
- Design scholarship programs to recruit additional Black students if African Americans are underrepresented on campus; in particular,

Figure 11.2. Self-Evaluation Checklist for Instructors

1. Are you asking questions that allow the personal experiences of students to inform their responses?

2. Have you created a nonthreatening, nonjudgmental environment that is conducive to free and open discussion?

3. Are students doing a dominant portion of the talking during question-and-response sessions?

4. Are you attempting to get all students involved in the conversation? (If the class is very large, are you attempting to get everyone involved over contiguous class meetings?)

5. Are you evaluating student responses and identifying weaknesses in knowledge base or logic? Are you using these evaluations for one-on-one developmental talks?

6. Are students coming to class prepared to engage in discussion? If not, are you attempting to motivate them to do so?

7. Have you determined (preferably on an individual basis) your students' desired outcomes from their educational endeavors?

8. Have you explained the connection of prescribed course performances to these desired outcomes?

9. Have you built into your course design opportunities for self-direction in the design of course performances based upon individual learning goals?

10. Do you present yourself as an educated person in mannerisms, speech, and dress?

11. Have you identified any similarities between your background and your students'?

12. Have you revealed these similarities to them?

13. Do you verbally encourage your students, thereby strengthening their self-efficacy?

14. Do you attempt to guide students to success by sharing personal insights from your own experiences?

15. Do you foster in your students a personal responsibility for the success of fellow African Americans?

enhance the recruitment of African American males to counter their low numbers in college

- Allow four-year colleges and universities to offer specific bachelor's degree programs at two-year colleges
- Create remote campuses and learning centers in areas of significant low-income populations
- Seek federal and state aid to offer a college education to prison inmates
- Promote programs delivered by technology at a distance
- Develop outreach programs that send a clear message to minority high school students—that college is within their reach and financial aid options are available

Figure 11.3. Challenges to Achievement, and Strategies to Close
the African American College Achievement Gap

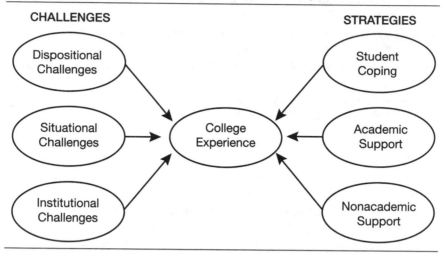

- Engage in K–16 partnerships that:
  - create and facilitate a going-to-college culture
  - allow colleges of education to partner with underperforming schools to improve student achievement
  - strengthen the preparation of students for a successful college education
  - provide knowledge about and assistance with the college application process

Promote High Student Persistence and Graduation Rates
- Commit to the goal of increasing African American student success
- Develop and implement an accountability system that assigns responsibility for learning
- Ensure closing the racial and ethnic achievement gap is a strategic priority of school planning
- Provide Black students with opportunities for leadership
- Implement programs for faculty understanding of the role of culture in learning
- Ensure that school culture reflects a multicultural rather than majority culture orientation by actions such as:
  - hiring, mentoring, and developing a culturally diverse faculty
  - evaluating campus climate and programs with the goal of

strengthening the overall climate so that African Americans feel that they are listened to, valued, respected, and treated fairly
- Strengthen the academic and social integration of Black students in the school through programs such as:
  - the freshman experience
  - initial on-campus residences for distance education programs
  - out-of-class school involvement and leadership participation
- Strengthen drop-out prevention programs by actions such as:
  - personalizing the college experience by creating meaningful personal bonds between students and other members of the school community
  - providing professional career counseling
  - giving students status and recognition
  - increasing self-esteem and school success
  - improving self-concept and academic skills
  - improving environmental conditions that in turn improve the quality of cross-racial interactions
  - providing counseling services to assist Black students in developing coping mechanisms and resilience in a potentially unfavorable campus environment
- Use organizational learning to institutionalize a philosophy of intentional cultural pluralism campus-wide that impacts every office
- Assist in meeting the financial, academic, and sociocultural needs of minority students
- Support a continuing research agenda regarding the achievement of Black students in order to:
  - identify best practices at predominantly White and historically Black colleges and universities
  - determine how online technologies are impacting learning processes and how they might improve learning outcomes and close the achievement gap
- Build and nurture a strong sense of school community

Academic Strategies

- Position teaching as a cornerstone of faculty activity
- Use organizational learning to support professional development toward inclusive educational transformation by focusing on topics such as:
  - the constructivist philosophy of teaching and learning
  - creating a student-centered learning environment

- best practices in adult learning
- effective instruction for culturally diverse students
- assessments for learning
- Organize academic programs and services for Black students around specific variables and challenges identified in this book that research shows to be important, such as:
  - remedial programs to close the preparation gap
  - tutorial and support programs that improve self-confidence and provide a range of assistance for students who desire to improve their academic performance
- Improve course design and teaching quality by using research-based methods matched to the particular course delivery medium (i.e., face-to-face or distributed) and to the cultural backgrounds of all students
  - respect and attend to the diverse talents and abilities/gifts of all students and their preferences for learning by teaching to diversity
  - build on students' prior knowledge and experiences and help them connect their learning experiences to their cultural experiences outside the classroom
  - teach learning strategies and thinking skills
  - create learning communities that facilitate the social construction of knowledge and understanding
  - provide systematic and frequent feedback to students, particularly in virtual classroom settings
- Ensure that curricula include contributions from underrepresented minorities in the United States; students of color benefit both psychologically and academically when their ancestors are mentioned as having played a key role in the formation of their country
- Adopt the roles of engager, motivator, model, and mentor; the most important attribute that Black men, in particular, need from their instructor is caring on a personal basis instead of representing a problem to be solved or a vocation/career to be planned
- Maintain a climate of high expectations for Black students
- Implement assessment for learning strategies that include:
  - performance-based, authentic tasks
  - the cultural characteristics and educational experiences of students
  - effective instructor feedback
  - collaborative student work
  - student self-assessment and reflection
- Build and nurture a strong sense of classroom community

REFERENCES

Banks, J. A., Cookson, P., Gay, G., Hawley, W. D., Irvine, J. J., Nieto, S., Schofield, J. W., & Stephan, W. G. (2001). Diversity within unity: Essential principles for teaching and learning in a multicultural society. *Phi Delta Kappan, 83*(3), 196.

Baron, S., Field, J., & Schuller, T. (Eds.). (2001). *Social capital: Critical perspectives.* New York: Oxford University Press.

Becker, G. S. (1994). *Human capital: A theoretical and empirical analysis, with special reference to education* (3rd ed.). Chicago: University of Chicago Press.

Becker, G. S. (2005). *A treatise on the family* (Enlarged ed.). Cambridge: Harvard University Press.

Bowen, W. G., & Bok, D. (1998). *The shape of the river: Long term consequences of considering race in college and university admissions.* Princeton, NJ: Princeton University Press.

Bowen, W. G., Kurzweil, M. A., & Tobin, E. M. (2005). *Equity and excellence in American higher education.* Charlottesville, VA: University of Virginia Press.

Bridglall, B. L., & Gordon, E. W. (2004, May). Nurturing talent in underrepresented students. *Pedagogical Inquiry and Praxis, 6.*

Chang, M. J., Astin, A. W., & Kim, D. (2004). Cross-racial interaction among undergraduates: Some causes and consequences. *Research in Higher Education, 45*(5), 527–551.

Cuyjet, M. J. (Ed.). (2006). *African American men in college.* New York: Jossey-Bass.

Erickson, F. (1987). Transformation and school success: The politics of culture and educational achievement. *Anthropology and Education Quarterly, 18*(4), 335–356.

Gaventa, J., & Cornwall, A. (2001). Power and knowledge. In P. Reason & H. Bradbury (Eds.), *Handbook of action research: Participative inquiry and reason* (pp. 70–80). Thousand Oaks, CA: Sage.

Gould, M. (1999). Race and theory: Culture, poverty, and adaptation to discrimination in Wilson and Ogbu. *Sociological Theory, 17*(2), 171–200.

Guiffrida, D. A. (2005). To break away or strengthen ties to home: A complex question for African American students attending a predominantly white institution. *Equity and Excellence in Education, 38*(1), 49–60.

Gurin, P., Dey, E. L., Hurtado, S., & Gurin, G. (2002). Diversity and higher education: Theory and impact on educational outcomes. *Harvard Educational Review, 72*(3), 330–366.

Hale, F. W. (Ed.). (2004). *What makes racial diversity work in higher education: Academic leaders present successful policies and strategies.* Sterling, VA: Stylus.

Hoffman, K., Llagas, C., & Snyder, T. D. (2003). *Status and trends in the education of blacks* (NCES 2003-034). Washington, DC: U.S. Department of Education Institute of Education Sciences.

Ibarra, R. A. (2001). *Beyond affirmative action: Reframing the context of higher education.* Madison, WI: University of Wisconsin Press.

Kitano, M. K. (1997). What a course will look like after multicultural change. In A. Morey & M. K. Kitano (Eds.), *Multicultural course transformation in higher education: A broader truth* (pp. 18–34). Needham Heights, MA: Allyn & Bacon.

Kuh, G. D., & Love, P. G. (2000). A cultural perspective on student departure. In J. M. Braxton (Ed.), *Reworking the student departure puzzle* (pp. 196–212). Nashville, TN: Vanderbilt University Press.

Mickelson, R. A. (2003). When are racial disparities in education the result of racial discrimination? A social science perspective. *Teachers College Record, 105*(6), 1052–1086.

Morey, A. I., & Kitano, M. K. (1997). *Multicultural course transformation in higher education: A broader truth*. Needham Heights, MA: Allyn & Bacon.

Morse, R. J., & Flanigan, S. (2005). *Using the rankings*. Washington, DC: U.S. News & World Report. Retrieved November 29, 2006, from http://www.usnews.com/usnews/edu/college/articles/brief/06rank_brief.php

Ogbu, J. U. (1991). Minority coping responses and school experience. *Journal of Psychohistory, 18*(4), 433–456.

Rovai, A. P. (2004). A constructivist approach to online college learning. *Internet and Higher Education, 7*(2), 79–93.

Spenner, K. I., Buchmann, C., & Landerman, L. R. (2005). The black-white achievement gap in the first college year: Evidence from a new longitudinal case study. In D. B. Bills (Ed.), *The shape of inequality: Social stratification and ethnicity in comparative perspective*, Vol. 22 (pp. 187–216). Amsterdam: Elsevier.

Swail, W. S., Redd, K. E., & Perna, L. W. (2003). *Retaining minority students in higher education: A framework for success* (ASHE-ERIC Higher Education Report: Volume 30, Number 2). San Francisco: Wiley Publishers.

Tinto, V. (1994). *Leaving college: Rethinking the causes and cures of student attrition* (2nd ed.). Chicago: University of Chicago Press.

Trueba, E. T. (1998). Race and ethnicity in academia. In L. A. Valverde & L. A. Castenell (Eds.), *The multicultural campus: Strategies for transforming higher education* (pp. 71–93). Walnut Creek, CA: Altamira.

Wills, E. (2005, February 15). Minority students make gains in higher education. *The Chronicle of Higher Education*. Retrieved November 29, 2006, from http://chronicle.com/weekly/v51/i25/25a03202.htm

About the Editors and Contributors

Joya Anastasia Carter is assistant professor of early childhood education at Georgia State University in Atlanta. Her current research, teaching, and service emphasize one central theme: producing an inclusive education for students from underrepresented populations by designing and delivering progressive teacher training in curriculum and instruction. This major field of scholarship in inclusive education also includes evaluation and assessment of students with disabilities; co-teaching and collaboration models; multicultural curriculum mapping and differentiated instruction; cross-cultural teaching and learning strategies; qualitative methodology; and Africana Feminist Theory. Carter received her B.A. from Hampton University, her M.Ed. from Georgia State University, and her Ph.D. from Syracuse University.

M. Gail Sanders Derrick is associate professor of education at Regent University in Virginia Beach, Virginia, where she teaches courses in adult learning and motivation in an online doctoral program. She received her Doctor of Education in Higher Education Administration from George Washington University. Her research interests are self-efficacy, motivation, and Adult Learning Theory, including the factors associated with learner autonomy. She is also interested in creating environments conducive to learning and facilitating learner autonomy in an online setting.

Louis B. Gallien Jr. is distinguished professor of education at Regent University. He teaches, directs, and advises doctoral students in the higher education cognate of an Ed.D. program. He coedited *Instructing and Mentoring the African American College Student: Strategies for Success in Higher Education* (with Marshalita Sims Peterson, 2004). In that same research vein he has written articles and presentations, and has advised a variety of collegiate institutions across the United States and Europe on the institutional impediments and successful strategies for improving the academic achievement levels of collegiate African Americans. He serves on the editorial board of the *Journal of College Values and Character* at Florida State University and is a reviewer for the *American Educational Research Journal* and *Choice Magazine* of the American Library Association.

JoAnn W. Haysbert is the 15th president of Langston University in Langston, Oklahoma. Previously, she was Acting President, Provost, and Assistant Provost for Academic Affairs at Hampton University in Virginia. She is also a former public school administrator who devoted more than 30 years of stellar service as a professional educator. She is a successful grant writer, an astute fundraiser, and is recognized by her colleagues and students for her excellence in teaching and strong leadership abilities.

Hope M. Jordan is professor of education at Regent University and has over 25 years experience in both K–12 and higher education. She teaches and directs the Special Education Master's and Educational Specialist in Special Education Leadership programs. Additionally, she has written and administrated several grants and is involved in several book- and article-writing ventures. Her academic background in psychology, general education, special education, administration and supervision, and organizational leadership provides her with a broad perspective of education from various levels.

Robert A. Lucking is professor of educational curriculum and instruction at the Darden College of Education at Old Dominion University in Norfolk, Virginia, where he serves as Graduate Program Director and Director of the Military Career Transition Program. He has been a Fulbright Lecturer in Denmark and a Fulbright Scholar in India. Additionally, he has written extensively on the use of technology in instruction.

Richard C. Overbaugh is associate professor of instructional computing at the Darden College of Education at Old Dominion University. He teaches courses in instructional design and technology in blended environments in the master's and Ph.D. programs, which he designed and implemented. His research interests focus on the efficacy of instructional strategies and collaborative tools in distributed teaching/learning environments as well as on hierarchical assessment of knowledge acquisition. Overbaugh also works with Old Dominion University's Academic Technology Services to design advanced distributed teaching/learning environments to support seminar-type graduate student collaboration. He has served on the editorial boards of five journals, and works with the Virginia Modeling, Analysis and Simulation Center.

Emery M. Petchauer is instructor of education at Lincoln University, Pennsylvania. His research and writing surround hip-hop as an emerging worldview in formal and informal educational settings and its implications on teaching and learning. He is a former high school teacher who has contributed to local communities of hip-hop in San Diego, California, and Norfolk, Virginia.

Marshalita Sims Peterson is associate professor of education and former chair of the Education Department at Spelman College in Atlanta, Georgia. Her research examines the teaching and learning process with focus on curriculum design/implementation, pedagogical constructs, academic achievement, student assessment, academic programming, and program evaluation. She presents internationally on various educational topics relating to her research, including quality education, student achievement, and innovative instruction for all students. One of her most recent publications as coeditor is *Instructing and Mentoring the African American College Student: Strategies for Success in Higher Education* (2004).

Michael K. Ponton is professor of education at Regent University, teaching primarily research courses in the Ed.D. program. He has published extensively in the field of self-directed learning, where his research interests include adult learning, personal initiative, autonomous learning, and self-efficacy. He serves on the editorial boards for the *International Journal of Self-Directed Learning* and *New Horizons in Adult Education and Human Development.* Before coming to Regent University, he was associate professor of higher education at the University of Mississippi. Prior to entering academe, he was an aerospace engineer for the National Aeronautics and Space Administration (NASA).

Nancy E. Rhea is assistant professor for the Department of Curriculum and Instruction at the University of Mississippi. She is involved directly with both the Secondary Teacher Education and TESOL (Teaching English as a Second Language) programs. She has taught for 19 years at both the secondary and postsecondary levels and has also served as program director for a postsecondary ESL program. Rhea's research interests lie in learning theories, language acquisition, cultural issues in education, and testing and assessment.

Alfred P. Rovai is professor of education at Regent University. He teaches research design, statistics, program evaluation, and assessment of student learning in a mostly online Ed.D. program. Previously he taught at Old Dominion University and at UCLA. He has written extensively on distance education topics and presently is the North American Regional Editor for *International Review of Research in Open and Distance Learning*, Consulting Research Editor for *Educational Technology Research and Development*, and is on the editorial boards of *Internet and Higher Education* and the *Journal of Computing in Higher Education*.

Helen R. Stiff-Williams is an African American scholar and professor of education at Regent University. She serves as coordinator for the K–12 School

Leadership Program in the master's and doctoral programs. Her areas of expertise include standards-based education, character education, instructional delivery, student assessment, school improvement for low-achieving students and low-performing schools, and educational policy and practices. Stiff-Williams's past professional experiences include being chairman of the Department of Education at Hampton University; division chief in the Virginia Department of Education; assistant superintendent; and experiences in school leadership at the elementary, middle, and high school levels. Currently, she is in demand for her interactive presentations and staff training sessions on "Infusing Character Education into Standards-based Teaching," "Upgrading Instruction for Low Achieving Students," and "Teaching and Learning Online."

D. Nicole Williams is assistant professor in the School of Business at Langston University. With her juris doctorate degree, she previously served on the legal team for Athens Legal Aid & Defender Clinic in Athens, Georgia, and the Civil Liberty Union of Maryland in Centreville, Maryland. As a new professional in academia, she recently chaired the committee on Hiring Procedures at Langston University. She is expected to continue her scholarly pursuits and her role as an effective classroom teacher.

Index

NAMES

SUBJECTS